Murderous Sussex

Murderous Sussex

The executed of the Twentieth Century

John J. Eddleston

The Breedon Books
Publishing Company
Derby

First published in Great Britain by
The Breedon Books Publishing Company Limited
Breedon House, 44 Friar Gate, Derby, DE1 1DA.
1997

ISBN 1 85983 081 1

Printed and bound by Butler & Tanner Ltd., Selwood Printing
Works, Caxton Road, Frome, Somerset.

Colour separations by Colour Services, Wigston, Leicester.

Jackets printed by Lawrence-Allen, Weston-super-Mare, Avon.

CONTENTS

ACKNOWLEDGEMENTS

I would like to express my gratitude to the following people for their invaluable assistance in the preparation of this book. First and foremost must be Yvonne Berger, who not only gave a great deal of her time helping with the research but also proof read the entire volume and helped trace illustrations, as well as providing much encouragement.

My thanks must go to the staff of the Public Record Office at Kew, and the now defunct Chancery Lane; also the staff of Colindale newspaper library, especially Fred Harwood, who always made us feel welcome. In addition, I am indebted to the staff of Brighton Reference Library and Eastbourne Reference Library, especially Mrs Heather Downie. Finally I owe a debt to Mike Greenwood at the Sussex Police Headquarters who assisted with some details of the careers of certain officers mentioned in these pages.

INTRODUCTION

IN MANY WAYS, the counties of East and West Sussex might well be described as the murder capital of the country. True, London has had more murders that ended in the death penalty but Sussex has seen many of the cases which captured the nation's headlines.

Amongst those famous cases are John Thorne, who killed his girlfriend and then buried her body on his chicken farm, Patrick Mahon, who cut his victim into pieces at a bungalow on the Crumbles, and Field and Gray who battered Irene Munro to death on that same stretch of shingle beach. The most famous case of all, though, must be that of John George Haigh, who earned himself epithets such as 'the Vampire Killer' or 'the Acid Bath Killer'. However, the lesser-known cases can be even more fascinating and these include a case which involves a house owned by a king. Sussex has them all.

This book tells the stories of all the murderers of the 20th century who either killed in Sussex, or had a strong Sussex connection, and who went on to pay the ultimate penalty. Decide for yourself if they all deserved that fate.

John J. Eddleston
Brighton, 1997.

CHAPTER ONE

A LOVERS' WEEKEND

BY the year 1899, Victoria had ruled over an expanding British Empire for 62 years. The old century was coming to a close and the new, promising 20th century was about to begin.

Of course, there were still problems. The Boers in South Africa were proving troublesome again and hostilities had broken out, but the genteel southern coast of England was far removed from such concerns. One of the most fashionable watering holes was the seaside town of Brighton, yet it was this same town of promenades, piers and bandstands, that was to play its part in a brutal and terrible murder.

At 9.45 pm on Friday, October 27th, 1899, Alice Rial, a chambermaid at a temperance hotel, Findlay's Hotel, at 36 Queen's Road, Brighton, checked a lady into room 11. The lady gave her name as Miss Brooks and reserved a second room, number 10, for her brother who was to arrive in the town the following day. Alice noticed that Miss Brooks carried a Gladstone bag and a small hold-all, bound up with leather straps. The new guest was also seen by the hotel proprietor, John Findlay.

The following morning, Miss Brooks enjoyed a leisurely breakfast in the hotel, later walking up to the railway station where at approximately 3.30pm she did indeed meet the man she later introduced as her brother. The two then returned to the hotel where Mr Brooks signed the register. The couple enjoyed the rest of the day together, although had Miss Brooks purchased a copy of the *Brighton Argus* published on that same Saturday, she might well have read a 27-line article on the back page which told of the body of a male child being discovered in the ladies' waiting room on platform three of Dalston Junction railway station in north London.

Mr and Miss Brooks took breakfast together in the coffee room of the hotel on the morning of Sunday, October 29th. Having paid their respective bills, they checked out that afternoon, walked back to the station, and caught the train back to London. What John Findlay and Alice Rial could not know at the time was that Miss Brooks was in reality 36-year-old Louisa Josephine Jemima Masset, and her 'brother' was 19-year-old Eudor Lucas, her lover.

Louisa Masset lived at 29 Bethune Road, Stoke Newington, having been there for some 18 months, earning her living as a day governess and teacher of French. The house was actually owned by Richard Cadisch, Louisa's brother-in-law, he being married to Leonie, one of Louisa's two sisters. On April 24th, 1896, Louisa had given birth to a son, whom she named Manfred. Although unmarried, Louisa steadfastly refused to reveal the name of the child's father, saying only that he was French, and that he had returned to his native land in August 1898. Still, mother and father remained in touch and it seems that he did take an interest in the boy's upbringing, certainly supporting Manfred financially.

Always a practical woman and perhaps not wanting her life to be ruled by an infant son, Louisa placed Manfred in the care of a nurse when he was only three weeks old. This nurse, Helen Eliza Gentle, had once been employed by a clergyman but since her widowed mother, Mrs Norris, had fallen into poor health, Helen had left that position and returned to the parental home at 210 Clyde Road, Tottenham, to look after her and it was here that she also took care of Manfred. The boy was certainly looked after very well and every Wednesday, his loving mother would visit him, often taking him out to Tottenham Green, a nearby park.

It was in that same month of August, 1898, when Manfred's father left for France, that Eudor Lucas first arrived in England. Seeking lodgings for himself, he had first moved into 31 Bethune

Road, taking rooms in a house next door to Louisa. Since she was half-French, there was perhaps a natural affinity between the two and despite their difference in age, they soon became close friends. That friendship continued even after Eudor had moved to new lodgings in Mildmay Grove, Islington.

It is impossible to determine exactly what Louisa wanted, or thought she wanted, from the friendship with the handsome, dark Frenchman. What is certain is that at Whitsun, 1899, Eudor, Louisa and two friends travelled down to Brighton and stayed in that same hotel run by Mr Findlay. There was, of course, no suggestion that anything improper took place between Louisa and Eudor, but they did grow ever closer until soon, in the September, she felt able to confide in him that she had given birth to an illegitimate child.

Eudor thanked Louisa for her frankness, telling her that it was very honourable to have presented him with the true picture, but adding that he wished to hear no more about it. Louisa never talked about her son in front of Eudor again, nor did the couple ever discuss possible future marriage plans. It seemed that both were happy to allow their relationship to develop naturally and not long afterwards, on Tuesday, October 24th, Louisa mentioned to Eudor that she was thinking of returning to Findlay's Hotel on the coming Friday.

Eudor was no fool and instantly knew what Louisa was suggesting. As a clerk in the City, he was unable to leave work early but said that he would be happy to join Louisa on the Saturday. Since discretion was to be the watchword, Louisa suggested using the name Brooks, arranged to meet Eudor's train, and made her plans for the forthcoming trip to the seaside.

Louisa it seems was also making other plans. On October 16th, she had written to Mrs Norris, Helen Gentle's mother.

The complete letter read, "Dear Mrs Norris, I thought I should be able to see Manfred last Friday but was obliged to meet his father who came over quite unexpectedly. Since I have seen him I must let you know that Manfred will soon be taken from your care as his father considers him a big boy now and quite old enough to make a change. He wishes him to be brought up in a cousin's family so that he can have him under his personal supervision and he must also start the French language which at his age can be picked up very quickly. I am very sorry to remove him from your loving care, but if I raise any objection I shall simply be interfering with his future welfare and prospects — shall be over on Wednesday and will talk matters over with you again, but thought it wise to give you as long a notice as I possibly could.

Was glad after all we had the doctor as I was satisfied that the little chap was not in for more than an indigestion and was able to tell his father, so love and kisses for him and kindest regards to you and your daughter. Yours truly. Louisa Masset." The letter carried a post script, "Will bring over the shoes he tried on lately for the house as his clothing will be seen to in his new home and there is no need for him to carry over too much luggage."

So it was that at 12.30pm on October 27th, a rather tearful Helen Gentle met Louisa outside the Birdcage public house on Stamford Hill. Here she placed Manfred in the care of his mother, also handing over a brown paper parcel containing some of the child's clothes, and one of his favourite toys, a small pair of scales. The last time Helen saw mother and child together, they were boarding an omnibus that would take them to London Bridge station.

It is certain that Louisa and Manfred did go to London Bridge. The bus conductor, Thomas Bonner, remembered the pair and stated that they alighted at the station at approximately 1.35pm. Two other witnesses also recalled seeing Louisa and the by now rather tearful child.

Georgina Worley was an attendant in one of the ladies' waiting rooms at London Bridge. She first saw Louisa at 1.42pm and noticed that she remained in the waiting room until about 2.30pm. Indeed, she even had a short conversation with the mother, who informed Georgina that she was waiting for someone to arrive at the station.

It was also around 2.30pm when the senior attendant of a different waiting room, Ellen Rees, came on duty. Some ten minutes later, Ellen noticed the mother and child and asked why the boy was crying. The mother replied that he was missing his nurse and after chatting for a few more minutes, the mother announced that she would take the boy to the refreshment room and buy him a cake. It was the last time anyone remembered seeing Manfred alive.

At 6.30pm Mary Teahan, a governess from Richmond, and her friend, Margaret Biggs, alighted from a train at Dalston Junction station and tried to enter the first cubicle of the ladies' lavatory on platform three. Something was blocking the doorway, making it impossible to open, and thinking that someone might have been taken ill, the two ladies took their story to the porter, Joseph John Standing. He, in turn, sought the assistance of his superior, the station master, David Bundy, and it was this gentleman who entered the toilet and found the battered body of a small boy.

Dr James Patrick Fennell was called from his surgery in Dalston Lane and he confirmed that the boy was indeed dead. At first it was thought that the poor infant had been stabbed but a subsequent post-mortem confirmed that the actual cause of death was suffocation. The child had also been battered and near his body lay two pieces of sharp clinker brick. It appeared that the boy had been stunned, smothered, and then stripped naked. Finally his assailant had thrown a black woollen shawl over the body before making good her escape. The examination of the body took place at 6.55pm and various estimates of the time of death put it at some time between 2.55pm and 5.55pm.

Reports of the death were widely published. Indeed, as has already been mentioned, a brief article even appeared in the Brighton paper. One of those who read those reports was Helen Gentle, who thinking that the description of the dead child sounded remarkably like her charge, took her suspicions to the police and later formally identified the dead child as Manfred Masset.

Whilst all this was going on, Louisa was, of course, enjoying her weekend of love in Brighton. From there she wrote letters to Helen, telling her that the crossing to France had been rather rough and she had been sick, but adding that Manfred was now happy in France and sent his love. These letters, once delivered, were immediately passed on to the police.

Brighton, however, provided still more evidence of Louisa's involvement in this tragic case. A few days after 'Miss Brooks' had left the hotel, John Findlay found a pair of toy scales in the room which Louisa had occupied. These were forwarded to the police and Helen Gentle confirmed that they were the ones that Manfred had taken with him. This proved yet another link in the chain.

Annie Skeats was an attendant in the ladies' room at Brighton railway station and at 3.30pm on the Saturday, she had found a brown paper parcel in the waiting room. She was certain that the parcel had not been there at 2.30pm when she had last been in the room and, of course, this was about the same time that Eudor Lucas had arrived in the town, to be met by Louisa. Annie took the parcel to the cloak room and when no one claimed it, the parcel was forwarded to London Bridge station. There it was opened by Detective Sergeant Richard Nursey who saw that it contained a child's coat and frock. Attempts had been made to remove some of the trimmings, perhaps to disguise the items, but Helen Gentle was still able to identfy them as being the same articles worn by Manfred when she had handed him over to his mother.

By the afternoon of Monday, October 30th, the police were anxious to trace Louisa Masset. Her behaviour, meanwhile, was exactly the same as usual. She remained at home until 1.30pm on the Monday when she left to attend to her regular routine and teach at various addresses around London.

By 5.15pm Louisa was at the home of Maximilian and Clara Haas, at Greencroft Gardens, West Hampstead. As usual, she left at 6.45pm and was described as being in her usual high spirits. By 11.00pm, though, things were very different, for it was at that time that Louisa knocked on the door of her other brother-in-law, George Richard Symes, who lived at Streatham Road, Croydon.

Louisa was now very upset, indeed, almost hysterical. She told George that she had seen a newspaper placard saying the child found at Dalston had been identified. Upon buying a paper she had read to her horror that the child was Manfred and that the police were now looking for her. She then explained to George that she had lied about the child going to France, had spent the weekend with Eudor in Brighton, but swore that she had nothing to do with the murder.

George Symes listened intently to Louisa's story, which took him until the small hours of Tuesday morning. Then he travelled across London, to Richard and Leonie Cadisch's house at Bethune Road, where he discussed the matter further. Staying there until it was daylight, George and Richard then returned to Croydon where they noticed two men were following them. They turned out to be Police Sergeant William Burch and Constable Allen who had been watching number 29 and had trailed the two men when they left the house. These two officers accompanied George and Richard to Streatham Road and took Louisa into custody.

The evidence against Louisa continued to build. Maud Clifford was an assistant in a draper's shop, McIlroy's, at 161 High Street, Stoke Newington. She said that she had sold a black shawl, similar to the one found with Manfred's body, to a woman fitting Louisa's description, on or about October 24th. The manager of that same shop, Ernest Hopkins Mooney, stated that he had only purchased 15 shawls on October 18th. Three of those were black and only one of these had been sold. The two that remained matched exactly the one the police showed to him.

The most damaging evidence, though, came from Ellen Rees, the ladies' room attendant at London Bridge station. She mentioned to the investigating officers, who included Inspector Frederick Forth, that not only had she seen Louisa in the afternoon of the day in question, but had seen her again that same night. At 6.50pm Louisa had again been in the waiting room and asked Ellen for a towel as she wanted a wash. Later still, Louisa asked Ellen what time the next train to Brighton left and was told that it was at 7.20pm. Ellen reported that Louisa finally left the waiting room at about 7.18pm, presumably to catch that train.

The case seemed to be clear cut. Louisa Masset had a relationship with Eudor Lucas. In September she had told him of her child and although he was not openly disapproving, he had said that he wanted to speak no more about the boy. In October, Louisa had given herself to him for the first time. This was a major step and if she wanted more, then surely the child was an encumbrance. This was why she had plotted her terrible course of action.

Telling Helen Gentle, and indeed her own family, that the boy was being sent to France, Louisa picked him up outside the Birdcage, took him to London Bridge, but then returned to Dalston Junction where she stunned him with the clinker brick and then smothered Manfred to death before stripping him and covering the body with a shawl. Later she returned to London Bridge, caught the 7.20pm train to Brighton which arrived at 9.18pm and then calmly walked to her hotel, arriving there at 9.45pm.

The next day, Eudor's train arrived in Brighton at 3.30pm. Louisa met him at the station having first deposited Manfred's clothing in the waiting room. As if further confirmation was needed, the brown paper taken from the parcel was shown to match with a piece which remained at Helen Gentle's house, and the clinker brick was very similar to others found in the front and back garden of the house at Bethune Road. What was Louisa's answer to all this damning evidence? The story she told was simple and yet difficult to substantiate.

According to Louisa, it was on Wednesday, October 4th, on one of her regular trips to Tottenham Green with Manfred, when Louisa first encountered two ladies. Manfred was happily playing on the grass with a little girl who said her name was Millie. This Millie was in the care of two ladies, eminently respectable, who sat together on a nearby bench. The three fell into conversation and quite naturally they spoke about the children. The ladies were sisters-in-law and Millie was the daughter of the younger one. Their surname, they informed Louisa, was Browning.

The Brownings were, it seems, considering opening a small school and asked Louisa if she was satisfied with the education Manfred was receiving. Once she had replied in the negative, saying that she felt Manfred was picking up some minor bad habits in his speech, an offer of a place in the new school was made and Louisa said that she would think about it. Arrangements were made to meet up on the following Wednesday.

October 11th arrived and the Brownings gave the address of the new school as 45 King's Road, Chelsea. Louisa had made her mind up. Manfred would indeed be enrolled for a fee of 10s a month for his education and £12 a year for his board and lodgings, the latter sum to be paid in advance when the boy was handed over.

Louisa was now faced with a difficult decision. She had no wish to hurt the feelings of the kindly Miss Gentle and so concocted the story of the boy being sent to France. In this way, there could be no reflection on Helen's teaching methods. Having picked Manfred up at 12.30pm, Louisa travelled to London Bridge where she was supposed to meet the Brownings at 2.00pm. From there the party would all travel to King's Road to see Manfred settled in before Louisa returned to London Bridge in time to catch the 4.00pm train to Brighton.

In the event, the two ladies did not turn up until just before 4.00pm. They apologised profusely for being late whilst Louisa gave Manfred into their charge, along with £12 in cash and the brown paper parcel of clothes which Helen had given to her earlier. Naturally, Louisa asked for a receipt.

The Brownings said that they did not have any paper but would go to the refreshment room to see if they could obtain some. Louisa returned to the waiting room to collect her bag and waited patiently for their return. When they did not come back, she simply boarded the train to Brighton. After all, the ladies were very respectable and Louisa did have their address.

The 4.00pm train arrived at Brighton at 6.19pm. Depositing her bag in the left luggage, Louisa said she then went for a walk down to the sea front. Here she enjoyed a meal in a restaurant known as Mutton's. From there she had thought of taking a walk to the West Pier but instead strolled down to the shops in West Brighton. Later, she returned to the station to collect her bag, passing the Jubilee Clock Tower at 8.45pm. As for the supposed sighting of her by Ellen Rees at 7.00pm, the lady must simply have been mistaken.

The police did, of course, check out Louisa's story. The address in Chelsea turned out to belong to a respectable businessman, Henry Willis, who had owned that property for ten years. He had never heard of the Brownings, or indeed Louisa Masset. It was going to be a question of who the jury believed.

Louisa's trial opened at the Old Bailey, before Mr Justice Bruce, on December 13th, 1899. Mr Charles Mathews led the prosecution, assisted by Mr Richard D. Muir, whilst Louisa's defence rested in the hands of Lord Coleridge and Mr Arthur Hutton. The proceedings lasted until December 18th, when the jury returned a guilty verdict and Louisa Masset was sentenced to death.

What really happened on that dark day in October 1899? Let us re-examine the evidence.

If Louisa was a murderess, then the only real motive could be that she felt her son was an encumbrance to the continuance of her relationship with Eudor Lucas. This woman, who everyone described as a devoted and loving mother, coolly planned how she could best dispose of her child. Yet this same calculating mind left the child's clothes where they would most certainly be found, murdered him in the railway station closest to her own home, used a brick which came from her front garden and came up with a totally unprovable and weak story to explain away the various time discrepancies.

The alternative is that Louisa was innocent. If so, then two scheming women, having taken and murdered Manfred, later planted clues to incriminate Louisa by travelling down to Brighton to plant the clothes in the brown paper parcel. They also used a brick similar to those in Louisa's garden, and left behind a shawl identical to one they knew Louisa owned. The Brownings' motive for this would, of course, be the sum of £12. At the time, other baby-farmers were killing children for much smaller sums. Which story is the most plausible?

Before coming to a final decision, consider the following: Ellen Rees, whose evidence was so damning, did indeed pick Louisa out of a line-up and positively identified her as the woman she had seen for a second time at 7.00pm on the evening of the murder. This same woman wore glasses to make this identification, yet she admitted that she was not wearing those glasses on the day in question. Of course, Ellen tried to explain this by saying that she wore glasses only for reading. Why then did she need them at the line-up? Further, she said that perhaps 200 women, many of them with children, would pass through her waiting room on an average day. Even more interesting, before she came forward to give her evidence to the police, Ellen Rees had seen pictures of the murdered boy and the accused woman in the local newspapers.

Maud Clifford and Ernest Mooney of the draper's shop both gave conflicting evidence. At one stage, Mooney said that he had not seen the particular pattern of the shawl anywhere before, yet in another part of his evidence, he admitted that it was a common pattern and might be obtained anywhere in London. Of course, it would be stretching the bounds of coincidence a little far to state that one of the Brownings had managed to purchase an identical shawl somewhere else in London. The evidence that Louisa ever bought such a shawl is, however, rather weak. Miss Clifford failed to pick Louisa out from a police line-up and even in court could not positively say that this was the woman to whom she had sold the shawl. Finally there was the evidence of Henry James Streeter.

Mr Streeter was a waiter at Mutton's restaurant in Brighton. When he read of the Masset case in his newspaper, he contacted a Brighton solicitor who in turn passed on the evidence he had given to Louisa's defence team. Unfortunately, Streeter was not called as a witness and his evidence was passed on only after Louisa had been sentenced to death.

Henry Streeter remembered the afternoon of October 27th, 1899. It was a dull, rainy day and as a consequence, the restaurant only had two customers all the time he was there. One was a gentleman, but the other was a young woman, dressed in black, who arrived not long after 6.00pm and stayed for 45 minutes. Both Streeter and the proprietor, Mr Mutton himself, swore that they could positively identify the woman. If that woman were shown to be Louisa, then she did indeed catch the 4.00pm train.

We know that Louisa was at London Bridge at 1.35pm, for she was seen by Thomas Bonner, the omnibus conductor. Indeed, Helen Gentle, who saw her get on to that bus, confirmed that Louisa had asked her to accompany her on the journey to London Bridge. Surely if Helen had agreed to that suggestion, all the cold calculating plans would have been thrown awry.

The medical evidence showed that the very earliest Manfred could have died was at 2.55pm. The return journey to Dalston would have taken about an hour, so if Louisa had simply turned around at London Bridge and gone straight back, she could not have arrived until 2.35pm which does seem to fit in with the earliest time of death. This, of course, is impossible, for Louisa was seen by Ellen Rees and the perhaps more reliable witness, Georgina Worley. According to Miss Worley, Louisa was certainly there until 2.30pm, meaning that she could not have arrived back at Dalston until 3.30pm. If she had killed Manfred at that time, it would still fit in with the medical evidence but Louisa could not have then returned to London Bridge until 4.30pm at the very earliest. Therefore, if she caught the 4.00pm train to Brighton, she was innocent.

Despite two petitions, one in England which raised 1,000 signatures and one in France that raised 1,200, there was no reprieve. At 9.00am on the morning of Tuesday, January 9th, 1900, Louisa Masset was hanged at Newgate by James Billington, assisted by his son William. More than 2,000 people had gathered outside the prison and they cheered as the black flag was raised to signify that the sentence had been carried out.

It has been said that Louisa confessed her guilt before she had died. In fact, her last words were, "What I am about to suffer is just, and now my conscience is clear." Those could just have easily have been the words of a loving and dutiful mother who felt that she had let down and abandoned the son she adored.

CHAPTER TWO

COLLECTING BLACKBERRIES

EDWARD Gifford took his position as gamekeeper to the Marquis of Camden very seriously indeed. There were, of course, local poachers to take care of, but there were other trespassers in the woods under his control, including children and courting couples.

It was 6.30pm on the evening of Friday, September 6th, 1912, and Gifford was patrolling his patch at the edge of Buckland Hill Wood, near Wadhurst. As he strolled along, admiring the rich autumnal colours, a number of screams rang out from the top side of the wood. They were obviously female screams and Gifford decided to investigate.

Walking along the side of the wood, Gifford failed to see anyone. There was a meadow at the top of the wood and here he crossed a bridge over a small stream and entered the wood itself. Once again he skirted the edge of the wood until he had walked perhaps 100 yards.

It was then he saw two people, a man and a woman, lying together amongst the trees.

"Come out of it," ordered Edward Gifford. For a few seconds there was no reply but then the man stood and shouted, "I will come out." The woman still did not move as Gifford carefully studied the man who was now quite close to him. He did not know the man's name, but did recognise him as someone he had seen before, in the nearby hamlet of Wood's Green.

Gifford ordered the man to bring the woman out but he merely answered, "It's all right, she knows her way out. She will come out presently." That was all very well but she had still not made any effort to do as she had been told. Gifford walked deeper into the woods, having first told the man to stay where he was. It was only when Gifford was close to the still figure that he realised it wasn't a woman but a young girl. She lay face down in the soil and when Gifford picked her up he saw immediately that she was beyond all help. The child's face was covered in blood, as was her hair, and she was most certainly dead. Clutched in her tiny hand was a man's red handkerchief and this too had bloodstains upon it. Placing the child gently back on to the earth, Edward Gifford turned to face the man but by now he had disappeared.

Gifford was unsure what he should do next. Of course, he needed to call the police, but should he leave the child's body where it lay. Luckily, within a few minutes, two gentlemen out for a stroll passed the spot and Gifford told them what he had seen and asked them to fetch a constable.

Police Constable McKean was very soon on the scene and Edward Gifford was able to give him a most detailed description of the man he had seen with the little girl.

According to Gifford he was quite tall, a typical countryman with dark hair and a bronze complexion. McKean knew all the locals very well and he soon came to realise that Gifford was describing Albert Rumens, a 44-year-old labourer who lived at Wood's Green, with his mother. McKean also knew the dead girl, Mabel Ann Maryan, who had turned ten only a few days earlier, on September 1st. Furthermore, McKean knew that the Maryan family lived next door but one to Rumens.

The body was taken to the nearest building, which was Wickhurst Farm, whilst Constable McKean went in search of Albert Rumens. Meanwhile, although no details were released at this early stage, rumours soon spread around the villages that a child had been found dead in the woods.

Albert Rumens, meanwhile, had not run very far. Henry Wickham, unaware at this stage that anything had happened, was walking towards Wood's Green. He saw Rumens and called out to him but Rumens failed to reply. From the direction he was travelling, Rumens was heading towards the Balaclava Inn. There was nothing unusual in that as Rumens was known to like a drink. It was actually around 7.15pm when Rumens arrived at the Balaclava for it was then that the barmaid, Clara Lofts, served him with a pint of beer. Rumens drained his glass and then without a word, left the pub and walked off towards his home.

It was just before 8.00pm when Rumens walked past the grocer's shop run by William Chapman. By this time, the story of a girl's body being found in the woods was common knowledge, as was the fact that Mabel had failed to return home and that Rumens had been seen talking to her earlier that day. The two incidents had not been officially linked but people in the village were beginning to draw their own conclusions.

Chapman called out to Rumens, "Alf, have you seen Maryan's girl?"

Rumens replied that he had seen her and that she had 'turned in by Fuller's Pond'. Chapman continued, "You go and tell Mrs Maryan, as they have lost their child, and heard that she had gone across the fields with a man."

With a cheery, "Righto! I will," Rumens continued on his way.

It was just after 8.00pm that Rumens knocked on the Maryan family's back door. It was Mabel's mother, Sarah Alice Caroline Maryan, who came to the door to be greeted with a shout from the man everyone had been looking for.

"Here is Albert Rumens. What do you want with him?"

Sarah had by now heard the description of the man seen with the body in the woods and she too believed that it might be Rumens. She therefore demanded to know what had become of Mabel. Rumens told her that he had met her in the woods and they had been searching for blackberries together. He finished, "I left her in the woods and she will be home presently." Sarah told Rumens she did not believe him and that the police would very soon be here to take him away. She then closed the back door in Rumens' face.

By 8.30pm Albert Rumens was at the public house in Silvers Lane. It was there that he approached John Manktelow, who lived at 18 Wood's Green and so also knew both Rumens and Mabel well. Rumens seemed to be rather concerned and said to Manktelow, "They said I killed Mabel and that 'Mac' would be after me."

A few minutes later, Mac, in the form of Constable McKean did indeed appear and asked Rumens if he could speak to him. A few men inside the public bar were approached and in due course a makeshift identification parade was arranged by the headlights of two cars. Edward Gifford, who had followed McKean into the village had no hesitation in picking out Rumens as the man he had seen with the dead girl. As a result of that, Rumens was immediately taken into custody.

The very next day, Rumens was taken before the Mark Cross Petty Sessional Bench where the magistrate, Mr H.G. Dixon, heard evidence of the arrest, given by Superintendent Criddle of Uckfield. The case was still in its early stages and so after a very brief appearance, Rumens was remanded until Friday, 13th September. Before that, the inquest on the dead child opened at Wickhurst Farm with the East Sussex coroner, Mr G. Norbury, in charge. Here some evidence of her daughter's movements were given by Sarah Maryan.

According to Sarah, Mabel had left home alone at around 4.50pm on September 6th. Her daughter had wanted to go blackberrying and Sarah said it would be fine as long as later she took a walk up Brickland Hill to meet her father, Frank, on his way home from work. Mabel promised that she would and left the house carrying a little can and a wooden stick. Those two items had been found close by Mabel's body.

The next person to give evidence was ten-year-old Harold Chapman, the son of William. He attended the same school as the dead girl and knew her very well. On the Friday evening in question, Harold and his younger brother had gone out to play. They were in a field at Stream Hill when they saw Mabel walk down the hill, from the woods at the top, carrying the can and stick. He also saw Albert Rumens emerge from the same wood and follow Mabel down the hill.

For a few minutes the children chatted, with Rumens standing close by. Then the group walked to the bottom of the hill. Harold and his brother went into a field owned by Mr Lees, whilst Mabel walked off towards the woods again. She had gone only a few yards when Rumens caught up with her and the last Harold saw of her she was walking off, with Rumens.

Perhaps the saddest evidence showed that the dead girl's father had actually seen her in the company of the man accused of killing her. Richard Rabson, who lived at 17 Wood's Green, was walking home with his brother, Charles, and Frank Maryan. As they trod through a field close by the woods where Mabel would eventually be found, Frank Maryan saw a man and a woman at the far end of the field. It was then about 5.40pm and the three workmates saw the man lift what Frank thought was a woman, over a fence at the edge of the woods. At the time Richard said he thought that the 'woman' was in fact Mabel but Frank said it couldn't be and walked on towards his home.

On September 12th, the inquest not surprisingly returned a verdict of wilful murder. On this same Thursday, the funeral of Mabel Maryan took place in the parish churchyard. The next day, Rumens again appeared before the Justices at Mark Cross.

Mr Dixon was again in charge, sitting with John Hallett and Mr T. Parsons. Rumens was not defended and Mr Harold Pearce appeared for the Director of Public Prosecutions. Here evidence was given by Edward Gifford, Constable McKean and others and at the end of the proceedings, Rumens was committed for trial.

The trial took place in the court house in the ancient county town of Lewes, on December 16th, 1912. Mr Justice Channell presided, the prosecution case being stated by Mr C.F. Gill and Mr Theobald Mathews. Rumens was defended by Mr Sutherland Graeme.

The early evidence related to the actual cause of Mabel's death. According to the medical evidence, given by Dr James Herbert Fazan, death was due to suffocation. The child had, it seems, had her face forced against the ground with such force that her nose was flattened. There was also evidence of very strong pressure on the back of her neck. So much so that a bone had been fractured and there were marks where her assailant's thumb had gone into her skin. There was no sign of any sexual assault.

Edward Gifford gave his testimony again but now added that the reason he recognised Rumens was because he had seen him just a couple of days before the murder. On that occasion he had been in the company of another gamekeeper, named Wells. Rumens had passed them and asked Wells if he had a match. After Wells had handed over a light, Rumens put his arm around his neck and kissed him! Under such circumstances it was hardly surprising that Rumens should stick in Gifford's mind.

Mary Gibb, who was Rumens' mother, identified two handkerchiefs as similar to ones she had given to Albert. One of these was the same one found in Mabel's left hand whilst the other was found on Rumens when he had been searched after being arrested. Mary also had to agree that one of her son's handkerchiefs was missing.

However, Mary also tried to show that there was insanity in the family by stating that one of Rumens' cousins was in an asylum and another had thrown himself under a train.

Constable McKean, in addition to his earlier evidence, pointed out that when Rumens was examined, it was seen that the knuckles of one of his hands were injured. Tests had also shown that there was blood on the sleeve of the coat he had been wearing and on both knees of his trousers. He went on to say that Rumens was known to be a very hard worker and a most inoffensive man when sober, but that a change came over him when he had been drinking. Later it was shown that Rumens had been drinking on the day of the murder.

The grocer, William Chapman, testified that he had served Rumens with a quart of beer early that morning. Having heard all the evidence, it took the jury only 20 minutes to return their guilty verdict.

There was to be no appeal against the death sentence. On the morning of Tuesday January 7th, 1913, a crowd of 40 or 50 people gathered outside Lewes prison. Rumens had spent a restless night, pacing his cell until 4.00am. He had then managed to steal a couple of hours fitful sleep, finally rising at 6.00am. Although breakfast was brought to the condemned cell, he was unable to eat any, although he did manage a drink.

At 8.00am, John Ellis and his assistant, Henry Pierrepoint, entered the death cell and pinioned the condemned man. The scaffold was a small wooden contraption positioned in a small green turfed area at the east end of the prison, a ditch having been dug to accommodate the drop so that the base of the scaffold was level with the ground. Rumens walked with a firm step and showed no resistance as the noose was placed around his neck. In a few seconds it was all over. It was the first execution at Lewes since that of Arthur Henry Wood on April 26th, 1892.

At the subsequent inquest on the dead man, the governor of the prison, Major Reginald Adams Marriott, stated that the drop was 6ft 6ins and there had been no problems with the execution. The usual verdict was returned and the body of Arthur Rumens was placed in a grave dug close by the scaffold. The only gravestone he would receive was a small stone tablet set into the prison wall.

CHAPTER THREE

THE MAN WITH MANY NAMES

IN October 1912 there were three ladies living at 6 South Cliff Avenue, Eastbourne. The house was owned by Countess Flora Ruth Sztaray, who had been there for eight years. Her close friend, Florence Fuller, had also been living there for the past 18 months. The third woman at number 6 was the countess's maid, Lilian Maud Chaplin.

Most evenings the countess and Florence would dine at the house but sometimes they would choose to have a meal at one of the many restaurants or hotels that dotted Eastbourne. One such occasion was to be on Wednesday, October 9th when the countess rang a cab company that she had used many times before and asked them to send a carriage to take them into town.

In fact there had been four people inside the house at South Cliff Avenue. Mr Bechstein, the countess's hairdresser, had called to attend to the two ladies and, as he left at around 7.15pm, the cab, a single-horse brougham, driven by David Potter, pulled up outside the house.

As Potter waited for his fare to appear, he happened to glance at the house. Over the front door was a sort of flat-roofed porch and, in the darkness, Potter detected a movement on the roof of that porch. Looking more closely, he saw in the shadows the unmistakable shape of a man's head and shoulders. A minute or so later the countess and

Florence Fuller appeared and climbed into the cab, the countess bidding the cabbie a welcome. "Potter, you are a stranger. You haven't been here for a long time. Drive me to the Burlington."

As the cab pulled away, Lilian Chaplin closed the door and went upstairs to light the fires in the bedrooms.

The cab turned down Silverdale Road and was almost at the junction with Compton Street when Potter stopped the brougham and told the countess what he had seen above her front door. There had been a number of burglaries in the area of late and the countess had no doubt that a thief was about to break into her house. She ordered Potter to return to South Cliff Avenue.

Arriving back at her home, the countess left Florence Fuller standing on the pavement whilst she dashed to her front door and rang the bell, hoping that the burglar, still positioned somewhere over her head, would simply lie still, believing that she might simply have forgotten something. A puzzled Lilian Chaplin opened the door to her employer who hurriedly explained what was happening and then rushed to the telephone.

Police Constable John Luck timed the first telephone call at 7.30pm. The countess identified herself and said, "Can you send a constable at once to 6 South Cliff Avenue, as there is a man lying on the porch over the front door, and we think he will get in a bedroom window?" Luck said that he would contact the police office on the Grand Parade and someone would be there within minutes.

The telephone at Grand Parade was answered by 44-year-old Inspector Arthur Walls, who said he would go to the address at once. Whilst he was on his way, Countess Sztaray rang for a second time and asked if anyone had been sent. Constable Luck said that Inspector Walls was on his way and would be there as soon as he could.

The countess was obviously in a state of panic, for a couple of minutes later she rang for a third time and Luck told her that by his calculations, the inspector should be there any second. As the countess replaced the receiver, Inspector Walls turned into South Cliff Avenue.

By now, Florence Fuller had also gone inside the house, at the request of the countess who was concerned for her safety. The only person left outside number 6, was the coachman, David Potter, who saw Inspector Walls rushing down from the top of the street. Walls was actually on the wrong side of the street so Potter made a low whistle to attract his attention and at that, the inspector came over to his cab.

"Is this number six?" Potter informed him that it was and pointed to where the mysterious stranger still lurked in the shadows. Walls had now seen his man and stepped forward to the gate of the house. The countess, meanwhile, was standing in her hallway and shouted, "There is a man over my door." Walls took a step back so that he should get a better view of the man and shouted for him to come down. There was no reply but the man on the porch roof did make some kind of movement.

Inspector Walls took another step to the right so that if the man did come down, he should not be able to run off, but at that same instant there was a flash of light and the unmistakable report of a gun being fired. Inspector Walls dropped to a stooping position but managed to right himself and stagger back towards the garden gate. Meanwhile, the noise of the shot had startled David Potter's horse and he was having trouble controlling it. In order to bring the animal to heel, Potter took the brake off his cab and allowed the horse to gallop off up the hill, whilst he gradually regained control and slowed the vehicle down.

When Potter was but halfway up the hill, the sound of a second shot rang out. Potter tried to raise the alarm by shouting at a gentleman on the corner, "There's a murder down the road. Give an eye and see if anyone comes this way." He then rode on to Grand Parade and told other cab drivers what he had seen. Within minutes, Potter and another cabbie, a gentleman named Plumb, were heading back to the scene of the shooting.

Meanwhile, back at South Cliff Avenue, the countess had heard the shots but was under the impression that the person who had been hit was Potter. She rang Constable Luck yet again to tell him that there was shooting. He said he would send Inspector Pratt, who leapt on to his bicycle and peddled furiously to the scene. Before

Pratt arrived, the countess had telephoned one final time to tell Luck that Walls had been shot.

A number of people rushed to aid Inspector Walls. Kathleen Sheathes was a domestic servant at number 3, a house almost directly opposite the scene of the shooting. She saw a small crowd of people gathered around a man lying on the pavement and told her employer, Mr George Beresford Noble Flanagan, who happened to be a surgeon. He, too, had heard the shots but had been enjoying dinner at the time. Once Kathleen had told him what she had seen he went to see if he could offer assistance. He found Inspector Walls lying in the road, on his back. He was still alive but died within minutes and never regained consciousness.

There was one clue to the possibly identity of the assassin. Close by the body, police found a trilby hat. Since this did not belong to the inspector, or any of the gentlemen who had tried to offer assistance, it was logical to assume that it had belonged to the killer. The hat was brown and inside, on a leather band, was stamped 'Kelvington'. There was also a ticket which read: 'No. 56 H.O. 62 P. 8/6'.

A massive search of the area was organised and throughout the region, many men were stopped and questioned, especially if they were not wearing a hat. All these inquiries led nowhere and the same night, a request for assistance was made to Scotland Yard. The following morning, Chief Inspector Elias Bower and Sergeant Hayman travelled down to Eastbourne. By 8.00am they were conferring with their Sussex colleagues.

This could have proved to be a very difficult case to solve. The police had no decent description of the man they were looking for and only the trilby hat could possibly be of assistance. However, by the end of that first day, the two Scotland Yard detectives had the name of a man who might well be the killer of Inspector Walls.

Edgar Power lived at 315 St Anne's Road, Haringay and had once been a medical student. On October 10th, he had walked into the police station at Eastbourne and asked to see the chief constable. The story he told proved to be most interesting. Power told the police about a friend of his who lived at 25 Queen's Road, Finsbury Park. That morning he had been at the house of his friend, who would later be referred to as John William Williams, when a letter from Eastbourne had arrived. This letter was from his friend's brother and was a plea for help reading something like, "If you would save my life, come here at once. Come to 4 Tideswell Road and ask for the name of Seymour. Bring some money with you. Urgent, urgent."

The two men travelled down to Eastbourne together and it was Power who was entrusted with the sum of £2 to help out the brother. On the way down, they read newspaper reports of the murder of Inspector Walls, and both had become suspicious, believing that this might have something to do with the tone of the letter. Arriving at 3.20pm, John William Williams had gone to the Royal Hotel for lunch whilst Power met the brother and handed over £1.00 of the money entrusted to him. In the course of their conversation, Power asked outright if the need for money had any connection with the murder of Inspector Walls. He was told that it had not, and was only needed to pay off his lodgings so that he could leave Eastbourne. The name Power gave to the police was that of John George Williams.

At this point, some explanation might well be justified of the fact that two brothers were apparently both named John Williams. As will become clear later, the two brothers were not named Williams. The man who had taken lodgings in Eastbourne had given a false name. In order to arrive at that name, he had taken his brother's first two names: John William. The letter 's' had been placed on to the end of the second name, to provide a surname, and the man's real first name, George, had been placed in the middle to give the name John George Williams. Later, when that man became involved in a murder trial, the brother, in order to protect the true family name, had been forced to give evidence under the same alias. Since his real Christian names were John William, he was now forced to go under the name of John William Williams.

Back at the police station, Edgar Power's statement was taken seriously and as he later caught the train back to London, accompanied by a young lady with whom John George Williams had been living, one Florence Seymour, police officers were watching his every move. It was Power, too, who told officers of a meeting he had arranged with John George Williams at Moorfields on the afternoon of October 11th. Power did not turn up for that meeting but Inspector Leonard Parker of the Eastbourne Borough Police, together with Chief Inspector Bower and others, did. John George Williams was arrested at 1.15pm and after being interviewed, was charged with murder the following day.

Meanwhile, on October 11th, the inquest of Inspector Walls opened at Eastbourne Town Hall before Mr G. Vere Benson. The foreman of the jury was Mr George Nicholson but only evidence of identification was given before the proceedings were adjourned until October 29th.

On October 12th, the man accused of the murder of the inspector was taken by train back to Eastbourne. The train had been supposed to arrive at 2.23pm but it was a very foggy day and as a consequence, Williams arrived back at 2.58pm. A large crowd had gathered to catch a glimpse of the accused but his head was covered by a piece of light blue cloth and he was bundled into a waiting police car without delay.

Williams' first appearance at the police court was on October 14th. Only evidence of arrest was given, but this included a statement that Williams had made in the police car on the way to Victoria Station. In this, Williams was alleged to have said, "I want you to do this for me. If you can inquire at the station you will find I went there to catch a train just after five on Thursday. I just missed it, and caught one about twenty minutes after. I paid excess fare on a third-class ticket. It was a big chap — the ticket collector. He must remember it. I left quite openly." This, of course, was implying that if he had been guilty of murder, he would have left the town secretly and not in such an open manner. Details were also given of other statements Williams had made including that he had been at the cinema on Wednesday, with his common law wife, Florence, at the time of the murder.

He was then remanded for eight days. Two days after this appearance in court, the body of Inspector Walls was buried after a service at All Souls' Church. The dead man, whose home had been at 40 Cavendish Avenue, had left behind a widow, a son and a daughter.

In the meantime, there had been another development in the case. Edgar Power and Florence Seymour, who was heavily pregnant at the time, had remained under police surveillance. On October

15th, these two had returned to Eastbourne and had been observed walking over the beach, searching for something. After watching them for some time, police took them both into custody and eventually, Florence made a statement which later proved to be highly contentious. The police, meanwhile, returned to the beach and continued the search which Florence and Power had started. In the early hours of the morning, that search paid off when Sergeant Hayman found a revolver.

On October 22nd, Williams made his second appearance at the police court, the case for the Director of Public Prosecutions now being put by Mr Cecil Whiteley. Details of Williams' movements since he arrived in Eastbourne were given, and of his relationship with Florence Seymour. A large number of witnesses were called but still the case was incomplete so proceedings were adjourned until October 26th when it was determined that Williams would be sent for trial.

That trial began at Lewes on December 12th, 1912, before Mr Justice Channell. Williams was defended by Mr Patrick Hastings and Mr C.F. Baker whilst the prosecution case would be put by Sir Frederick Lowe MP, and Mr Cecil Whiteley. The case lasted for three days.

Evidence was given by Dr James Adams, who had examined the body of Inspector Walls. He found a wound between the second and third ribs, on the left side of the chest. The heart bore two wounds, the fatal bullet had entered the upper part of the heart, exited at the bottom and had finally come to rest in the under surface of the right kidney.

Attempts were made to reconstruct the movements of Williams and Florence Seymour. They had apparently arrived in Eastbourne on the afternoon of October 2nd and had taken lodgings with Mrs Lily Daniels at 6 Bolton Road, Williams using the name Seymour and saying that they wanted a bedroom and dining room for a week.

Whilst staying at that address, Mrs and Mrs Seymour visited the cinema a number of times and once remarked to Mrs Daniels that they had seen a film called *Dante*. Mrs Daniels went on to say that during the week, she only ever saw the gentleman wearing a hard felt hat, never a trilby.

On October 9th, the week was up and at around noon, the Seymours left Bolton Road. At the time, Mr Seymour was wearing a grey overcoat and a black bowler hat and announced, "We are going to London and then to St Albans to stay with some friends there."

In fact, Williams did not leave for London, for at 10.00am, before he had even checked out of Mrs Daniels' establishment, Williams had called at 4 Tideswell Road where the door was opened by Miss Annie Frances Jones, a friend of the landlady, Mrs Emily Jane Man. Once again he was asking for accommodation and took a bedroom and sitting room saying, "I may not require them for more than three days. I have a law case on."

Here, Williams used the name of Sinclair and left saying that his wife was at the station and he would return presently with her.

At 12.30pm Williams, alias Sinclair, was back at Tideswell Road, this time with Florence. It was noticed that he was carrying a white cardboard hat box amongst his luggage. Soon after they had deposited their bags in their room, Williams and Florence went out again. By the time they returned, at around 6.15pm, Williams had changed his clothes and was now wearing a dark jacket suit. Fifteen minutes later, the couple were out again and Annie Jones testified that Williams was wearing a trilby hat.

When she had been arrested on Eastbourne beach, and taken to the police station, Florence Seymour had made a full written statement. In this document she had stated that after leaving Tideswell Road at 6.30pm they walked along the front and sat upon a bench near the bandstand. After resting for some ten minutes, she and Williams then walked up to the top end of South Cliff Avenue where again they rested on a seat. After a few minutes, Williams had made some excuse and left her there alone. He was gone for about 30 minutes and when he returned, he was not wearing his hat. They then walked down towards the bathing pool where he told her to throw away a brown paper parcel she had been carrying for him. This parcel contained a length of rope. Later they went to the pictures yet again and on the way there, Williams posted a letter to his brother in London.

The following morning, Williams and Seymour had taken

breakfast at 9.00am, when he had read a couple of newspapers carrying details of the shooting of Inspector Walls. After they had eaten, Florence saw Williams cleaning a revolver in their bedroom but almost as soon as he had finished, he told her he was going to throw it away. At 10.00am they went for a walk near the Redoubt and he mentioned that he was expecting his brother down later that day. They took a stroll along the beach and finally sat on the sand. Williams then took out the revolver, broke it into two pieces and buried these. Then they returned to Tideswell Road where they had lunch at 2.00pm.

If all that testimony was true, then Florence was saying that Williams had left her alone, at the end of South Cliff Avenue, minutes before the murder of Inspector Walls. Now, however, she claimed that her statement had been made under threat of arrest and she had been pressurised not only by the police, but also by Edgar Power.

Florence now said that she and Williams had gone for a walk to the end of South Cliff Avenue, but this had been on the last night they slept at Bolton Road which would be October 8th, not the 9th. On the 9th, they had gone to the pictures where they had arrived at 6.45pm, staying until about 8.30pm. However, this new testimony was seriously damaged by two witnesses. Albert Edward Birkett of the Post Office gave testimony that for a letter to be delivered at an address in London on the morning of October 10th, it would have been posted in Eastbourne on the 9th.

The other witness was Ernest Charles Bowers, a chef, who said that at around 7.00pm on the night of October 9th, he saw a woman who fitted Florence's description, sitting on a seat at the top of South Cliff Avenue. He also said that she had been holding a medium-sized parcel wrapped in brown paper.

The time came for Edgar Power to give evidence. In addition to what he had already said at the police court, Power admitted that after arriving in Eastbourne, he was given £2 by Williams' brother, to hand over. He told of his meeting with Williams at 3.15pm and how, suspicious of what he had read in the newspapers, had asked Williams directly if he was concerned in this murder. Williams replied that he was not, whereupon Power had asked him why he had bothered to send that letter and drag them down to Eastbourne. Williams thought for a few seconds and then muttered that being known to the police, he was sure to be picked up even though he had nothing to do with the killing. Power scoffed that this was ridiculous but Williams was not to be convinced.

After meeting up with Williams, Power was asked to escort Florence back to London and they caught a train after 7.00pm. Williams and his brother had already left, on the 5.30pm train. Arrangements had first been made for the three men to meet up again at a café in Leicester Square.

That meeting took place at 10.30pm Florence having been safely deposited at the Devon Hotel on Vauxhall Road. Power was now to claim that at the meeting in the café, the subject of shooting had come up and he had mocked Williams saying that he couldn't hit a haystack in a lobby. Williams had replied, "That was a good shot anyhow," and when asked to explain what he meant had added, "The shot all this trouble is about."

The three men parted just after midnight, Power having arranged to meet Williams the next day. Meanwhile Power delivered a letter to Florence which Williams had written.

It read, "Darling Florence — Have had bad news. Must go to Paris tomorrow. Have booked room for you at the old hotel. Have you enjoyed yourself at the seaside? Am longing to see you — Love and kisses. George."

Interestingly enough, when he was questioned, Williams' brother would say he had no recollection of any discussion about shooting at the café meeting. It appeared that Power was doing all he could to incriminate John Williams.

Williams did give evidence on his own behalf. The letter delivered to Florence he had written, but only at Power's suggestion and dictation. It made him look as if he was running from something but the truth was that it was Power who had made it look that way. As for the reason for moving from one address to the other in Eastbourne, that was easily explained. It had been his intention to return to London but Florence's condition was rather delicate and on the morning they were to leave, she felt ill. He had already been told that the rooms would be needed for someone else so he took the lodgings at Tideswell Road, just so Florence could have time to recover before she made the tiring journey back to London. He did not shoot Inspector Walls but suspected that a gang who he knew to be in Eastbourne might well be responsible.

This did not, however, explain two other vital pieces of evidence. The gun found on the beach was scientifically tested by Robert Churchill. Bullets fired from it showed markings which matched those on the bullets recovered from Walls' body, and the trilby hat, which was of a rather large size, was traced to a consignment sent to Bournemouth. Williams and Seymour had stayed at Bournemouth only a few months before, using the name Ashton.

The jury retired at 6.15pm on December 14th and it did not take them very long to decide that Williams was guilty as charged. The death sentence having been given, it was now possible to say something more about the history of John Williams. An article in the *News of the World* stated that Williams was not the man's real name and that he had a long criminal record. The son of a parson, Williams had served in the Boer War where he had been wounded. In 1902, he had received a sentence of two years in prison for stealing from a comrade in camp. Later still he served 18 months for robbery and receiving at Kimberley. A third sentence lead to his deportation from South Africa in the spring of 1907.

Back in England, Williams continued in his old familiar ways. In October 1907, at Wells, he got nine months' hard labour for house-breaking. Less than a year later, in September 1908, he got 21 months for burglary and finally, in November 1910, he received 12 months for breaking into a flat in Jermyn Street, London.

Williams' appeal was heard on January 13th, before the Lord Chief Justice, Lord Alverstone, and Justices Ridley and Phillimore. New evidence was given that Williams had asked his landlady at Bolton Road whether he could stay for three more days or not, and details were given of the times that the film *Dante* were shown, but it did not change the basic facts of the case and the appeal was dismissed.

In the interval since the trial itself, Florence Seymour had given birth to Williams' daughter. On the last visit Florence made to see Williams in jail, the child accompanied her and Williams pressed a piece of bread into the little girl's hand saying, "Now nobody can ever say your father never gave you anything."

On the morning of the execution, Wednesday, January 29th, 1913, a dense mist hung over Lewes jail. More than 100 people had gathered along the east wall and as the clock struck 8.00am, the distinct sound of the trap doors could be plainly heard. John George Williams had been despatched by John Ellis, who had been assisted by William Willis, and had been given a drop of 7ft 6ins. Only now was it revealed that John Williams, who had also used the names Seymour, Ashton and Sinclair was in reality George MacKay, thus finally revealing his brother's true name as John William MacKay.

CHAPTER FOUR

DEATH ON THE RAILWAY

ONALD Ashford Palmer, who lived at Ivyholt in Wood's Green, was looking forward to visiting Brighton. The train journey had been pleasant enough thus far and gazing out of the window at the latest stop, he noticed that they had reached Horley. It wouldn't be long now.

It was around 7.20pm on Saturday, April 25th, 1914 as the train pulled out of Horley. It had not gone very far when Donald heard a cry which appeared to come from the next carriage. This cry was followed almost immediately by what seemed to be a laugh but there was no mistaking what came next: a bloodcurdling and prolonged scream.

Donald Palmer lowered the window of his carriage and leaned out to look into the next car. The noises had come from the rear so looking backwards, Donald tried to see what, if anything, was the problem. To his horror he was able to see a woman, lying on the floor of the next carriage. Her back was towards the engine and a man was leaning over her, although Palmer was unable to see what the man was doing to her. Upon closer inspection, he saw that the man was holding a knife in his raised hand, so wasting no time, Donald pulled the communication cord in order to alert the guard that something was wrong.

Alfred Hillman, the guard, saw the signal and quickly looked out of his compartment but could not see anything awry. There obviously was some kind of emergency but whatever it was did not appear to affect the train's safety directly and by now, they were very close to Three Bridges station. Whatever was amiss, Hillman thought that it might be better dealt with at the station. Hillman could not speak with the driver directly, so he signalled by means of a flag, instructing him to continue to Three Bridges which was the next station.

The alarm system in operation on the train was such that once a communication cord had been pulled, the signal was constant until it was re-set. This meant that once it had been tripped, it remained tripped until the matter was dealt with. Back in his carriage, Donald Palmer was not aware of this fact and as far as he was concerned, his attempt to stop the train had been ignored. Seeing that the attack in the next carriage was continuing, Palmer pulled the cord twice more and it was with much relief that he finally felt the train coming to a stop as it reached Three Bridges.

When the train finally stopped, Donald Palmer saw a man jump down from the next carriage. The man was of medium height, perhaps 5ft 7ins tall, but he was stoutly built and looked like he might be very strong. As if this was not enough, though, the man carried in his right hand a knife which was dripping with blood. Donald knew that this man had to be detained at any price.

He followed the man up the platform and saw the guard, Alfred Hillman, approaching him. Quickly Palmer explained what he had seen and Hillman then bravely grabbed the man. For a few seconds the man offered no resistance but he soon began to struggle and tried to pull away from Hillman's grip. At one stage, Palmer had to shoulder-charge the man and push him into the stationary train but the man's strength was such that eventually it took eight men to control him and pin him to the platform.

Alfred Smart, who lived at 121 Shanklin Road, Brighton, was the rear guard on the train. He saw the commotion and ran down to offer his assistance. Once the man had finally been subdued, Smart turned the handle of the carriage the man had left and opened the door.

Inside he finally saw the reason for all this trouble. A woman's body lay on the floor of the carriage, with her head leaning against a window. The floor was saturated with blood and it was obvious that the poor creature had been stabbed and her throat cut. The attack upon her must have been sudden and she could not have put up much of a struggle, for she was still wearing her hat and spectacles.

The assailant was still trying to free himself and from time to time made various statements. William Tiller, the ticket collector at Three Bridges heard him shout, "I hope I shall be strung up and I deserve it. She was a good girl. I did what I wanted and I am satisfied."

It was clear that something had to be done to make sure this man did not escape. The station master, Mr J. Carey Harmer, gave instructions for ropes to be brought and supervised the binding of the still writhing figure. As this was being done, Harmer heard the man say, "You deserve the Victoria Cross for getting me." The job finally being completed, Harmer ordered the man to be taken to the waiting room. It was there that William Tiller heard him say, "Is she dead? If she is I am satisfied. If not, I am not satisfied."

The police and a doctor had been called. In due course, Superintendent Isaac Budgen arrived at Three Bridges, with two constables. He spoke briefly to the man who steadfastly refused to give any information about who the woman was. Meanwhile, Mr Matthews, a doctor from Crawley, had examined the woman and certified that life was extinct. She had been stabbed in three places, twice in the breasts and once in the back, and her throat had been gashed. The knife used had a six-inch long blade, was pointed towards the end and had one serrated edge.

The assailant had by now been taken to East Grinstead police station where he was formally charged with the murder of an unknown woman. When he was searched the police found a quarter bottle of whisky, still more than half full, and two single third-class tickets from Horley to Three Bridges. This indicated that he had boarded the train at Horley and inquiries would be made there. In addition, both the man and the dead woman had been wearing Burnley football colours. The Burnley-Liverpool FA Cup Final had taken place at the Crystal Palace earlier that day — the opening of

Wembley Stadium was still some nine years away — and it was thought that the couple might have been at the big match. Finally the woman, whose body had been taken on a stretcher to the Fox Hotel, was searched and two half-return tickets from Horley to London Bridge were discovered. Eventually it would be discovered that the couple were from London and were simply taking a trip to Sussex.

The police soon managed to identify the man involved in this tragic case, since he was more than happy to talk about himself, although he steadfastly refused to name the woman. The assailant turned out to be 32-year-old Herbert Brooker, who lived at 85 Albert Road, North Woolwich, London and worked as a lock-gate keeper at the Royal Albert Docks. Brooker had previously served in the Royal Navy for 12 years, where he had been a gunner. When Brooker had been on leave, he had lodged with the Mates family at Crawley and this complicated the inquiries somewhat. Mr and Mrs Mates had two daughters and one of these, a deaf and dumb girl named Florence, had been very friendly with Brooker. She was away from home at the time and at first, police believed that Florence Mates was the dead girl. However, when she was found to be alive and well, further inquiries revealed that Brooker had also been friendly with a married woman named Ada Stone.

Ada, who was 29 years old and separated from her husband, had been a waitress at the California Hotel on the Albert Dock Road. That was where she had first met Brooker and the relationship had been maintained when Ada left the hotel and took employment at a restaurant at 120 Powys Street, close to where Brooker worked. Ada's sister, Maud Newsted, who lived at 1 Johnstone Road, East Ham, was traced and it was she who identified the dead woman as Ada Stone.

Brooker had still been talking freely about what he had done. In the cells at East Grinstead, Constable John Andrews was supervising Brooker when he said, "I intended to do it, but did not intend to do it in the train. We had both been drinking and dancing and were pretty well oiled up, when something cropped up and I did the deed. If I had waited another quarter of an hour they would not have collared me — at least not so quick. I have been carrying the knife for this last week down my leg, so that she could not see it."

Brooker's first appearance in court was at the East Grinstead petty sessions on April 27th. The proceedings lasted only seven minutes and about the only drama occurred when the magistrate noticed a man in the corner of the courtroom, holding up a camera in an attempt to get a picture of the accused man. The man was forcibly ejected and Brooker was remanded until May 4th.

On his second appearance, Herbert Brooker was committed for trial. Two days later, on May 6th, the inquest on Ada Stone returned the verdict that she had been murdered by Herbert Brooker. The jury, however, expressed a desire to add a rider that under the circumstances, Alfred Hillman, the guard, was justified in not stopping the train immediately the communication cord was pulled. In certain circles there had been criticism of his actions, and even suggestions that had he acted promptly, the life of the deceased might have been saved. In adding this rider, the inquest jury were exonerating Hillman from any blame.

The trial took place at Lewes on July 7th, 1914, before Mr Justice Darling. Brooker was defended by Mr Barrington Ward, who was assisted by Mr Stormouth Darling, whilst the prosecution case was put by Mr Rowland Harker and Mr St John Hutchinson. Brooker's plea was that he was so drunk at the time of the attack that he had not the reason or the intelligence to appreciate what he was doing. He claimed not to have any recollection of the period in question and that these circumstances should reduce the charge to one of manslaughter.

The prosecution showed that Brooker and Ada had first met at Christmas, 1913. A relationship had developed and marriage had been discussed. Indeed, in one of his early statements to the police, Brooker himself had said that the banns had already been called. The problem, though, was the fact that Ada already had a husband and before she could remarry, he would have to be traced and a divorce arranged. Brooker had said that he would place advertisements to see if the husband could be found but this did not seem to be enough for Ada. She complained about these efforts and also claimed that she never saw enough of Brooker. This, in turn, led to a number of arguments between them.

Detective Sergeant Henry Tarbord of the Metropolitan Police, had visited Ada's lodgings at 41 Rope Yard Rails, Woolwich. He had found a letter there, from Brooker, which admonished Ada for a letter she had apparently sent to him, once more pressing him to do more about getting them together. Emma Annie Fisher, who had a room at the same lodging house as Ada, said that the victim had only moved there on April 23rd, two days before she died, so the letter must have been a very recent one. She also gave evidence that on the morning she died, Ada had told her that her young man had asked her to go to Brighton with him. Ada went on to tell her that she expected to be back home by 2.00pm on the Monday.

Testimony was given that the couple appeared to be very friendly towards each other before the attack took place. Charles Payne, who lived in Crawley, had met the couple in an inn at Horley, around 6.45pm. Brooker was in an excellent mood and bought a glass of whisky for Payne. Charles Adsett was a railway porter at Horley station. He saw Brooker and Ada alight from the London Bridge train at 2.52pm. They were laughing and walked out of the station arm in arm. He saw them again at 7.15pm in the booking office.

They were still on friendly terms and even sang a song together — *You made me love you, I didn't want to do it.* The last time he noticed them they had boarded the Brighton train and were sitting together, facing the engine. Mrs McKay, who lived in Tooting, had been a passenger on that Brighton train. She remarked that when the train reached Earlswood, three ladies who had been in her carriage got out, leaving her alone. When the train arrived at Horley, she saw Brooker with a young woman, walking along the platform and looking into the carriages. She thought at the time that Brooker was very much the worse for drink and hoped he would not choose to get into her carriage. As it was, the couple got into the next carriage. Mrs McKay did not hear any scream, possibly because the noise of the train would have carried it away from her, but she did hear the noise of the bell which rang when the communication cord was pulled.

More telling perhaps was the testimony of Charles Scott of 85 Albert Road, London. He had known Brooker for some eight months and at one stage, the accused man had lodged with Scott's mother.

On Friday, April 24th, Scott met Brooker, who at one stage in the conversation suggested he was thinking of going back to sea. He went on to say that he had quarrelled with his young lady and would have satisfaction, one way or the other.

The jury retired at 5.45pm and after a short deliberation found Brooker guilty of murder but with a recommendation to mercy on account of his previous good character and his service to his country.

Brooker, a sailor who had made several trips on the *Lusitania*, remained in excellent spirits after his death sentence. He firmly believed that the jury's recommendation would carry the day and he would receive a reprieve. When, however, he received news that there was to be no reprieve, not surprisingly he became very depressed indeed.

He did, however, manage to sleep soundly on the night before his execution. Shortly before 6.00am on the appointed day, he rose and ate a breakfast of eggs and bacon. Meanwhile, outside the prison, a crowd estimated to be as large as 200, were gathering in the sunshine.

At 8.00am on Tuesday, July 28th, 1914, Herbert Brooker was hanged at Lewes by John Ellis who was assisted by Thomas Pierrepoint. He was given a drop of exactly 7 feet.

CHAPTER FIVE

A NICE WEEKEND BREAK

THOMAS Upton simply could not understand it. Having come home from work at 3.00pm he found that the curtains in his front room were still drawn. Weren't those lazy so-and-so's up yet?

Thomas entered his house at 57 North Road, Brighton, and pointed out what he had just noticed to his wife, Mary. She confirmed that she had not seen their guests all morning. She had taken them two cups of tea at 8.00am and the woman had shouted her thanks but since then she had seen and heard nothing. Well actually, that wasn't quite true. At 12.30pm Mary had heard two loud reports following very quickly upon each other. She had just assumed it was a car tyre bursting somewhere in the street.

At Thomas' request, Mary knocked on the front room door but there was no reply. Somewhat reluctantly she opened the door. At the sight that confronted her she screamed out for her husband. Although the room was rather dark, Mary could make out two figures sitting in the bed. Both were covered in blood.

Thomas Upton rushed into the room and went to draw back the curtains. As he did so, his foot caught something hard which he accidentally kicked across the room. It was a revolver. Having shed more light into the room, Thomas saw that both occupants of the bed were in their night attire. On a table near the bed stood an empty whisky bottle and near this table, lying on the floor, was a pillow which was saturated with blood. Without hesitation Thomas ran off to fetch a policeman.

The first officer on the scene was Police Constable Frank Miller who saw that both people had been shot. The woman had been hit in the left temple and the man in the right. The bedding was also heavily bloodstained. It looked as if the woman was beyond all help but the man was still alive and indeed, was semi-conscious. Miller summoned further police help and also called for a doctor and an ambulance.

The date was Tuesday, April 7th, 1913, and in those distant days, procedure was perhaps not all it should have been. Another officer, Constable Holman, was soon on the scene and it was he, along with Miller and Mr Upton, who dragged the wounded man out of bed and dressed him. Attempts were then made to revive the woman, until Dr H.C. Maguire arrived and took over. He pronounced the woman dead and accompanied the badly injured man to hospital. By now, he had slipped into unconsciousness and would remain so for eight days.

Thomas and Mary Upton had let out rooms for some time but the arrangements were always rather informal and as a result, they had no idea of the names of their two guests. All they could say was that the couple, whoever they were, had arrived at 12.45pm on Saturday, April 4th, stating that they wished to take a room until the following Tuesday. They had been given the front room on the ground floor.

For the most part the couple had kept to themselves. That same Saturday they had gone out for a few hours and then returned in order to take tea. Later that evening they had been out again and upon their return, the woman told Mary Upton that they had been to the second house at the Hippodrome. They then stayed in bed until midday on Sunday, but by 1.30pm were out again. Returning at 4.30pm, the busy holidaymakers stayed in for a few hours but were out drinking from 7.00pm until 10.00pm when they retired for the night.

On Monday, April 6th, the visitors rose earlier and left the house from 9.30am until noon, when they again took tea. Leaving again at 1.30pm they came back very late. Indeed, Thomas Upton was waiting for them at the front door at 11.15pm. He could see that both were under the influence of drink but was at least pleased that they hadn't needed to rouse him from his bed. Thomas said, "The missus thought you were lost." The couple both laughed and the man replied, "We have had a jolly evening." It was then that the 8.00am cups of tea were ordered for the following morning. After all, it was the day they would be leaving.

When 8.00am came on the Tuesday, Mary Upton had taken up the teas and knocked on the door. From within she heard the woman call out, "All right, thank you." That was the last time anything was heard until the two reports which it was now obvious had been the shots which killed one and badly wounded the other.

Once the mysterious man had been admitted to hospital, his clothing was searched and two letters were found. One was addressed to the coroner of the district and the other to a Mrs Clifford at 72 Isledon Road, Holloway, London. On the back of this second envelope, the same hand had written, "Wife used to live somewhere about Kensington S.W." It was these letters which enabled the police to finally identify the two people. The dead woman was 24-year-old Maud Clifford and the unconscious patient was her estranged husband, 32-year-old Percy Evelyn Clifford, an engineer by trade.

The inquest on Maud opened at Brighton's Town Hall on April 9th, before Mr Bush. Little evidence was taken and the proceedings were adjourned. Meanwhile all efforts were made to revive Percy Clifford and when he did finally recover, he was discharged from hospital and immediately arrested and charged with murder. During his first appearance at the Brighton police court, Clifford was heavily bandaged. He was defended by Mr W.D. Peskett who explained that Clifford had once been a theatrical artiste before serving in the South African war where he had been wounded in the foot but little further evidence was given. The proceedings were adjourned until May 8th.

It was on May 8th that much more information was revealed. The prosecutor, Harold Pearce, stated that the dead woman was a particularly attractive young lady and had first met Percy Clifford in 1909. At the time, and indeed for the next couple of years, Maud earned her living as a prostitute, until, in 1911, on the day before her twenty-first birthday, the couple were married.

For the next year, the newlyweds lived at various addresses in London but there were problems between them, mainly due to the fact that Maud was still a prostitute and Clifford strongly objected to this way of life. He started to beat her and she was often seen to be sporting bruises. Once, Maud even took out a summons against him although he managed to persuade her not to proceed with it. In October 1912, Clifford and Maud finally split up and she moved to a new address which she did not pass on to her husband.

Clifford certainly tried to find his wife. When his clothing had been searched at the hospital, a newspaper cutting had been found. This was an advertisement which had been placed in the personal column and read, "Dimps. Do come, Belgrave, 10 Friday, Brighton, Saturday." Dimps was the nickname Maud had been known by.

Other evidence was given in the police court and at the end of the day's proceedings it was decided to send Clifford to the next Lewes assizes on a charge of wilful murder.

The trial was to last only one day, July 8th, 1914. The case was heard by Mr Justice Darling, with Mr Barrington Ward and Mr Miles Hansell handling the prosecution whilst Clifford was defended by Mr Stormouth Darling. From the very beginning there was drama. As the jury were being sworn one of them announced, "I have a conscientious objection to ..." The judge interrupted impatiently and said, "Oh, yes, let him go."

Percy Clifford, wearing a grey suit and a deep black tie, was placed in the dock and the prosecution case began. Augusta Walton was the mother of the dead girl. She stated that her daughter had married Percy Clifford on January 7th, 1911, at St Pancras Registry Office. The couple had then had various addresses until they parted, whereupon her daughter took a furnished flat in Brixton, not far from where Augusta herself lived. She went on to claim that the reason they had separated was that Clifford never did any work and her daughter was forced to sell herself on the streets in order to bring in some money. She went on to deny that her daughter had continued in this line of work after she had left Clifford and said there was no truth to stories that Maud had been seeing three other men at the same time.

Susan Hughes gave her address as Copenhagen Street, off Caledonian Road, London. She had lived with Clifford from 1903, and in 1909, when Maud came out of prison after serving a short sentence for prostitution, she came to live with them. It soon became clear that Clifford had fallen for Maud and in due course, they moved out and set up home together.

Susan recalled seeing Clifford just before Christmas, 1913. He was very short of money and told her he was no longer living with Maud. He seemed to be very depressed and said he was thinking of finding Maud, shooting her and then killing himself. In January, 1914, Clifford had called on her again. This time he had a revolver in his possession and again he said he wanted to shoot Maud and himself. Concerned for his well-being, Susan allowed him to stay with her for a few weeks. Once he had gone, Susan found the revolver hidden amongst some linen but the very next day, Clifford had returned and asked for it to be given back to him.

It was then that the letters Clifford had written were read out in court. One had been addressed to his mother, Ellen Clifford, of 72 Isledon Road. In one part this read, "I am writing this as I am nearly on the verge of distraction." It went on to allege that his wife was seeing three other men and ended, " What I do now I do not because I am afraid but because nobody will laugh at me and say 'I knew his wife, the way she is going on' I don't want to live any more, I feel quite sick."

The letter to the coroner was in much the same vein. It began, "Sir, I am putting some work in your way." It went on to name the three men Clifford believed his wife was seeing and was signed, "I am sir, Yours sincerely, Percy Evelyn Clifford."

The letter carried a postscript, "I have tried to induce my wife to return to me and live happily, but she says her mother has told her not to, but to be by herself. Please remember that the home and everything else is mine, and I leave it all to my mother to bury us both."

For the defence, a number of witnesses were called. Jacob Carr who lived at 28 George Street, Brighton, had known Clifford and his family for 20 years. He knew Clifford by the nickname 'Oscar' and although he had seen only him three times in the previous 11 years, they remained on good terms. When Clifford and Maud travelled down to Brighton, they met up with Jacob who, on the Monday night, had a few drinks with them in a public house in East Street. He said they seemed to be on the best of terms and Clifford told him they were going back to London the next day.

A more telling witness was Clifford's mother, Ellen Clifford. She stated that her son had been wounded in both the shoulder and the leg whilst serving as a dispatch rider in the Imperial Yeomanry during the Boer War. As a result of those wounds, her son's right hand was paralysed, for which he received a pension of 2s 6d per day. After leaving the Army, Clifford had driven a cab for a short time and had also worked in the betting industry. She went on to describe Maud as a bad tempered woman whom she had once seen throw a milk jug at Clifford, simply because he was a few minutes late coming home. Having said that, Clifford was passionately fond of his wife.

There could, of course, be no denying that Clifford had killed Maud, but was he responsible for his actions? Susan Hughes had already agreed, under cross examination, that Clifford often behaved strangely and sometimes suffered from fits.

Clifford's mother said he was very excitable and had threatened once or twice to throw himself from a window. Finally, when interviewed by the police, Clifford had claimed that he had no memory of anything from the Sunday night before the shooting until he woke up in hospital.

However, all such avenues of mental problems appeared to be closed off by the evidence of Dr Dow from the prison. He agreed that some of the prisoner's answers were slow in coming but that could well be due to his injuries as the bullet he had fired into his brain was still there, it being much too dangerous to remove it. In Dow's opinion, Clifford was perfectly sane, suffering from nothing more than double vision.

The jury retired at 2.33pm, returning at 2.58pm to announce that

Clifford was guilty. An appeal was submitted and this was heard on July 27th before the Lord Chief Justice, Sir Rufus Daniel Isaacs, and the Justices Coleridge and Avory. The defence asked for leave to call further medical evidence but permission was refused and the appeal was dismissed.

On the morning appointed for his execution, Clifford enjoyed a good breakfast, asking for three eggs, two rashers of bacon and a pint of beer to wash it down. As he ate, John Ellis and his assistant, who was never named, waited to perform their terrible task.

Tuesday, August 11th, 1914, was, by all accounts, a beautiful sunny day with no breeze at all to stir the trees. A few days earlier, Britain had gone to war with Germany and there were apparently very few people waiting outside the east wall of Lewes prison as the clock began to strike at 8.00am. Those who were there swore that they heard the dull thud as the scaffold doors were thrown open and Percy Clifford was hanged. It was the tenth and last execution at Lewes since the prison had opened in 1873.

CHAPTER SIX

DEATH ON THE BEACH

THIRTEEN-year old William Weller from Lewisham was enjoying his holiday in Eastbourne. He and his mother had already seen many of the sights and now, on the afternoon of Friday, August 20th, 1920, his mother had promised him a picnic on the beach.

William would never be sure exactly what time the picnic finished or what time he and his mother were making their way back to the guest house.

What he did remember is that some time between 3.00pm and 4.00pm as he played amongst the shingle, he fell over a black object sticking up out of the pebbles.

Picking himself up, William went to examine his discovery and recoiled when he saw that it was a woman's foot. He dashed to his mother who, after confirming for herself her son's grisly find, rushed back to the guest house at 32 Manifold Road, and told the landlord, Mr Clement James Lamb, what they had seen.

One might reasonably think that there would be some urgency about the possibility of a body being buried on the beach, but, remarkably, the Wellers and the Lambs sat down to tea before Clement Lamb and William Weller returned to the beach and located the protruding foot. In fact, it was around 6.45pm when Lamb arrived, scraped away some of the shingle and confirmed that there was a woman there. He guarded the body whilst William ran for a policeman.

By 8.00pm, Inspector Ernest Cunnington, alerted by a telephone call from a constable, had arrived at the murder scene, a desolate spot to the north-east of the town, an area of shingle and scrub known as the Crumbles. The body lay in a hollow in the pebbles and the scene was well protected from prying eyes along the cinder track that led to Langney and Pevensey, and the small mineral railway that ran along the top end of the beach, parallel to it.

The body was that of a young woman, and she was lying on her left side. Her right leg was fully extended, as was her left arm. The right arm was bent under the left armpit and she was fully clothed apart from the fact that her right shoe was missing and her skirt had been folded back high on to her hips, exposing her right leg as far as the thigh. A black straw hat, somewhat crushed, covered the face and when this was removed, the police saw that the poor woman's head had been badly battered.

Other officers were called to the beach, including Superintendent Willard. Once the body had been removed to the mortuary, Willard carefully scraped away the pebbles where the head had lain, to discover that blood had soaked into the shingle to a depth of 18 inches. There was no identification on the body and the only other clues were a bunch of keys, some 500 yards away, and a large ironstone brick, heavily bloodstained, which it appeared, had been the murder weapon.

The body was first examined by the police surgeon for the district, Dr Ernest Stanley Radford Cadman. He arrived at the beach some time after 10.20pm and as he made his examination he actually sat on the ironstone brick. Dr Cadman noted a number of cuts and small puncture wounds on the head, especially around the lips. He also saw that some teeth had been knocked out. The woman, whoever she was had apparently received a blow which stunned her and knocked her to the ground. Then, whilst she lay there, helpless, the assailant had picked up the heavy brick and dropped it on to her head before covering the body with shingle. The Eastbourne police wasted no time in calling in the expertise of Scotland Yard and on August 21st,

Chief Inspector Mercer travelled down to Sussex. Meanwhile, the unfortunate woman had been identified.

Reports of the crime published in the local papers, together with a description of the woman and the clothes she had been wearing, including a green coat with a fur collar, led Mrs Ada Wynniatt to come forward. Ada ran a small hotel at 393 Seaside, a curiously named thoroughfare that runs parallel to the sea front. She reported that one of her tenants was missing and had not been seen since the afternoon of Thursday, August 19th. This young woman had worn a distinctive green coat and once Ada had viewed the body, she was sure that it was indeed her guest, Miss Munro.

Irene Violet Munro was 17 years and nine months of age and lived with her mother in Queen's Gate, South Kensington. A shorthand typist, Irene had been working for a company in Oxford Street and had hoped to go on holiday to Scotland, with her mother, to see her grandmother. Irene's mother had just gone up to that beautiful part of the country, but Irene had only discovered that she could take a holiday a few days before and by then it was too late to find accommodation in the north. As a result, she had chosen to go to Eastbourne instead and had arrived at 393 Seaside on the afternoon of Monday, August 16th.

Although Irene had taken rooms at Ada Wynniatt's house, these were actually occupied on the first night, so Ada arranged for Irene to spend that Monday at a friend's house: Martha Balcombe's establishment at 1 Norman Cottages, Worthing Road. Martha later confirmed that Irene was with her that one night, going to bed around 9.30pm and leaving after breakfast on the Tuesday, at around 10.00am.

On Tuesday, August 17th, Irene had taken her luggage to Ada Wynniatt's house. She was in and out at various times that day: leaving at 11.00am returning at 1.00pm and then going out again around 2.00pm. Irene returned for the night at 9.30pm, telling Ada that she was going up to her room to write a letter. On the Wednesday, August 18th, Irene was out again after breakfast. She came back to Seaside at some time between 1.00pm and 2.00pm but was back out by 3.00pm. She was late home that night, not getting back until 10.00pm and in fact popped out again, albeit briefly, to post a letter.

On Thursday, the day she vanished, Irene had left at 10.30am saying that she was going to Hampden Park. Whether she went there or not was never discovered but by 2.00pm Irene was back to change her clothes. The weather was quite bright and Irene left again at 2.45pm. However, just a few minutes later, she was back saying that it was rather chilly and after picking up her green coat, Irene walked out of 393 Seaside, never to return.

Although she was somewhat concerned that night, Ada had heard from Irene that she had some friends in Brighton so she believed that Irene might have visited them and stayed there for the night. Ada became somewhat more concerned when she hadn't heard anything by Friday night and had determined to go to the police the following morning, unless Irene turned up for breakfast. When on Saturday, there was still no sign of Irene and the newspapers were full of stories about the body on the beach, Ada knew she could wait no longer.

In fact, Ada Wynniatt's statement led the police to two more witnesses. Frederick George Rogers was a builder and decorator and at this time he was painting 393 Seaside, assisted by his apprentice, Charles George Verrall. These two had spoken to Irene a couple of times whilst she had been staying at Mrs Wynniatt's and they recalled a conversation with her on the day she disappeared.

Both men saw Irene return for her green coat on the afternoon of August 19th, and Rogers saw her leave the house and walk off in the direction of Hampden Park, to the west of the town. A few minutes later, though, Charles Verrall saw Irene walk past again, now heading in the opposite direction, towards the Crumbles, and now she was in the company of two men. Verrall later became rather confused over the ages of the two men, sometimes saying that they were middle-aged and sometimes stating that they were in their mid-20s, but he was able to give reasonable descriptions of the clothes they had been wearing.

The publicity the case received caused other possible witnesses to come forward, including a group of railway workers who had been on the Crumbles on the afternoon of August 19th. Charles Standen,

Samuel Hancock, his brother, Arthur Hancock, Martin Funnell and Horace Marchant, were enjoying a tea-break just before 3.00pm. On the beach, not very far from where Irene's body was subsequently discovered, lay an old upturned railway carriage which the workmen used as a hut. These five men were sipping their tea when they saw, coming from the direction of Eastbourne, two men and a woman.

The woman was walking arm-in-arm with the shorter of the two men and, as they strolled, they suddenly came across a small kitten. The woman crouched down to stroke the kitten and after a minute of so, one of the men picked up the animal and carried it with them as they continued the journey. The group passed very close to the railway carriage and as they did, the man with the kitten dropped it into the hut, saying, "There's a kitten for you." Shown photographs of the dead woman, all five men swore that this was the woman they had seen with the two men, one of whom was carrying a walking stick with some kind of animal's head as a handle.

On August 23rd, the inquest on Irene Munro opened at the Town Hall before Mr G. Vere Benson. By now, Irene's mother, Flora, had arrived in the town and she gave brief details of her daughter. Irene had been an only child and Flora had last seen her alive on August 14th when she had gone up to Scotland. She had since received a letter from her daughter, postmarked Eastbourne and dated August 18th, saying how much she was enjoying her stay but pointing out that she was a little short of money. Part of the letter detailed some of Irene's movements, "I went to Beachy on Tuesday night and lost myself. I did not get back until nearly 11 o'clock. Yesterday I went to Pevensey Bay, walked there and back ..." Mrs Munro was also able to state that her daughter had with her a faded blue handbag. Since this had not been recovered, it was now assumed that robbery was a possible motive for the murder, even though Irene must have only had a few pounds on her when she died. The proceedings were then adjourned until September 6th.

On August 24th, the funeral of Irene Munro had been due to take place but it was postponed at the last minute so that further examination of the body could take place. The same day, Irene's clothing was placed on to a dummy and photographed in the hope that the pictures might jog someone's memory. More importantly, it was announced that the police had two men in custody, helping them with their inquiries. At the time, the names of these two men were not revealed because of course, they had as yet not been charged with any offence, but they were 19-year-old Jack Alfred Field and 29-year-old William Thomas Gray.

Jack Field was an ex-navy man who had been discharged in February 1920 and now lived with his parents in Susans Road. William Gray was not British and had first come to England when he had been serving in the South African Heavy Artillery. He had been discharged from the Army in October 1917, as medically unfit and lived in Longstone Road, with his wife.

There were two witnesses which led to police first becoming interested in Field and Gray. George Blackmer was a bus conductor and he had travelled to the Archery Tavern, close to Irene's lodgings in Seaside, at around 2.45pm. On the same bus were Field and Gray, two men he knew quite well. In fact, Field had actually spoken to George because he was wearing a brand new uniform and Field joked that he was too good to speak to them now. George saw the couple get off the bus in Seaside and soon afterwards, an attractive girl walked up to them and said, "Hullo Jack ..." The three then walked off together, towards the Crumbles.

Charles Dyer had also seen Field and Gray — although he knew Gray only by name — walking past St Agnes's Church with a dark haired woman between them. The woman was hanging on Gray's arm and Dyer, knowing him to be a married man, said that he 'should be shot'. The problem was that these two witnesses could not positively identify the woman as being Irene Munro. However, if Field and Gray were put into an identification parade, perhaps the railway workmen, who had identified Irene as being the girl on the beach, would now be able to say that these were the men they had seen with her.

The identification parades took place on August 25th, but none of the railwaymen could pick out either Field or Gray. After further questioning, both suspects were released on August 26th, although the police did keep a walking stick with a dog's head belonging to

Field's father but often carried by Jack, and a hat belonging to Gray.

Meanwhile, on the same day that the abortive identification parades took place, Irene Munro's body was finally laid to rest in the small cemetery at Langney Point, her grave overlooking the spot on the beach where she had been brutally murdered.

The police tried every avenue of investigation. On September 1st, a local medium, Miss Goebel, held a seance on the beach and made a series of disclosures which matched facts in the case not revealed to the public. Another seance was organised and Miss Goebel claimed that Irene had been murdered by a married man because she had threatened to expose him. Unfortunately, this information, although quite detailed, did not lead to any arrests. However, soon afterwards, a witness came forward who was finally to break the case.

William Putland was a stoker in the Royal Navy and had been on leave in Eastbourne at the time of the murder. He had returned to his ship on August 23rd but had subsequently read of the murder and approached his commanding officer with some information he had. As a result of his statement he was sent back to Eastbourne, where he repeated his story to the police. Following this, he was escorted along the sea front where he saw two men at a coffee stall and identified them as the men he had seen with Irene Munro.

William Putland said he had first seen Irene Munro on August 17th, whilst he was with his cousin. Irene had been lying on the beach and he noticed her because she was particularly attractive. At the time she was wearing her green coat, a black straw hat and black stockings.

The following day, Putland saw Irene again, close to St Andrew's Church but now she was with two men. The day after that, August 19th, William saw these three again. He was now with a friend, Frederick Wells, outside the Arlington Arms and he pointed them out to Wells who said he knew one of the men by sight. At a loose end and with nothing else to do, Putland and Wells followed the two men and Irene along the cinder path near the Crumbles. They saw them meet up with a kitten and one of the men pick up the kitten and drop it into a railway hut. Later that same day, Putland saw the two men again. There was now no sign of Irene.

When Frederick Wells was spoken to, he agreed with Putland's story. He, too, was taken along the sea front by the police and he, too, picked out the man he knew by sight. Between them, Putland and Wells had positively identified Jack Field and William Gray. On September 5th, both men were arrested and charged with the murder of Irene Munro.

There were a number of appearances at the police court, the first of these being on September 6th. Both of the accused men seemed to be quite indignant about being in custody and on various occasions both made vociferous complaints. On September 9th, for instance, told that they would be remanded again, Field said, "I think it's really time they went on with it. I've been hanging around for a fortnight and I'm fed up with it."

At a subsequent hearing, Field was airing his thoughts again: "I should like to say I think it is about time some of you knew what you were doing. We have now been here for 16 or 17 days. We were pulled up once, we were detained for almost two days, and asked to make a statement as to where we were. We made a statement and the statement was proved correct, and we were released on that. Now we are charged again on the same charge. You have no evidence against us at all. There is nothing against us. Mr Mercer said he had a sailor to identify us. I have never seen him, neither has my friend. Nobody has identified us ..."

By September 23rd, both the accused men had managed to obtain legal representation. Field was represented by Mr Robert Brennan and Gray by Mr Herbert Baron. The following day, the inquest returned a verdict of wilful murder against Field and Gray and by the end of that same month, both men had been sent for trial.

The trial of Field and Gray opened at Lewes, before Mr Justice Avory, on December 13th, 1920. The Crown lined up three barristers: Mr C.F. Gill, Sir Henry Curtis Bennett and Mr Cecil Whiteley. Field was defended by Mr James Dale Cassels and Mr G.P. Robinson, whilst Gray's team were Sir Edward Marshall-Hall and Mr John Flowers. The jury consisted of men only and the proceedings lasted until December 17th.

On the very first day there was drama in court. The prosecution having made their opening speeches, the court adjourned for lunch and upon reassembling, it was announced that one of the jurors had been taken ill. The sick man was attended to by two doctors before being discharged. Another juror was selected, the entire jury re-sworn and the proceedings started anew.

Dorothy Ducker was a barmaid at the Albermarle public house and she had known both Field and Gray as customers ever since she had been transferred from the upstairs bar to the public bar which they frequented. On August 19th, they had first gone into the Albermarle at a few minutes after noon. They had stayed until 1.30pm and during that period of 90 minutes, Gray had asked her to go to the pictures with him, but she had refused.

At 1.45pm the two men returned, staying until 2.30pm. Both men were drinking bitter and complained that they had little money, Gray asking for a free pint. Dorothy had, of course, refused this request whereupon Gray had added that they would have money by that evening.

That was certainly true, for at 6.45pm they were back again and seemingly flush with cash. Gray asked Dorothy and another barmaid, Elsie Finlay, to have a drink with them, Field ordered a Bass and Gray had a Guinness, both drinks being more expensive than the usual draught bitter. Dorothy was also offered a cigarette and commented on the fact that they were expensive Egyptian Abdulla rather than the usual Woodbines.

Dorothy did not see Field and Gray again until August 26th when they admitted that they had been held by the police in connection with the murder on the Crumbles. Until this point, Dorothy had only known the two as Billy and Jack and she told the two men that she had just been reading about their arrest in the newspaper. Gray snatched the paper off Dorothy, scanned the article quickly and then marched out of the pub without comment. That same night, Dorothy had visited the Hippodrome and noticed Field and Gray behind her in relatively expensive seats.

Elsie Finlay backed up Dorothy's testimony and added that Gray paid for all the drinks and was seen buying other rounds for friends he saw through the night. Elsie had known both men for much longer than Dorothy and said that they had been coming into the public bar for perhaps ten or 12 weeks.

William Knowles also knew both men and he had met them outside the Pier Hotel on the night of August 30th. Saying that it was a while since he had seen them, Gray told him that they had been hauled up over the Crumbles affair. Field added, "Yes, we were down that way in the afternoon with a girl, but since she's come forward and proved it." Unfortunately for Field and Gray, this latter statement simply was not true.

Both men had given the same basic outline of their movements on the afternoon of August 19th, the day that Irene disappeared. Field had called at Gray's house and they had left there together at 2.05pm. From there they walked along Seaside, over the Crumbles and along to Pevensey Bay where they visited the castle. They stayed there about 15 minutes and met up with a young lady they knew, Hilda Baxter. At 4.00pm they all left Pevensey together and walked back to Eastbourne, arriving there at 5.10pm. If this was true then they were not the men seen with Irene Munro.

Hilda Baxter, though, did not support this alibi. Hilda was a scullery maid and although she admitted that she knew Field and Gray, she had only met them for the first time at around 8.30pm on the day Irene's body had been discovered, when she went out to post a letter. The two men had said good evening to her and asked to escort her home as it was quite late. She saw them once more, on August 22nd, when Field mentioned that on the day of the murder he and his friend had been to Pevensey, but she certainly had not been with them. In fact, Hilda Baxter had never even been to Pevensey. Faced with this, Field said that he must have been mistaken about Miss Baxter, but persisted in his claim that he and Gray were at Pevensey when Irene Munro was seen on the beach with two men.

There was also evidence that Field and Gray had sought to escape from the Eastbourne area. Sergeant Herbert Hubble of the Royal West Kent Regiment testified that on the morning of August 21st, both men had approached him at Summerdown Camp, and asked to speak to the recruiting sergeant as they wished to join up. Hubble advised them to go to Chichester and enlist there.

Medical evidence was then called. The post-mortem had been carried out by Dr James Adams and Dr Reginald Robert Elworthy. They testified that Irene's lower jaw was broken with two teeth broken inwards. The upper jaw was more badly damaged, with four teeth being completely broken away. The injuries to the head were consistent with an early blow, sufficient to stun, and then the ironstone brick being dropped from a height of a few feet. However, Irene, although not a virgin, had not been raped. The clothing was disarranged but it was likely that this was caused by Irene being dragged deeper into the hollow after she had been stunned.

Some of the most damning evidence was given by Archibald Thomas Darrington. Archibald was a native of Eastbourne but had been arrested for stealing a bicycle and on September 12th, was being held on remand at Maidstone prison. It was on that day, whilst on exercise, that Gray approached him and after finding out that Darrington had been in Eastbourne on the day of the murder, asked him to say that they had been together that day. Darrington refused to help, saying that he did not want to get into more trouble, but Gray would not be dissuaded. A few days later, Gray approached him again and asked him if he knew the name of the sailor who was to give evidence against them. Darrington said he did, whereupon Gray asked Darrington to say that he had seen the sailor struggling with the girl on the Crumbles beach.

Field went into the dock to give his testimony. The money he and Gray appeared to be splashing about after the murder was easily accounted for. He had drawn 29s unemployment benefit on the morning of August 19th, and Gray had an Army pension which he had also drawn that day. They were not guilty of murder and had never even met Irene Munro. Gray did not go into the box but in his statement he denied that he had ever engaged the convict Darrington in conversation. The prosecution, though, called two warders, Herbert Hillier and Robert James Jukes, both of whom said that they had warned Gray and Darrington about speaking whilst on exercise.

After listening to 53 prosecution witnesses, and hearing Field's story of what he said had happened, the jury retired, at 2.05pm on December 17th. They returned at 3.08pm having found both men guilty but recommending them to mercy because in their opinion, the crime had not been premeditated.

The appeal opened on January 17th, before the Lord Chief Justice, Sir Rufus Isaacs and Justices Bray and Acton. The proceedings lasted two days and had the distinction of allowing new evidence to be called.

Field was the first to give evidence on his own behalf. He now admitted that he had lied at the trial and had known Irene Munro. He and Gray had first met Irene on August 14th whilst they were walking along the sea front. After some discussion she asked them to accompany her to Beachy Head and after returning late, they all arranged to meet up again on the Thursday.

On August 18th, they met Irene at around 2.30pm. They went for a walk and Field said that she seemed to want to be alone with Gray. However, at the end of the day, all three arranged to meet up on Friday afternoon. On the Friday, August 19th, he and Gray did catch the bus to the Archery, met up with Irene and went for a walk along the Crumbles. They did see the kitten and all the evidence given by the various witnesses about that encounter was true. However, very soon afterwards, Gray made it plain that he wanted to be left alone with Irene. Field, taking the hint, walked on to Pevensey alone.

Returning later, Field saw Gray coming towards him and asked him what had happened to Irene. Gray had replied that they had argued and she had gone home. Later that same day, Field noticed that Gray had more money and asked him where he had got it from. Gray told him to shut up and mind his own business. A couple of days later, when the news of the murder was plastered all over the newspapers, Gray had admitted that he had struck Irene and left her on the beach after covering her with shingle. It had been Gray's idea to join the Army and throughout the entire period up to and including the trial, Field had supported his friend's story because he didn't want Gray's wife to be hurt and because Gray had promised him that if they got into serious trouble, he would own up and clear Field.

When it was time for Gray to give evidence, he denied all of Field's story and said that in fact it was Field who had admitted to him that he was responsible for Irene's death. According to Gray, after they had been sentenced to death at Lewes, the two prisoners had been held in the station master's office at the railway, waiting for the train to take them to London. Field apologised for lying in court and admitted that he had struck Irene and left her for dead. He had left Field alone with Irene at around 3.30pm, had not set foot on the Crumbles and any witnesses who said they saw him with her after that time, were either mistaken or lying. As for the money, after the murder had taken place, he had stolen a wallet from the swimming baths that same morning. Gray also denied having any conversation with Darrington at Maidstone prison.

Gray's story was soon shown to be false. All four prison warders who had been with Field and Gray at Lewes station swore that no conversation had taken place between the two men and James Woolgar, an attendant at Eastbourne baths, said that no complaint of a missing wallet had been received on August 19th. The judges decided that on the testimony given, there was no reason to discriminate between the two men and both appeals were dismissed.

What was the truth in the death of Irene Munro? On the evidence of the many witnesses and Field himself, both men met Irene Munro on the day that she died and both men were with her close to the spot where her body was discovered. Gray's story had been shown to be a tissue of lies, meaning that it was almost certainly he who struck Irene in the face, rendered her unconscious and then dropped a large brick on to her head, killing her instantly. But was Field present at the time and did he play any active part in the crime? What is certainly true is that knowing his friend was involved, Field lied for him, covered up for him and maintained his story until the appeal. He may well have been equally guilty but if he did tell the truth about walking with Irene and Gray on the beach, he may well have also been telling the truth about being on the way to Pevensey at the time Gray was battering Irene Munro to death.

It was too late to save the life of either man. At 8.00am on the morning of Friday, February 4th, 1921, Jack Alfred Field and William Thomas Gray met again for the first time since the appeal when they stood side by side on the gallows at Wandsworth prison. There they were hanged by Thomas Pierrepoint, who was assisted by Robert Baxter and William Willis. The governor of the prison, Major Read, reported that neither man made any confession before he died.

Jack Field, though, did leave a message. Seconds before he was executed he handed a letter to the chief warden. This letter thanked him and all his staff for their kindness to him whilst he had been in the condemned cell. It ended, "...I have no complaint to make about anything or anyone."

CHAPTER SEVEN

LEFT LUGGAGE

JESSIE Mahon knew her husband well. In fact, she knew him far too well for her own peace of mind. Ever since they were married on April 6th, 1910, there had been problems and by the end of April, 1924, she had convinced herself that Patrick Herbert Mahon was involved in yet another extra-marital affair.

Like many other suspicious wives, Jessie decided that she needed some hard evidence if she was going to face her husband and demand the truth, so, she searched his clothes. About the only thing that might have yielded further information was a cloakroom ticket from Waterloo station. What could he have possibly deposited in the left luggage that he didn't want her to see? The only way to find out was to redeem the luggage and see what it contained.

Jessie Mahon did not see herself playing the role of detective and thought it would be better if she got a friend of hers, who happened to be a former policeman, to collect the bag for her. The ticket was duly handed in and a small Gladstone bag received. Once the bag was opened, though, the friend realised that he might well be dealing with something much more serious than a mere affair. The bag was put back into the left luggage, the ticket returned to Mahon's pocket, and the police contacted. It was just after 7.00pm on May 1st, when Chief Inspector Percy Savage and Detective Sergeant Frew, arrived at Waterloo station. They, too, checked the contents of the bag and then Savage ordered a watch to be kept on the cloakroom.

The police vigilance was soon to be rewarded. At 6.40pm on May 2nd, Patrick Mahon handed in his ticket, number J2413, to the attendant, Henry George Boniface. Having collected the bag, Mahon headed for the York Road exit but was stopped Detective Mark Thompson, and taken into custody. It was 8.30pm by the time Chief Inspector Savage arrived at Kennington Road police station to interview him.

At first Mahon said that he was unable to open the bag as he had lost the key. In order for the investigation to be conducted properly, Savage escorted Mahon, and the Gladstone bag, to Scotland Yard, arriving there at some time between 9.00pm and 9.30pm.

Here Mahon confirmed that the bag was indeed his, although he still claimed not to have the key. Of course, Mahon was only delaying the inevitable and the police simply removed the straps and the bag was opened by pulling the sides out, thereby revealing its contents.

The first item to be removed was a pair of lady's bloomers, heavily bloodstained. Also inside were two pieces of white silk, also heavily stained, a blue silk scarf with blood on it, and a sharp cook's knife. Finally, the bag yielded a brown canvas bag with the initials E.B.K., stamped on it, and a bath towel. All the items in the bag had been liberally doused with a proprietary disinfectant called Sanitas.

Asked to explain how these items had come to be bloodstained, Mahon replied, "I am fond of dogs and I suppose I have carried home meat for the dogs in the bag." Savage then pointed out that in his opinion the stains were human blood and Mahon would be detained pending further investigations. At this Mahon fell silent, placed his head in his hands, and seemed to be deep in thought.

For a full 15 minutes he was quiet and then he said softly, "I wonder if you can realise how terrible a thing it is for one's body to be active and for one's mind to fail to act." He then fell silent again for 30 minutes before saying, as if to reassure the officers, "I am considering my position." Finally, after another 15 minutes of deliberation, Mahon announced, "I suppose you know everything. I will tell you the truth." He then went on to make a long statement which was taken down and later signed by him.

As a result of what Mahon had said, Chief Inspector Savage

contacted his colleagues in Sussex and on Saturday, May 3rd, he travelled down to the Royal Oak Hotel at Pevensey where he met Inspector Thomas Hall and Inspector William McBride. These three officers travelled on to a bungalow known as the Officer's House, at Langney Bungalows, Westham. The scene was close to the Crumbles beach at Eastbourne, not far from where Field and Grey had murdered Irene Munro in 1920.

The door to the bungalow was locked, but Savage had found the key amongst Mahon's property. A cursory search showed a sitting room and three bedrooms, the third of which was locked. When this door was unlocked and opened, the first thing Savage and the others noticed was a most offensive smell. The window blinds were drawn and these were pulled up so that light could flood into the room.

At the foot of the bed was a large trunk which, like the canvas bag, carried the initials E.B.K. This was opened and the first thing the police noticed was a shoe tray holding three pairs of shoes and a pair of slippers. When this was taken out, four parcels were discovered and it was found that each of these contained human remains.

Many other clues were found in that initial search. A saw lay to the right of the fireplace and two empty tins which had once contained Sanitas were discovered. In the dining room was a two-gallon saucepan which was two-thirds full of a reddish fluid. To the right of the fireplace stood a three-legged coal cauldron, one leg of which had been bent underneath. A large quantity of charred human bones lay in the fireplace and in the scullery there were more bones in a dustpan, a coal box, a bath, a bowl and a saucer. In all, there were hundreds of pieces of flesh, skin and bone to be collected together.

That same evening, Chief Inspector Savage returned to London, and at 8.00pm he again interviewed Patrick Mahon. As a result of that interview, Mahon made a further statement amending some dates and times from the first, but largely containing the same information. Earlier in the day, Mahon had spoken at length to Detective Sergeant Frew who had been left to guard him. Frew made copious notes in his pocket book and later read those notes in court. They made chilling reading.

"I boiled some of the flesh in a pot. I burnt the head in an ordinary fire. It was finished in three hours. The poker went through the head when I poked it. The next day I broke the skull and put pieces in a dustbin. The thigh bone I burnt. It is surprising what a room fire will burn. There is one in the back sitting-room and one in the front sitting-room. You will find some bones there. Her clothes are still there. The reason for going for the bag was because I was returning to the bungalow that night to get some more flesh ... It was ghastly. I used the silk and cloth to wrap the pieces of flesh in, boiled flesh. The silk was in the trunk and the bloodstains will be through the body which I put in there." Yet the man who made this statement was denying that he had committed murder. It had all been an accident, he said, and the poor woman he had disposed of was Emily Beilby Kaye.

Emily Kaye had been 38 years old when she had died, having been born on November 26th, 1885. The family had been rather unlucky in general. Both parents had died 15 years before and two brothers had also passed on. Emily's only surviving close relative was a sister, Mrs Elizabeth Beilby Harrison, who lived at 12 Albert Road, East Hale, Cheshire. Mrs Harrison, who had last seen Emily on April 5th, later identified a large number of items as having belonged to her sister. She also said that Emily had told her that she was engaged to be married and that the object of her affections was a man named Patrick Derrick Patterson. There was also a suggestion that Pat, as he preferred to be known, and Emily would be emigrating to South Africa once the knot had been tied.

Mahon, meanwhile, was ready to give the police more information. On May 5th he made further detailed statements to Chief Inspector Savage who, on that same day, handed Mahon over to the custody of Superintendent David Sinclair of the East Sussex Police. Mahon was then driven down to Hailsham, where he made his first appearance in the police court at 3.45pm on May 6th, being represented by Mr C.W. Mayo of Eastbourne. Mahon was remanded until May 15th.

Previous to this, on May 4th, there had been further visitors to the bungalow on the Crumbles. A horrified Sir Bernard Spilsbury had arrived to find police officers picking up pieces of decaying human flesh with their bare fingers. This occurrence would lead, at Spilsbury's suggestion, to the introduction of the 'murder bag' for all future cases.

Spilsbury's examination of the scene was masterful to say the least. In all he found something between 900 and 1,000 pieces of bone, together with such other gruesome items as a saucer containing solid human fat, boiled flesh in a saucepan, and body portions including part of the left pelvis and the right shoulder. It was this last section which was to prove most interesting, for Spilsbury found a severe bruise on that shoulder. He was able to say that it had been inflicted during life and shortly before death. Was this connected with Emily Kaye's demise?

Most of the internal organs were found and Spilsbury was able to say that the dead woman had been strong and healthy. She had also been pregnant. Further, since there were no duplicate body portions, there was only one victim represented. Briefly, Spilsbury's conclusion was that the police were looking at an adult female, pregnant for between one and three months, who had been cut to pieces by means of a sharp plain knife and the bones divided by means of the saw they had discovered at the scene.

There was one more crucial fact. Mahon was claiming that Emily's death had been accidental. During a struggle, she had struck her head on a cauldron used as a coal-scuttle and died almost instantly. Conspicuously, no trace of the head could be found, so an accurate cause of death was impossible to determine. Spilsbury, however, was able to confirm that she could not have died in the way that Mahon had described. No matter how hard Emily struck her head against the cauldron, the fracture produced by that single blow would, at the very least have taken an hour or so to kill her. An instantaneous death was impossible. It was much more likely that Emily had been deliberately battered to death.

At the same time, John Webster, the senior official analyst to the Home Office, was examining various items. He examined, amongst other things, pieces of the doors, pieces of carpet, an axe, a saw, a knife, the coal cauldron and the items found in the Gladstone bag deposited at Waterloo. He found only two small spots of blood on the cauldron, close to the bent leg, something simply not compatible with Mahon's description of the event. The carpet had been cleaned but tested positively for human blood. The knife and saw also showed definite reactions, as did the items in the Gladstone bag.

His findings were further indication that the story Mahon was telling was simply not true.

Patrick Mahon's account was a relatively simple one. In effect, he had first met Emily Kaye in the summer of 1923. Mahon's own wife had been the company secretary to Consols Aerated Ltd, where he had been employed first as a salesman and later as a manager. In May 1922, the company had gone into liquidation and the firm of Robertson Hill & Co had been appointed as receivers. The matter was handled by one of the members, Mr Hobbins, whose clerk was Emily Kaye. As a result of the winding up, Patrick Mahon and Emily Kaye had worked together and in due course they started to see each other. Emily, according to Mahon, was fully aware that he was a married man.

The affair continued and soon Emily was trying to bring them even closer together. She suggested to Mahon a business deal involving the purchase of some French francs. Apparently she knew of a way to make money by speculating in this currency and sought to involve him in the transactions. He agreed and handed over £125 of his own money, for her to invest on his behalf.

In February, Emily gave Mahon a £100 note which he later cashed at the Bank of England, changing it into notes of smaller denomination. He admitted that he endorsed the note with a false name and address since he was a little suspicious about the currency deals and did not want them to be traced back to him. Eventually, three such notes were handed over and the proceeds shared between Emily and himself.

All this time, Emily was busily trying to persuade Mahon to live with her on a permanent basis. He, of course, resisted this as he was a married man but eventually Emily told him of an advertisement she had seen, for a bungalow near Eastbourne. She suggested that it would be a good idea if they went down there for a few days so that they could see what married life would be like together. They called this their love experiment.

George Bell Muir lived at 55 Greencoat Place, Ashley Gardens, London. He and his wife were close friends of Mrs Hutchinson who owned the Officer's House, and she told him that he could do as he wished with the property whilst she spent some time abroad. It was Mr Muir who, on April 4th, placed the advertisement in the *Daily Telegraph*, offering the bungalow for rent and he agreed that on April 5th, Mahon, who was using the name Waller, had come to see him about the matter. Eventually, 'Waller' had agreed to take the bungalow from April 11th to June 6th, at a rent of three and a half guineas a week. When asked to explain why he had taken the lease for such a long time when Miss Kaye had only suggested a few days for their 'love experiment', Mahon replied that his wife had been ill and he thought that after Emily had departed, he would take her, Jessie, down to Eastbourne where she could make a full recovery.

Margaret Nevin of 69 Princes Gate, London, was the cook-housekeeper to Mrs Hutchinson and she was last at the bungalow on April 11th. She testified that at that time, all the legs on the coal cauldron were straight. This would prove to be significant for the rest of Mahon's story.

Mahon took possession of the bungalow keys on Friday, April 11th, 1924, but slept at home with his wife that night, at their lodgings at 2 Pagoda Avenue, Richmond. Miss Kaye, meanwhile, had travelled down to Eastbourne on April 7th, where she stayed at the Kenilworth Court Hotel. On April 12th, he went to Victoria station in London where he had intended to catch the 1.20pm train. However, he realised that he would have to buy some things for the bungalow so sent a telegram to Miss Kaye, telling her that he would catch the 3.15pm train, arriving in Eastbourne at 4.49pm. There is no doubt that Mahon was met at Eastbourne by Emily. Reginald Stanley Marley, a taxi driver, testified that he had driven Mahon and a young lady from Eastbourne station to the Officer's House, on Saturday, April 12th.

Almost from the first, there was trouble between Mahon and Emily at the bungalow. Until recently she had been staying at the

Green Cross Club, a residential club for young women workers, situated at 68/69 Guildford Street, Russell Square, London. Emily now informed Mahon that she had given up her room there and had told people, including the secretary, Ada Constance Smith, that she was engaged to a man named Patterson. She was apparently burning her bridges and trying to force him into making the decision to live with her permanently.

On the Sunday, April 13th, Emily suggested a trip to Paris together. Mahon told her that he did not have a passport, so she insisted they travel up to London together so that could he could obtain one. They arrived at Victoria, where they separated for an hour. Once they met up again, Mahon told her that he had been to the passport office but on the train back to Eastbourne he admitted that this was a lie. This led to a further argument, which simmered until they arrived back at Eastbourne.

That evening, as Mahon made up the fire in the living room, Emily told him that she had written two letters, which she then produced. One was to a friend of Mahon's at the Richmond Bowling Club. Mahon was the assistant secretary there and the letter was tendering his resignation. The second letter was to a friend of hers at the Green Cross Club, Edith Mary Warren, known as Phiz. Edith knew Mahon, too, and this letter was telling Edith that Emily and he were off to Paris. Emily asked Mahon to sign both of these letters but he refused.

This denial of her wishes caused Emily to rekindle the argument about them being together. Tired of all this, Mahon announced he was going to bed, whereupon she threw an axe at him. The weapon caught him a glancing blow and continued on to strike the door. Before Mahon could react, Emily had leapt across the room and thrown herself upon him. They fought together and at one stage fell over a chair on to the floor, near the fireplace. Emily was underneath and it was then that she struck her head on the coal cauldron, buckling the leg. Then she lay still. Mahon recovered himself and then realised that Emily was dead. The fact that the cauldron leg had been buckled during their stay would apparently indicate that Mahon might well be telling the truth but this was negated by forensic tests which showed only two small spots of blood on the cauldron, hardly consistent with a blow severe enough to cause death. Mahon went on to say that in a panic, he put the body into the second bedroom. Over the next few days he would begin dissection and disposal of the body.

There was, however, a further complication to this story. At 10.00pm on the night of April 10th, 1924, Mahon had encountered Miss Ethel Primrose Duncan. Ethel Duncan lived at 55 Worple Avenue, Isleworth, with her sister and on the night of April 10th, she had no umbrella and as it was pouring with rain, she was soaked to the skin. It was then that she met a kind gentleman named Pat, who offered to walk her home, sheltering her under his own brolly. Pat was none other than Patrick Mahon.

As they travelled back to Isleworth, Pat told Miss Duncan of his unhappy married life. He told her that he lived at Richmond, and ended by asking her out to dinner the following Wednesday. Ethel accepted and he said he would send her a telegram arranging the exact details.

On April 15th, the telegram was sent and arrangements were made to meet at Charing Cross Station at 7.50pm. They enjoyed a pleasant evening together which concluded with Pat asking her to go down to a bungalow he had taken at Eastbourne. Ethel agreed and provisionally arranged to catch the 11.15am train on April 18th. Pat said he would send another telegram if there were to be any changes to the plans. On April 17th, Ethel received a telegram which read, "Catch train as arranged — Waller." Accompanying this was a telegraphic money order for £4 to cover her expenses.

Now it should be remembered that Pat Waller, alias Patrick Mahon, had, by Sunday April 13th, the day he claimed Emily Kaye had died, already arranged to meet Ethel Duncan, in London, on the coming Wednesday, April 16th. He did not change those plans and, indeed, invited his latest conquest to come back to Eastbourne with him, where the body of his previous love still lay in a locked bedroom.

Before Ethel Duncan travelled down to Eastbourne, Mahon had started the disposal process. First he cut off Emily's legs so that he could get her body into her trunk. He found he was still unable to do so without removing the head, which he then did. The portions were then put into the trunk which was locked in bedroom number two.

Ethel Duncan arrived in Eastbourne on April 18th. They had lunch and dinner in the town before travelling on to the Officer's House at 10.00pm. Here they slept in the first bedroom whilst the trunk stood next door. The following day, Ethel went into Eastbourne to do some shopping whilst Mahon visited Plumpton races. This was proved by the evidence of Edward Charles Buckland, a taxi driver of Pevensey Bay, who drove him there and back. Mahon and Ethel met up again in Eastbourne and dined at the Sussex Hotel before going back to the bungalow. The following day Mahon read a telegram to Miss Duncan.

Although he had sent this to himself, it purported to come from a business contact and requested that he return to London the next day. On Monday, April 21st, Mahon and Ethel travelled back to London together, parting at around midnight. Finally, Mahon maintained that at no stage had he known that Emily was pregnant.

There were a number of appearances in court before the matter was sent for trial. The inquest opened on May 7th, before the deputy coroner for East Sussex, Dr W.A. Dow. This initial meeting took place at the Officer's House and was mainly to allow the jury to view the various remains which had been placed on display in the scullery. The second convening of the inquest was at the more convenient Westham Drill Hall on June 4th, and finally concluded on June 11th when the jury came to the conclusion that the dead woman was indeed Emily Beilby Kaye and that she had been murdered by Patrick Herbert Mahon. As for the Hailsham police court, Mahon made his sixth appearance on June 5th. The hearing was carried on to the next day when it was decided to send Mahon for trial at the next Sussex assizes, due to open in July. That trial finally opened at Lewes on July 15th, 1924, before Mr Justice Avory. The prosecution team was led by Sir Henry Curtis Bennett, assisted by Mr Cecil R. Havers and Mr H.R. Howe. The defence was led by Mr James Dale Cassels MP, who had with him Mr Thomas Gates and Mr C.R. Collingwood. In addition to these learned gentlemen, Mr Paul Bennett, instructed by Mr Alfred Johnson, watched the case in the interests of Ethel Duncan.

A good deal of evidence was heard on that first day, witnesses being able to refer to a model of the Officer's House which stood on the solicitor's table in front of the judge. This wooden model had a detachable roof so that individual rooms could be inspected in relation to each other.

To begin with, much of the evidence concerned Miss Kaye's financial concerns. The prosecution were, of course, arguing that part of the motive for Mahon murdering Emily, was so that he could appropriate her funds. Bertram George Cookman was employed as a securities clerk at the Midland Bank, 59 Coleman Street, London, where the dead woman had maintained an account. He produced a copy of her various banking transactions which showed that at the time of her death, she had a credit balance of £71 4s 8d. However, on February 10th, that balance had been more than £475. On that day Emily cashed a cheque for £404. She was given four £100 notes and four £1 notes.

Charles Neville Curtis was a clerk at the Bank of England. He confirmed that three of those £100 notes had been exchanged at the bank: one on February 19th, the second on March 24th, and the third on April 17th. All had been endorsed, as banknotes had to be at this time, with what proved to be false names and addresses and later, Inspector Thomas Hall of New Scotland Yard gave evidence that in his opinion the writing on all three was Mahon's. The first had been endorsed: ' A. Lowe, Firleigh, Glossop Road, Sheffield', the second: 'J.H. Edge, St Elmo, Staines', and the third, "J.B. Peters, 271 Hadleigh Road, Birmingham."

Next, evidence was given by Frederick Charles Stoner who, until May 14th, had been employed as a salesman by the Staines Kitchen Equipment Company, based at 94 Victoria Street, London. He identified a bill produced in court as a copy of that given to Mahon when he purchased a cook's knife and a saw. The company had a procedure whereby any item sold was entered into a book in trip-licate. The top copy of the bill was given to the customer, the second to the cashier as the bill was paid and the third kept for the company records. This particular bill was not dated but, if anything, that help-ed Stoner to pin down when the actual sale must have taken place.

The previous entry was dated April 12th, and the subsequent one dated April 14th. This meant that the items could only have been sold on or between those two dates. However, the fact that it was undated meant that the transaction almost certainly took place after the cashier had left for home. In other words, the shop had officially closed for the day and the transaction was taken after hours. The shop closed early on Saturdays, at 1.00pm, so in all probability, the sale of the knife and saw took place after 1.00pm on Saturday, April 12th. This meant that Mahon had bought the tools he needed to dispose of Emily's body even before they had arrived at the Officer's House.

On the second day of the trial, proceedings were held up for some time when one of the jurors fainted. The poor man had fallen forward and cracked his head on the bench in front of him. Sir Bernard Spilsbury, who was in court to give evidence, attended to the man and in time, the trial was allowed to continue. After a further ten minutes, however, the same juror fainted for a second time and eventually it became clear that he would be unable to return to court. At the same time, a second juror announced that he, too, might not be able to continue as he suffered from lumbago. Two new jurors were sworn in and the case began all over again.

Perhaps the most chilling part of the trial occurred when Mahon gave his testimony. He told how he had disposed of parts of Emily's body and that he finally disposed of the head by burning it on a fire in the living room. As the flames licked around the head, there was a sudden clap of thunder and at that precise moment, Emily's eyes opened and her hair flared into flame. Mahon had fled from the room in sheer terror. It has been said that as he related this part of the story, a clap of thunder resounded outside the courtroom and the defendant paled visibly inside the witness box.

The trial lasted until July 19th. Edith Mary Warren had given evidence that the dead woman had the most placid temperament and was most certainly not the type of woman to hurl an axe at someone. Portions of the doors from the bungalow had been examined and no marks found that were consistent with an axe hitting them with some force. Witnesses were called to show that Emily had not died when

Mahon suggested but was almost certainly killed on Tuesday, April 14th. She was certainly alive on the 13th, when she paid a butcher for some meat he had delivered. She was alive, too, on the afternoon of the 14th, when she called at her old hotel, the Kenilworth Court, to see if any mail had been delivered for her since she had left.

The jury retired at 12.10pm and returned with their verdict at 12.53pm. Asked if he had anything to say before sentence of death was pronounced, Mahon said to the judge, "I feel conscious of the bitterness and unfairness of the summing up you have uttered that I may say nothing except that I am not guilty of murder."

The appeal was heard on August 19th before the Lord Chief Justice, Sir Gordon Hewart, and Justices Swift and Branson. The grounds were that the judge had misdirected the jury in that he failed to point out that Emily's death might have been an accident and was also wrong in directing that women should not serve on the jury. The appeal was dismissed.

Before he faced his final penalty, a little of the history of Patrick Mahon became known. Soon after he had married Jessie, Mahon had received a prison sentence for embezzlement. In June 1916, at Surrey, he received a second sentence, this time of five years, for battering a maid, Olive Kate Wickens, during a robbery. He had struck her over the head with a hammer and it was said at the time that she was lucky to survive.

Patrick Herbert Mahon was hanged at Wandsworth on Wednesday, September 3rd, 1924. Thomas Pierrepoint officiated and was assisted by William Willis. Something like 1,000 people had gathered outside the prison to see the execution notice pinned to the gates.

The execution proved perhaps that the gentlemen of the press can sometimes be rather economical with the truth. It was reported at the time that there was not the slightest hitch with the proceedings but this did not agree with the findings of Spilsbury, the pathologist who carried out the post-mortem. Splisbury stated that there had been two dislocations of the spine: one between the fourth and fifth vertebrae and another between the fifth and sixth. The reason for this was that as Pierrepoint drew the bolt and the trapdoors opened beneath Mahon's feet, he leapt backwards in a desperate attempt to avoid his fate. Mahon struck the back edge of the trap with such force that it snapped his spine. Only then did gravity carry him into the pit, causing the rope to become taut, breaking his spine a second time. Spilsbury would later describe Mahon as being 'doubly hanged' giving the cause of death as coma, followed by asphyxia.

CHAPTER EIGHT

THE EVIDENCE OF ONE MAN

DONALD Gilchrist Cameron was a very worried man. A commercial traveller of 86 Clifford Gardens, Kensal Rise, London NW10, Mr Cameron had become concerned over the apparent disappearance of his daughter, Elsie Emily Cameron, on Friday, December 5th, 1924.

Elsie Cameron was 26 years of age and had, relatively recently, become engaged to her sweetheart, a gentleman named Thorne. John Norman Holmes Thorne, who preferred to use his second name, Norman, was a local man but in 1922, unemployed and unable to find work for himself, he had borrowed £100 from his father and purchased a field in Crowborough, East Sussex. Here, Thorne had built a few huts, bought in some hens and started his own poultry farm which he had given the name Wesley Poultry Farm, although in reality it was still little more than a field at the end of a muddy lane. Elsie had been in the habit of visiting Thorne on a regular basis and had often taken lodgings in the nearby village. Her latest visit had supposedly taken place on December 5th, but the circumstances were curious to say the least.

Donald Cameron had last seen his daughter at around 8.20am on that cold grey Tuesday. They had breakfast together before he left for work and Elsie seemed to be in excellent spirits. The same was said of her mood throughout that morning. The Camerons shared their home with Bertha Motture and her husband, Charles William. Bertha reported that she had spoken to Elsie at 9.00am. They had chatted for about half an hour before Elsie went to do some shopping. Bertha saw her again at 11.30am in Chamberlain Road as Elsie returned home with some new clothes she had just purchased and when Bertha saw Elsie for the last time that day, at noon, Elsie showed off a new style that she had just had done at the hairdressers. Although Bertha did not see Elsie again, she did hear her leave the house at about 2.00pm.

Donald had returned home from work that night and found a letter waiting for him. This was a hurriedly scribbled note, in Elsie's hand, announcing that she had gone to Crowborough. At this stage there was, of course, no cause for concern. It was something Elsie had done many times before, although admittedly she usually gave much more notice when she planned one of her trips to Sussex. She would undoubtedly spend the weekend with her fiancé and then return home, most probably either Monday or Tuesday.

The Monday came and went, as did the Tuesday, and still Elsie had not returned home and in the meantime, a couple of letters had arrived for Elsie apparently from her fiancé. Puzzled as to what was going on, Donald Cameron then sent a telegram to Norman Thorne on December 10th. It read, "Elsie left Friday. Have heard no news. Has she arrived. Reply." In due course, a reply did indeed arrive but the message it carried did nothing to clear things up. It read, "Not here. Open letters. Can't understand. Thorne."

When Mr Cameron did open the letters from Thorne he found one, dated December 7th, saying that he had expected to have received a letter from her by now since she had not met him, as arranged, on the previous Saturday. Now concerned for his daughter's safety, Donald Cameron reported her disappearance to the police.

It was December 12th by the time Police Constable Beck paid a visit to Norman Thorne's poultry farm. As they were speaking about Elsie, whilst leaning on the gate of the farm, a local man, Robert John Cosham, happened to stroll past and could not fail to notice the talk between the two men. In due course, reports of the missing girl began to appear in the local and, indeed, the national papers and it was then that information began to flow.

On December 15th, one of the detailed newspaper reports was seen by George Adams, a nurseryman of 2 Grovehurst Villas, Blackness. He and another worker, Albert James Sands, had left the nursery at 5.00pm on Friday, December 5th. The two men walked home together and their route took them down the lane which ran alongside Thorne's farm. It would have been sometime between 5.10pm and 5.20pm when they reached the farm and both men had seen a woman, who looked very much like the published description of Elsie Cameron, some ten yards from Thorne's gate. Indeed, the lane was very muddy at the time and the two men stepped to one side to allow the lady to pass them. As Adams read on, he noted that the missing woman was believed to be carrying a small attaché case and he recalled just such a case being held by the woman he had seen.

Having first spoken to Albert Sands, Adams went to speak to Florence Mary Cosham on December 16th. Florence lived at 'Corona', Luxford's Lane, Crowborough, and she had known Elsie very well, as she often stayed at 'Corona' on her weekend visits to Sussex. Norman Thorne heard through the grapevine that Adams had been speaking to Florence about Elsie and that same night he called at Adams' house and said that he had heard that there might be some news for him about Elsie. Adams told Thorne about the woman he and Sands had seen. Thorne said that he didn't believe the woman could have been Elsie, for she had never arrived at his farm, but if it was her, she might have found that he wasn't there and had perhaps wandered away in a sort of daze and possibly lost herself in Ashdown Forest. The two men conversed for about an hour, and Thorne left at about 7.00pm.

On that same December 16th, Elsie Cameron's mother wrote a letter to Thorne, part of which read, "...Whatever has happened to her? We get no rest day or night. If it had been a week or two before, I might have thought she had done something rash." That last sentence implied that at this stage, even Elsie's family had at least considered the idea that their daughter might have done away with herself. It was, however, something which they would soon come to deny had ever crossed their minds.

Meanwhile, the police were taking her disappearance very seriously. The case was but a few days old when Scotland Yard, in the form of Chief Inspector John Gillan and Detective Sergeant Ambrose Askew, were called in, although the investigation was still led by Superintendent Isaac Budgen, who was normally based at Uckfield. On December 18th, Budgen interviewed Thorne at Crowborough police station, having informed him that two men had reported they had seen a woman, believed to be Elsie, arriving at his farm on the day in question. Thorne said he had heard this story himself and thought they must be mistaken but invited the police over to the farm to search the buildings for any sign of Elsie Cameron.

Superintendent Budgen, together with Inspector George Edwards of the Crowborough force, visited the Wesley poultry farm that same day and made a careful examination of the premises. They found nothing to arouse their suspicions and left after Thorne had made a statement. In that document, Norman Thorne said he had last seen Elsie on November 28th. She had not turned up on the Friday and in fact he had received a letter from her saying that she was travelling down to Groombridge on the Saturday. He had gone to meet her train but there had been no sign of Elsie, so after doing some shopping he had returned home, expecting to hear from her in due course. Unfortunately he had since burned that note.

As the investigation progressed it soon became clear that Norman Thorne might not be the concerned lover he claimed to be. Elsie's father informed officers that a couple of months ago, Elsie had come to him and announced she was pregnant. He had stormed around to see Thorne's father and both men agreed to bring pressure to bear on the young man to do the 'proper thing' and marry the girl. There was, however, a further complication. Not only did Norman Thorne apparently have a pregnant girlfriend, but he had also been seeing another young lady, a local girl named Elizabeth Ann Coldicott, who lived with her mother at 'Springhill', South View Road, Crowborough.

Thorne had first made the acquaintance of Miss Coldicott at a village dance some time around Whitsun, 1924. They had seen each other a few times after that and Elizabeth had been fully aware of

Thorne's ties with Elsie, he even introduced them to each other around a month after he and Elizabeth had first met. From September 1924, onwards, though, Elizabeth Coldicott had taken to visiting Thorne at his farm on a regular basis, often staying until late at night. He had finally told her that he wished to marry her but would have to be careful how he broke off the engagement to Elsie as she was a rather highly-strung person and he was not sure how she would take it.

Now that they knew the true situation, the police came to think that Elsie may well have arrived at Thorne's farm and that he might well know a great deal more about her disappearance than he had thus far volunteered. On December 26th, Thorne was interviewed again.

Faced with the new evidence, Thorne now admitted that there had been some trouble with Elsie over her condition. Rather delicately explaining their relationship, he described how he had been intimate with Elsie but not in a way that could have caused her to conceive. He therefore did not believe that she was pregnant but had told her that if she was in that condition, he would, of course, marry her.

It was now only a matter of time before a proper search of the farm and its environs took place. On January 14th, 1925, a number of officers, including John Gillan and Sergeant Askew, again visited the poultry farm. As they arrived, Thorne was writing a letter to Elizabeth Coldicott part of which read, "…The police have got to work. Don't worry. I have a clear conscience. Yours as ever. Norman." He was then taken to the police station and whilst he was being interviewed, officers with shovels and spades began to dig up the farm.

January 15th was an absolutely foul day. Not only was there a heavy mist over Crowborough but rain fell incessantly. This did not make things any easier for the officers but even so, at 8.25am the first breakthrough came.

A shout rang out that something had been found, about 18ins down. The muddy soil was scraped away and it was seen that the object, located by Police Constable John Philpott, was an attaché case. The case was opened and seen to contain a number of articles of women's clothing as well as a pair of ladies glasses. Although formal identification was made later, the clothing fitted the description of some of Elsie Cameron's garments.

Back at the police station, Thorne was told what had been found and then informed that he would be held in custody and probably charged with being responsible for the death of Elsie Cameron. By then it was 9.30am. Thorne made no reply to the officer's remarks and the police returned to their digging.

The initial excavation ended at 11.00am, whilst the police took a break from their efforts and enjoyed a brief respite from the appalling weather. They resumed after lunch and came to an end for the day at 5.00pm. Nothing of significance was found and plans were made to return the following day. Matters, however, would be taken out of their hands, for at 8.00pm Thorne said that he wished to make another statement.

That statement deserves to be reported in detail and read, "I, John Norman Holmes Thorne, after being cautioned, wish to tell you the truth of what happened on 5th December. Between 5.15pm and 5.30pm Miss Cameron entered my hut carrying her suitcase and that was all. I asked her why she had come unexpectedly, and she said she wanted some tea. I asked her where she intended to sleep and she said, 'In the hut,' and furthermore, that she intended staying until she was married. I asked who would support her and she said, 'You will have to.' I said I had to talk it over with mother and father. She insisted on being married at once. I went to the Cosham's, leaving her in the hut, at 7.30pm to see if I could arrange for her to sleep one night.

"I returned saying she would have to sleep in my bed. I proposed sleeping in a large chair myself. There was an argument between us as to her coming down without making arrangements, and she said it made no difference as we were to be married. I told her I had arranged to meet Mrs and Miss Coldicott at the station to carry their suitcases, and told her to go to bed. I went to the station, and when I returned at 11.30pm the dog came down to meet me. When I opened the door I saw Miss Cameron hanging from a beam by a piece of cord used for a washing line. I laid her across the table and lay by her for about an hour. I was intending to inform the police, but then, realising the position I was in, I went to the workshop and chained up the dog.

"I returned to the hut, and took off her clothes, and put her on the table naked. I got my saw and some sacking, tore up her clothes, and burned them in the hut. I laid the sacks on the floor and sawed off her head by the glow of the fire and put it in a sack. I put parts of the body in the sack, intending to carry them away, but my nerve failed me and I put them in the workshop. The next morning, as soon as it got light, I buried them in the chicken run. I then went into the hut and had some coffee and tried to build up evidence to protect myself. I buried her suitcase near the potato patch."

Having been told exactly where they would locate Elsie's remains, the police returned to the farm and at 10.00pm the digging began again, this time by moonlight and torchlight. One hour later, at 11.00pm on January 15th, 1924, Elsie Cameron was finally found.

The body was in fact in four pieces. The head, as Thorne had described, had been severed and placed in sacking and then packed tightly into a biscuit tin. The trunk, with the arms still attached, was wrapped in sacking and the two legs, hacked off at the upper thighs, were wrapped together in another piece of sacking.

On January 16th, at 2.30pm Norman Thorne was brought before the magistrate Mr John Hallett, at Crowborough police station and charged with murder. He was then remanded until January 24th, when he was due to appear at Mark Cross. Meanwhile the body was removed to the premises of Mr H.F. Webb, an undertaker of Beacon Road and it was at that location where, the following day, those remains were examined by Sir Bernard Spilsbury. It was perhaps the evidence of this one man which would settle the fate of Norman Thorne.

It is amazing that whilst such shattering events take place, families can do their best to carry on. Thorne's father travelled down to Sussex and, nothing if not a practical man, one of his first tasks was to tie up any loose ends at the farm. So it was that all the stock was sold to a local dealer, Mr Woolnough, whilst Thorne's two dogs and his cat were put to sleep by a vet when Mr Thorne senior came to feel that they would not settle at any other location.

On January 19th, the inquest opened at the Oddfellows' Hall, before Mr W.A. Dow, the deputy coroner for East Sussex. At this early stage, only evidence of identification was called, Elsie's father being the only witness. Proceedings were then adjourned until February 11th.

With such a complex case involving a great deal of public interest, there were inevitably a number of such adjournments. Thorne appeared at the Mark Cross petty sessional court, where he was represented by Mr E.A.R. Llewellyn, on January 24th, January 31st, and February 7th, when he was finally sent for trial. At these latter hearings, Thorne was now represented by Mr Cecil Oakes, whom Mr Llewellyn instructed, whilst Mr George Peevor appeared for the Director of Public Prosecutions. In the meantime, on January 24th, Elsie had been buried at Kensal Green Cemetery.

The trial opened at Lewes on March 11th, 1924, before Mr Justice Finlay. Thorne's defence was led by Mr James Dale Cassels, assisted by Mr Oakes and Mr C.T. Abbott. The Crown's case would be put by Sir Henry Curtis Bennett, assisted by Mr R.E. Negus.

Much of the early evidence was designed to prove what Norman Thorne now admitted, namely that Elsie Cameron had been involved in a relationship with him, that she had visited him on December 5th, and that she had perished in the hut on his farm. So it was that the early history of that relationship was first outlined. Thorne and Elsie had first met at the Wesleyan Chapel they both attended in Kensal Rise. By the end of 1921, they were sweethearts and in August 1922, Thorne had purchased the farm. To begin with he cycled back and forth from London to Crowborough so that he could see Elsie on a regular basis and also attend to business on the farm. This was, of course, highly inconvenient so not long afterwards, in October, he had moved into the small hut which Thorne had called home for the next couple of years. From this time onwards, Elsie visited Crowborough every three weeks or so. When down in Sussex she would stay at one of two locations: 1 Pasture Villas, a house owned by Agnes and Edwin Piper, or 'Corona', the home of Florence and Robert Cosham.

In the early days, Elsie usually stayed with Mrs Piper. Indeed,

Thorne himself had occasionally lodged there during the months when he was still commuting between London and Sussex, so Agnes Piper knew both of them very well. When giving her evidence, Agnes Piper recalled one particular occasion when Elsie had stayed with her in 1923. The visit was supposed to last for two weeks but Elsie actually stayed for six. Towards the end of that time, Agnes said that Elsie appeared to be very nervous. On the last night, she was so bad that Edwin Piper had to take her back to see Thorne. She then stayed at the farm for a couple of nights before Thorne had to escort her back to London where he gently handed her over to the care of her sister, Margaret Blomfield.

Florence Cosham gave evidence that she had spoken to Thorne several times about his continuing relationship with Elsie whilst he was seeing Elizabeth Coldicott. He had made it plain to her that he wished to end the relationship with Elsie but added that he was waiting for her nerves to get better before he broke off the engagement. Thorne had visited her house on the day he received the telegram from Elsie's father and at the time, suggested that Elsie might have thrown herself into the River Thames. This, of course, was put forward as an explanation when Thorne was well aware of what had really happened to his fiancée.

Florence's husband, Robert, stated that on the morning of December 5th, he had mentioned to Thorne that he was going to a whist drive that evening. In Thorne's statement he had claimed that when Elsie arrived at the farm he had gone to the Cosham's to try to find lodgings for her. The prosecution were suggesting that Norman never made that journey because he already knew that they would not be at home. In cross examination, though, Robert Cosham admitted that whilst Thorne might have remembered that he would be out, he made no mention of whether his wife would be at home or not.

Evidence was now given of the new relationship, that with Elizabeth Ann Coldicott. Two letters were produced, both written by Thorne and sent to Elsie. The first of these was dated November 21st, with the second following a few days later on November 25th. In these Thorne told Elsie that he had been seeing someone else and described himself as being, "...between two fires ..." Elsie answered both letters and those replies were also read out in court.

The first letter, which Elsie wrote on November 24th, read, "My Own Darling Norman, Your letter received last night, and I am returning it in this letter, although I don't see why you wanted it back. It was too late to send it on last night. Why should you not go this week as really Norman every day makes a difference to me. You must realise that this worry is dangerous for the baby.

"Why are there one or two things you have not told me, and in what way does it concern me? I don't know I have ever kept a single thing from you, and I don't think it is fair for you to keep things from me. Why did you not tell me everything last Friday?

"What do you mean by 'between two fires?' I want to be married before Christmas and C.D., is only a month tomorrow, and it will also be perfectly obvious to everyone after that: also you must let your people know as soon as you can. I feel ever so worried about things now.

"Please do get married quickly. I can't write any more now. Fondest love and kisses, yours ever."

The second letter, which followed about a week later read, "My Own Darling Norman, I received your letter. If at any time anyone would say anything against you, I would always have stood up for you. You are engaged to me, and I have first claim on you. Your love to me should have kept you true to me.

"It is a poor thing for a man to let himself go because he has a girl who has nerves badly. The doctor told me the way you had gone on was the cause of my nerves being as they are. Am I to take it you have got this other girl into the same way you have me? You say you must have time to think.

"Whatever this girl thinks of me I have first claim on you. Had you been a raving lunatic I would never have betrayed your trust and gone with another man.

"I have stood by you and loved you all the way through. My baby must have a name. Oh! you have deceived me! My heart is nearly broken. I have been told many times that you can't trust one man. If anyone but yourself had told me, I would not have believed it."

Now the prosecution were suggesting that these letters proved that although Thorne was trying to end the relationship, Elsie was having none of it. She had eventually travelled down to Sussex to confront her fiancé face to face and, probably in the course of an argument, Thorne murdered her. The defence, in their turn, tried to suggest that the same letters proved that Elsie was very depressed, admitted she was a nervous kind of person and having travelled to Sussex, felt so rejected when her lover went to meet the other woman, she took her own life. Elizabeth Coldicott had already given confirmation that she and her mother had been to Brighton on December 5th, and Thorne had arranged to meet them at the station. Their train pulled in at 10.15pm and after escorting them home, Thorne chatted to her at the garden gate. By the time he left it was around 11.30pm.

Other witnesses were called to give opposing views of Elsie Cameron's character. Her family, of course, despite what Elsie's mother had written to Thorne about her daughter possibly having: 'done something rash,' denied vehemently that Elsie was unstable enough to have taken her own life. Margaret Blomfield, Elsie's married sister, who lived at 21 Ravensworth Road, Kensal Rise, said she had last seen Elsie on December 3rd, when she was in good spirits. She admitted that Thorne had once handed Elsie over to her care at Victoria station in London, and at the time, Elsie had appeared to be distressed, but denied that Thorne had told her at the time that she had said she wanted to throw herself from the train on the way back. Added to this, of course, was the evidence of Elsie's father that she was in an excellent mood on the morning of December 5th, and the words of Bertha Motture who saw Elsie on a number of occasions that same morning and also said she appeared to be very happy.

To counter this, the defence called Alice Mary Hawksworth, a book-keeper from Willesden. She had been a Sunday School teacher at Kensal Rise Wesleyan Church and knew Elsie well. She recalled a day in September 1924, when Elsie said she was very nervous about her work. She went on to say that she thought people in the office were looking at her and laughing at her, as were people in the street.

One day she had even grabbed Alice's arm and told her she thought she was going off her head.

Rose Blythe and Mildred Pearson were shorthand typists and had worked in the same office as Elsie, also a typist, in the Minories. Although the work was very simple, Elsie seemed unable to grasp what she was supposed to do and as a result, worked with them for only six days, most of that time spent in a state of nervous exhaustion. Rose had spoken to Elsie who had told her that her head felt funny and, in a state of collapse, Elsie was taken to the cloakroom to rest. Rose and Mildred were asked to escort Elsie home and at the railway station they had to hold her back from the edge of the platform.

Samuel Hedley Robinson was called as a character witness for Thorne. He said that he had known Norman since 1913. He described the accused man as amicable, courteous and unselfish and considered that he would rather help others than look after his own interests. He had also known Elsie and described her as a girl who seemed not to enjoy life.

Norman Thorne had claimed that Elsie had committed suicide by hanging herself and that his only crime was the disposal of the body. It appeared that the outcome of the case would rest on the medical evidence and the prosecution called the famous pathologist Sir Bernard Spilsbury to testify about his findings.

Spilsbury's initial evidence was based on his first examination of the four separate pieces of the body. He then went into detail about eight bruises he had found on Elsie, the most telling of which seemed to be one of the right side of the back of the head and another covering a large area over the right cheek. The tissues beneath the skin had been pulped in this area and this was consistent with a crushing blow being delivered. Two Indian clubs had been found in Thorne's hut and Spilsbury agreed that a blow with one of these could have been the cause of death. More importantly, Spilsbury said that he had found no evidence of asphyxia which would have been the case had Elsie died as Thorne described. It was true that there were two creases in the neck but these were the natural folds found in a woman's throat. There was no groove as would have been caused by a washing line cord digging into the flesh. He was also able to confirm that Elsie had not, after all, been pregnant.

The police, of course, had been thorough in their investigation. After Norman Thorne had been charged, they had returned to the farm and conducted an experiment. A rope had been thrown over a beam as Thorne had described and a weight attached to it, to represent the body of Miss Cameron. The experiments had produced traces of rope fibre on the beams yet no such fibres had been found before this. Indeed, the top beams were covered with dust and cobwebs, although the one below this was clean, having been used as a storage place by Thorne. The defence, though, got the officers to agree that had the rope happened to hit a knot hole, there might well have been no fibres found.

The defence were not to be outdone on the medical evidence either. On February 24th, Elsie Cameron's body had been exhumed and in the presence of Sir Bernard, a second post-mortem examination had been carried out by Dr Robert Matthew Bronte and Dr John Smith Gibson. Both men were to give much the same evidence and their conclusion was that Elsie had a particularly thin skull. If death had been caused as Sir Bernard Spilsbury described, the head would have been crushed like an egg-shell. There were no injuries whatsoever to any of the bones of the skull. Both doctors also found two grooves on the neck, some three eighths of an inch apart, extending across the upper part of the neck. The tissues below these areas were examined in great detail, microscopic samples being taken. Those tissues showed crushing and in conclusion, both men agreed that the most probably cause of death was shock, due to attempted hanging. They held that Elsie had been alive when Thorne cut her down but had died very soon afterwards. Thorne had described how Elsie had at one stage fallen and struck her suitcase. This could well have accounted for the bruises Spilsbury had described.

Sir Bernard was recalled on the fifth day of the trial. He restated that in his opinion, the grooves in the neck were not caused by a cord, and that the evidence of haemorrhage in the neck tissues beneath was nothing more than tissue degeneration. He did, however, agree with the judge that if he were wrong in that belief, then the tissue slides did indeed show evidence of some injury to the neck. He also agreed that the skull bones were abnormally thin.

Dr James Woods, a lecturer on mental diseases at St George's Hospital and the London Hospital, was then called to the stand. He said that the descriptions of Elsie's behaviour were consistent with certain mentally neurotic conditions. The moods of elation, followed soon afterwards by depression were symptomatic of psychosis and he believed that especially in times of stress, Elsie would have suicidal tendencies. Questioned about what Elsie's reaction might be upon arriving at the hut to arrange her marriage to Thorne, only to see him leave to meet up with the girl who was her rival, Woods answered that he thought this could cause a sudden suicidal impulse.

Added to this was the testimony of Elsie's own general practitioner, Dr Watson Walker, who said that he had known Elsie as his patient since June 15th, 1921. He had treated her a number of times for neurasthenia, the last time being in November. Shortly after this she had come to his surgery saying that she had missed two periods and believed she might be pregnant. He was unable to confirm or deny this and suggested she returned the following month when things would be somewhat clearer. She was due to return to his surgery on December 18th.

There the evidence ended. Either Thorne was telling the truth and Elsie had killed herself, or he had somehow managed to strangle her without leaving any apparent signs, or had battered her to death causing her tissues to be pulped but causing no damage to her unusually thin skull. It was for the jury to decide.

On March 16th, 1925, the jury retired to consider their verdict. It took them only 30 minutes to decide that Norman Thorne was guilty and he was sentenced to death. The evidence of Sir Bernard Spilsbury had carried the day.

Thorne's appeal was heard before the Lord Chief Justice, Sir Gordon Hewart, and Justices Shearman and Salter. It opened on April 6th and the main grounds were alleged misdirection by the trial judge. The verdict was not given until the following day and when it was announced that it had been lost, Thorne was visibly moved. On the way down to the cells afterwards he was heard to sob and cry out that he was innocent of this charge.

There was even disquiet at the resumed inquest. Heard on April 16th, the foreman stated that whilst the cause of death was in accordance with the medical evidence, one of their number was not satisfied with that evidence and dissented. After being told by the coroner that a majority verdict was not acceptable and that the trial had decided that Thorne was guilty of murder, the lone juror assented and the inquest was complete.

Last-minute attempts to secure a reprieve were made. Even Sir Arthur Conan Doyle, the creator of Sherlock Holmes, expressed the opinion that there was some doubt, albeit faint perhaps, that the verdict was the correct one. None of this was to save Thorne from the gallows.

On Wednesday, April 22nd, 1925, John Norman Holmes Thorne was executed at Wandsworth by Thomas Pierrepoint, who was assisted by Robert Wilson. He walked bravely to the scaffold and died as he had told his father he would, 'like a man'. It was a significant date, for April 22nd would have been Elsie Cameron's 27th birthday.

Still the controversy was not over. At the inquest on Thorne, the jury asked if he had confessed his guilt before he died. Major Hugh Cochrane MacTier, the prison governor, refused to answer the question either way, saying he had received instructions that no such information was to be given out. This caused Thorne's father to pen a letter to the Press Association. Written on April 23rd, it was published the following day and read, "I consider that the accounts given in certain papers suggesting that a statement pertaining to a confession was made by my son, Norman, are baseless. He has made no confession, for he had nothing to confess, and I have this information on high authority.

"I still consider that he is the victim of a grave miscarriage of justice. Perhaps no one is to blame, but a combination of circum-stances has brought my son to an untimely end. He has won, however, the esteem of all by his bravery and fortitude right to the end under most distressing circumstances, and has now gone to that world where no mistakes are made and no wrong judgements given."

With that the town of Crowborough tried to return to peace and anonymity, but it was not to be. Only two days after Thorne had paid the ultimate penalty, ten-year-old Joan Annett was found battered to death and with her throat cut, in the grounds of Bridge Castle, the seat of Lord Henry Neville, close by Crowborough. George Jeffrey was arrested for the murder and tried at Lewes on July 8th. Found guilty, he was sentenced to be detained during His Majesty's pleasure since he had been only 15 years old at the time of the murder and therefore too young to hang.

CHAPTER NINE

A DAY IN BRIGHTON

IN the year 1927, Mr Geoffrey Holland, a successful man by all accounts, lived in Plummers Plain House, close by the village of Lower Beeding, situated about a mile from Handcross, midway between Crawley and Haywards Heath. Mr Holland employed a number of servants and two of these, Annie and James Gillon, were brother and sister.

Annie Gillon, who was 28 years of age, was a housemaid, and had started work in the house in May. Her brother, who was two years older, and had arrived at Lower Beeding a month or so after Annie, was officially the under-gardener but he also had other duties of a more general nature and one of his jobs was to look after the electricity generator which supplied the house with power. Although Gillon enjoyed most of his work, and did it with great enthusiasm, he was not too happy about having to repair the generator whenever it broke down, something it did with great frequency.

Annie Gillon had a room inside the main house whilst James, whose remit lay more in the open air, lived in what was termed a cottage but in reality was little more than a hut, in the grounds. Each day, in addition to her paid duties, Annie was in the habit of preparing meals for her brother. By all accounts the couple, who originated from Glasgow and had worked together at Plummers Plain since June, were very close and Annie appeared to enjoy looking after James, doing everything she could to make him happy and content. Indeed, it was Annie who was responsible for Gillon having his job at all. On June 17th, Geoffrey Holland had written to James.

'Sir, I hear from your sister that you would take a job here. Before I decide anything, will you please let me know whether you would take charge of a petrol engine of 5 h.p., and whether you have done any gardening work.

'Your duties would be mainly gardening, (digging, weeding etc.) besides running the engine and you would also have to clean windows, cut up wood and other odd jobs.

'Wages would be 32s from which would be deducted the cost of board and lodging, amounting to about £1.'

On Sunday, September 18th, Annie mentioned that the next day she had been invited to take a trip into Brighton. George Frederick Mercer, a man who filled the dual role of chauffeur and butler, was driving into the town to transact some business for Mr Holland. He had asked Lilian Blanche Crouchman, the cook, to go in with him and she in her turn had kindly asked Annie if she would like to go with them. Annie was delighted to accept the invitation and as a matter of course, told her brother James of her trip.

James Gillon was far from pleased and put his opinion quite firmly. He did not want Annie to go into Brighton and after the two had argued fiercely, Gillon insisting that Annie stay at the house. For her part, Annie, who rarely went against her brother's wishes, was determined to go and told Lilian Crouchman that she would see her the following morning.

Monday came and George Mercer brought the car around to pick up Lilian and Annie. The two ladies climbed into the vehicle, watched by James Gillon. There was, however, no scene between the two. Just before the car pulled away Gillon was heard to say, "So you are going to Brighton after all." It would later be said that there was no tone of malice in his voice and it seemed to be nothing more than a caring brother bidding his sister farewell. The car drove off and James Gillon returned to his duties.

It was 9.00pm by the time Annie returned to Plummer's Plain House. It had been a lovely day and she had thoroughly enjoyed herself. George Mercer put the car away and Annie and Lilian returned to the servants' hall.

Soon afterwards, though, James Gillon was in the same hall, asking Annie if she had had an enjoyable time. She replied that she had, whereupon Gillon said that he had eaten nothing all day and asked Annie if she would get his supper for him. Annie, remembering the argument over her trip to Brighton, refused, saying, "No, not after the way you treated me," before retiring to her room. Gillon asked Lilian Crouchman to go up to Annie's room and ask her to come down and talk to him. Lilian did as she had been asked but when she returned, the news she bore was not good. Annie had flatly refused to come back downstairs. There seemed to be nothing else James Gillon could do. Reluctantly he returned to his cottage.

The next morning, Tuesday, September 20th, 1927, the servants were all up and about early, attending to their various duties. Lilian Crouchman and Annie Gillon were both in the kitchen when Gillon strolled in and asked Annie if she was going to cook his breakfast for him. Annie's mood of the previous night had not improved. She turned to face her brother and said, "No, I have finished with you," and once again went upstairs to her room. By the time she returned a few minutes later, Gillon had left the kitchen so Annie returned to her duties, going into the servants' hall.

She may well not have heard Gillon come into the hall. Lilian Crouchman later said that she did not hear him return but she certainly heard the scream that filled the house seconds later. James Gillon had collected a sharp knife and a razor. With the latter he had slashed his sister's throat and with the knife he had stabbed her a number of times. Indeed, so severe was his attack that part of the knife blade broke off in Annie's back. Lilian Crouchman and George Mercer rushed into the servants' hall in time to see Gillon draw the razor across his own throat. The floor was awash with blood.

Surprisingly, Annie Gillon was not dead. Dr Greville Brend Tait, who lived at Ashpoles in Handcross, was sent for and arrived at the house at about 8.30am. He saw that Annie was badly injured and after making her as comfortable as possible he had the presence of mind to ask her if she wished to make a statement which he then took down in writing. According to this, Annie had said, "He came to me and asked me to get his breakfast. I said I would not. He then came for me and kicked me and then stabbed me and cut me with a razor." The doctor dressed the wounds of both his patients and then travelled with them in the ambulance to Horsham Hospital.

Brother and sister were seen by Dr John David Cruickshank. James Gillon was not badly injured and it was plain that he would be released from hospital in due course, no doubt to be interviewed by the police. Annie, though, was in a much more serious state and there were grave concerns for her health.

On September 22nd, Annie was X-rayed. When the pictures were examined, a portion of the knife blade was seen to be embedded in her back, between the third and fourth dorsal vertebrae. It was felt that the position of the blade was such that any attempt to remove it would result in instant death. The knife had severed the spinal cord and as a result, poor Annie was paralysed below the fourth rib. All that could be done was to try to make her as comfortable as possible and hope that she would become stronger in due course.

James Gillon was discharged from medical care on September 30th. That same day, at 9.45am, he was interviewed at the hospital by Superintendent Beacher who told him that he would be charged with feloniously wounding Annie Gillon with intent to murder her, and with attempting to commit suicide, which of course was a criminal offence in those days. Gillon then made a written statement in response, whereupon he was taken into custody. He later appeared before Mr Gatland at the Horsham police court, and was remanded in custody.

There were two more brief court appearances in October. On the 7th of that month, little formal evidence was given and Gillon was remanded until October 11th. On that date, he was back before the magistrates, the case now being prosecuted by Mr J.R. Dell. As a result, James Gillon was sent for trial at the next assizes but before that trial could take place, things took a much more serious turn.

At 8.20pm on Friday, October 28th, Annie Gillon told Sister Eva Holland that she was feeling very ill, believed she was going to die and was quite ready to meet her maker. Shortly afterwards, she slipped into unconsciousness. Just ten minutes later, despite all the efforts of Sister Holland and Dr Cruickshank, Annie died and the charge against James Gillon became one of murder.

The inquest on Annie opened on November 2nd and was conducted by the deputy coroner for West Sussex, Mr F. Fraser Haddock. This was soon adjourned until November 14th but at the end of the proceedings, Gillon, who had been present, asked to see the body of his sister. He was escorted to the mortuary and after viewing Annie's corpse, was taken back to prison in a state of semi-collapse.

The trial took place at Lewes on December 12th, 1927, before Mr Justice Horridge. Gillon was defended by Mr Thomas Gates, whilst the prosecution case was handled by Mr John Flowers. The proceedings would end that same day.

Police Sergeant William John Drabson had been one of the first officers on the scene after the attack had taken place on September 20th. He described how the servants' hall was in great disorder, the walls and furniture being covered in blood. The sergeant went on to report how he had found an open razor on the mantelpiece and close by an Army jack-knife, the blade of which had been broken off. He also gave evidence on Annie's background, stating that she was the daughter of Michael and Rose Ann Gillon and had been born on June 8th, 1899.

The servants gave evidence of the various discussions and arguments between James and Annie over her trip to Brighton and the subsequent refusal by Annie to cook any of her brother's meals. More important, perhaps, was their evidence about the attack itself.

Lilian Crouchman, the cook, who was by now employed at Mr Holland's town residence at 42 Chelsea Park Gardens, said that she was in the kitchen when Gillon stabbed Annie. Upon hearing the scream, she ran into the servants' hall in time to see the latter part of this attack and at one stage had tried to pull Gillon from his sister. He had then roughly pushed Lilian away shouting, "You dare come between us. I'll do you if you don't leave us alone." She had then run for help and met up with George Mercer who was already running towards the scene.

Mercer said that by the time he arrived in the hall, the jack-knife was in Gillon's hand. He had apparently already cut his own throat since his shirt front was saturated with blood. Mercer stood back as Gillon placed the weapons down, sat upon a chair, and dragged Annie on to his knee. He was in this same position when Dr Tait arrived upon the scene.

Dr Tait testified that as he attended to Annie's injuries, Gillon sat close by and repeatedly kept crying and shouting, "How are you Annie? I am sorry Annie." This apparent concern was somewhat negated by the rather nonchalant way that Gillon lit a cigarette and watched with interest as Annie's wounds were dressed.

William Matthews was the head gardener at Plummers Plain House. He, too, was soon upon the scene on the morning of September 20th. In fact, the attack was over by the time Matthews arrived but, fearful that Gillon might attack his sister again, he had asked him to leave the room. Gillon had snarled in reply, "Get out of it or I'll slash you." Then, almost immediately after this, Gillon had turned to George Mercer and said, "Let her alone. She is dying: so am I." Later still, Matthews had seen the razor and the knife lying on the floor and it was he who placed them on the fireplace, out of harm's way.

Dr Cruickshank gave evidence that after Annie's death he had finally removed the knife blade from her back. In fact, the broken part of the blade had split into two pieces, one much smaller than the other. He went on to describe Annie's other wounds which included an incised wound in her neck, two puncture wounds in the back and several minor cuts between the thumb and first finger of each hand. The cause of death was hypostatic pneumonia, brought on by the injury to Annie's spinal cord.

Annie had made two statements and these were both read out in court. The original statement, made to Dr Tait, has already been referred to. The other, much more detailed, statement had been taken by the police, some days after the attack. Here Annie described how Gillon had come back into the servants' hall on the morning of the 20th, shouted, "You are not going to make my breakfast?" and had then grabbed the back of her neck. He must have cut her throat at that very moment, for she felt all the power going out of her body.

Half turning, Annie saw the razor in Gillon's hand, had tried to take it from him, cutting her hands in the process, and that was about all she could recall.

James Gillon did not go into the witness box to give evidence on his own behalf. Instead the defence, hoping to prove that Gillon was insane at the time of the attack upon his sister, called Dr Frederick Ryott Percival Taylor, the resident medical superintendent of the Hellingly Mental Hospital.

Dr Taylor related how at school James Gillon had not been an able pupil. He had attained only the fifth standard, had made no friends, played no games with other children and left at the age of 14. From there he had joined the Navy as a stoker and a report showed that this too had ended ignominiously when Gillon deserted after striking a petty officer. For that offence he had been imprisoned.

Leaving the Navy, Gillon had then worked in a coal mine before entering his present occupation. Dr Taylor came to the conclusion that Gillon was what he would call a high grade mental defective who probably suffered from dementia precox or a premature degeneration of the nerve cells in his brain. Gillon believed that he was inferior to other people and had developed delusions of persecution. For example, he had come to believe that the constant breakdowns in the electric generator at Plummers Plain House was caused by other members of staff deliberately interfering with the mechanism in order to cause him problems. Finally, as if all this was not enough, Gillon's mother and another sister had both been patients at the Morningside Asylum in Edinburgh so there was a definite history of mental instability in the family. In summation, the doctor said that at the time of the attack upon Annie, Gillon was quite definitely insane.

To counter this evidence, the prosecution called Dr William Riddell Kemlo Watson, the senior medical officer at Brixton prison where James Gillon had been held. He simply stated that after observing the prisoner since his incarceration, he found no evidence whatsoever of insanity. The jury were out for only 15 minutes before returning their guilty verdict.

James Gillon's appeal was heard on January 12th, before the Lord Chief Justice, Sir Gordon Hewart, and Justices Avory and Branson.

The main grounds were that the trial judge had not adequately dealt with the plea of insanity. The appeal was dismissed but at these same proceedings it was stated that James Gillon had once been charged with the crime of incest. In fact, he had faced his trial, at Edinburgh, on January 31st, 1921, when he had been charged that he '...had incestuous intercourse with his sister, Annie, in consequence of which a female child was born.' For that offence, Gillon had been sentenced to three years in prison.

James Gillon was hanged at Wandsworth at 8.00am on Tuesday, January 31st, 1928. By all accounts he walked firmly to the scaffold where he was despatched by Robert Baxter who was assisted by Thomas Phillips.

CHAPTER TEN

A DEADLY DUO

POLICE Constable Peters was having a fairly quiet night. His patrol around the streets of Portslade had been free of incident thus far, and then, as he strolled down North Street, he saw something that made him suspect that all was not well.

It was 10.00pm on the night of Monday, November 13th, 1933, and as Peters reached the end of North Street, where it joined Clarence Street, he saw that old Mr Bedford had left a good deal of stock outside his shop.

Eighty-year-old Joseph Bedford had run the corner shop for as long as people could remember. Selling all sorts of ironmongery, earthenware and general tools, it was Bedford's habit to stack piles of goods outside the shop each day it was open for business. Then, at around 8.00pm each evening, the goods would be taken back inside and the shop locked up for the night.

This night, although the door was indeed locked, the piles of buckets, pans and pots made Constable Peters think that something might be wrong inside.

Peters knocked on the door but knew this was probably of little use. Not only was Mr Bedford suffering from poor sight, but he was also rather deaf. The police officer took out his torch and shone it inside the shop. Initially he saw nothing out of place but thinking that the torch might attract Joseph Bedford's attention, Peters repeatedly flicked it on and off. Still there was no sign of anyone inside. Peters then climbed on to the window sill but he was unable to see into the back of the shop where he knew Mr Bedford had a small kitchen, and was perhaps most likely to be.

It was then that the policeman saw a sight he was unlikely ever to forget. The torch beam played upon the shelves inside the shop and suddenly picked out the staggering figure of Joseph Bedford. As Peters watched, the old man, his face covered in blood, came into the main part of the shop and then fell forward on to a glass display case, shattering it into a myriad of pieces. Without further hesitation, Peters forced open the shop door and tried his best to render assistance.

Joseph Bedford was semi-conscious but seemed unable to say what had happened to him. His face was badly bruised and a deep wound in his head was still bleeding profusely. Rushed to Hove Hospital, Mr Bedford arrived there at 11.00pm that night but despite medical attention, he did not recover and died at 5.45am the following morning.

At first there was a body of opinion that this had been a sad accident, but by then the police had already realised that they were dealing with a case of murder. A pool of blood lay on the floor of the passageway which led to the kitchen. On a table in that room lay a copy of that day's *Evening Argus*, and that too was heavily bloodstained. Lying on the floor was a detachable shirt front and a neck-tie, both showing signs of blood, and a human tooth was found close by. Behind the counter there was a button which still had a piece of material adhering to it. Near where Joseph Bedford had fallen, his spectacles were found broken, and finally a large tin which Mr Bedford had used as a till, had been forced open and coins were scattered about the shop floor. Someone had battered Joseph Bedford, robbed him and left him for dead.

Initial inquiries painted a picture of Joseph Bedford as a kind but reclusive sort of man who seldom ventured out. The only relative living nearby was a nephew, Charles Harold Bedford, who lived at 15 Crescent Road, Worthing, just up the coast, and even he had not seen his uncle since June. The only other relatives anyone knew about were two nieces who lived at separate addresses in Maida Vale, London.

If anything, Joseph Bedford had been closer to his neighbours. His next-door neighbour, James Goble, spoke kindly of the dead man, saying that he was widely known as someone loved by the local children, including Goble's own son, Desmond, who often ran errands for him. Goble also informed newspaper reporters that Bedford had been a very talented man, able to play a dozen musical instruments.

Another neighbour, Alice Sandells, who lived at 8 Ellen Street, Portslade, had for the past 15 years taken Mr Bedford his evening meal and on the day of the attack, had done so at 5.15pm. This same lady, who also happened to be James Goble's aunt, had returned to the shop at around 8.40pm to post the newspaper through the letterbox. This, too, was something Alice did every evening and on this particular night, she noticed that the front door was open about six inches or so.

The police soon realised that they were looking for two men. Kathleen Elsie Jane Russell, who lived at 22 Gladstone Street, had been in Bedford's shop at 8.00pm. As she left, she saw two strangers standing outside. One of them spoke to her and she swore that she would recognise both men again. This timing fitted in with what was known about the approximate time of the attack and, of course, due to Joseph Bedford's regular habits, the shop would normally have been locked up immediately after this time.

On November 17th the body was examined by Sir Bernard Spilsbury. He agreed with the doctor who had conducted the original examination, stating that death was due to shock, brought on by a fractured skull. Spilsbury said that a number of blows had been inflicted but one in particular had been extremely violent. Some object had been brought down on to Joseph Bedford's head so hard that it made a marked dent in the hat he had been wearing at the time, crushing the fibres. On that same day, November 17th, Joseph's nephew, Charles, placed a placard in the window of his uncle's shop. It read:
"No one cares if I live or die
"The hurrying crowd is passing me by
"I yearn and I long to stop and think

"To gather while raiment of thought to drink
"At the fountain of wisdom and light
"There is no one cares if I die outright."

The funeral of Joseph Bedford took place on November 20th, and amongst the few people present was one lone figure dressed entirely in black. This woman turned out to be Mrs Sarah Harwood, an old girlfriend of the dead man, now 70 herself. When she had been just 26, Joseph had asked her to marry him and although she refused, they had always remained friends and kept in touch. Now she bade her old friend a sad farewell.

The local police wasted no time in calling in the assistance of Scotland Yard. Two officers, Detective Chief Inspector Ambrose Askew and Detective Sergeant Gillan, were sent to Sussex and they were capably assisted by Superintendent Fairs of the East Sussex police force. What these officers could not know as they began their investigations was that the killers were already held in police custody.

At 11.05am on November 15th, the day after Joseph Bedford had died, Constable Desmond George Lovell noticed a man outside Loaders' a shop in the High Street at Worthing, almost directly opposite the police station. Very shortly afterwards, this man was joined by another and they seemed to be very self-conscious. Lovell followed the men, saw them darting into shop doorways in an attempt to lose him and, finally satisfied that they were up to no good and should be questioned, he took them into custody. The two men gave their names as Frederick Smith and Jack Williamson. They said they had only just arrived in Worthing, having been given a lift from Croydon by a lorry driver. They were looking for work and had no intention of committing any crime. Yet it was noted that both these apparently unemployed men were wearing new suits. Where had they got the money to pay for those clothes?

It was Jack Williamson who gave the police the breakthrough they needed. During routine questioning by Inspector Lewis, Williamson made a verbal statement in which he admitted that he and another man had knocked down an old man in a shop in North Street, Portslade, on the Monday night at around 8.00pm. At that time, he did not know that Joseph Bedford had died and that his statement would soon lead to a charge of wilful murder.

Williamson, who had by now given the police his real name of Frederick William Parker, was interviewed by Chief Inspector Askew on November 17th. That interview began with Askew stating that he was investigating the death of Mr Bedford. Parker looked astonished and, realising that the charge would be much more serious than he had first thought, he now decided to name his accomplice. Parker then made a written statement in which he said that Frederick Smith, who was in reality Albert Probert, was his partner and that they had committed the crime together.

According to that statement, Parker and Probert had decided to rob the shop. He, Parker, was armed with a revolver which was not loaded, whilst Probert held a tyre lever which was wrapped in a stocking. At first, Parker had waved his gun at the old man and demanded that he put up his hands. Initially Bedford had made no move to comply so Probert stepped forward and struck him, very hard, behind one ear. Bedford fell to the floor but Probert had not finished. Falling on to Bedford, Probert repeatedly beat the man's head against the floor before finally taking him into the back room where, presumably, the beating continued. Parker, meanwhile, had found the till which he forced open. He stole some £6 in notes and coin, letting some loose change fall to the floor as he did so. Finally, he and Probert left the shop, walked to Portslade station and from there caught the train back to their lodgings in Worthing.

When faced with this statement, Probert simply denied that he had been at the shop or that he had been involved in any way in the robbery and murder. Parker might well have had a partner, but it was not him. Later still he made a written statement to this effect and Parker made a second, more detailed statement, outlining what he claimed had happened. Despite Probert's denials, both men were charged with murder. They made their first appearance at a special sitting of the Hove County bench, on November 23rd.

Meanwhile, other evidence was building up against both men. George Gunn, a landscape gardener of St Andrew's Road, Portslade, had already handed to the police a tyre lever he had found in one of the gardens he was working on. The lever, wrapped in a stocking, had been found in the garden of 16 Albany Villas, Hove, and appeared to be the weapon Parker had referred to. Other witnesses were able to help the police piece together the movements of the two accused men from the time they had first come to the area.

Mrs Payne, who ran a lodging house which was also in St Andrew's Road, Portslade, said that the two men had first arrived at her establishment on November 7th. They told her that they had no money but agreed to pay her 15s a week rent. Only 7s 6d of that money had ever been paid and the two men had left on November 13th.

On November 11th, two men had called at a shop run by Joseph Howard Smith at North Street. One of the men remained outside the shop whilst the other came in and tried to sell Smith a sweepstakes ticket. Smith was later to pick out both men at an identification parade, saying that Parker had been the one who spoke to him whilst Probert remained outside.

Mrs Parker, who was no relation to the accused, said that on the same day, November 11th, the two had actually sold her one of their tickets at the shop she ran in Church Road. Later on, those same two men returned to her shop and tried to borrow money for which they wished to leave an overcoat as security. She refused to help them and, like Mr Smith, she too picked out both defendants from a line-up.

On November 13th, Parker and Probert were back at Mr Smith's shop, where they tried to sell the overcoat. Mr Smith was not interested but suggested that they should try Mr Bedford's shop as he might buy such an item. That same gentleman saw them close by Mr Bedford's premises some time before 8.00pm.

The next sighting of Parker and Probert was at Worthing. At 9.45pm on the night of the 13th, both men called at a tea room run by Beatrice Tuck, in High Street. They rented one room, for which Probert handed over 4s in cash. The register was signed in the names of Franklin and Minall. The following morning her two guests gave a farthing to one of her children. That might not appear significant perhaps but the police had discovered that Joseph Bedford had a fondness for those coins and always had quite a few in his shop.

More of the farthings were discovered when Parker's and Probert's lodgings were searched after they had been arrested.

On the morning of the 14th, Parker and Probert entered the gentleman's outfitters run by Richard Oliver, on Brighton Road. Both men ordered a new suit of clothes and other items for which each paid 38s in cash. During their time in the shop, Probert had mentioned that he had lost a button from his old jacket and the tailor found one that seemed to be a good enough match and sewed it on whilst Probert waited. Finally, the old clothes were parcelled up for them and the two men left the shop looking very pleased with themselves, wearing the new clothes they had just paid for.

At 4.15pm on that same afternoon, Parker and Probert walked into another lodging house, this time at 9 York Road, Worthing, owned by a Mrs Mitchell, where they took rooms, stating that they would want them for about two months. These were the same two men who not long before had been trying to sell a coat to raise a few pennies.

After their arrest, the rooms Parker and Probert had occupied were searched. The farthings have already been referred to, but police also found an automatic pistol, along with the old clothes the tailor had parcelled up for them. Subsequent forensic examination of these clothes showed that although no blood was found on Parker's clothes, a good deal of staining was found on Probert's suit and overcoat. The blood was definitely human and of the same type as Joseph Bedford's.

Parker and Probert appeared at the police court a number of times, and were remanded as a matter of course. Both men were represented at this stage by Brighton-based solicitors: Probert by John Bosley and Parker by Stanley Cushman. The case only got under way on December 15th, when Mr Gerald Paling began to outline the case for the prosecution. As he began speaking, Parker collapsed in the dock and had to be treated in the well of the court. In all, over the days the case was being heard, Parker collapsed a total of eight times. He was not the only person to fall ill during this stage, though. One day, January 4th, 1934, Chief Inspector Askew fainted and he too had to receive medical treatment. Finally, after a number of adjournments, the magistrates decided that there was a case to answer and the two defendants were committed for trial at the next assizes.

At this stage, it is necessary to clear up what appeared to be a mystery. When the robbers left Joseph Bedford's shop, they left his front door open. This was shown to be the case when Alice Sandalls posted the newspaper, yet when Constable Peters came upon the scene, all the doors and windows were locked, the gas light had been turned down and the premises were secure. How could this be the case? Perhaps the most reasonable explanation had been given by Sir Bernard Spilsbury. He suggested that Bedford had been beaten unconscious but had eventually come round. At the time, he was so confused and dazed that he might not even have been aware that an attack had taken place. A creature of habit, he then automatically carried out his usual routine until finally his injuries caused him to collapse again when his shop was lit up by the beam from Constable Peters' torch.

The trial of Parker and Probert opened at Lewes on March 14th, 1934, before Mr Justice Roche. Sir Henry Curtis-Bennett and Mr R. Maxwell Turner appeared for the prosecution. Parker was defended by Mr James Dale Cassels and Mr Alban Gordon, whilst Probert had engaged Mr John Flowers and Mr Thomas Gates. The proceedings were to last for three days.

Both men were smartly dressed in court. Parker wore a brown suit with a pale mauve shirt and a grey tie with black stripes. Probert, separated from his companion by two prison warders, wore a dark blue suit, a white shirt with a blue collar and a grey and blue tie.

Amongst the first speeches was a request from Mr Flowers for an alleged verbal statement by Probert to Inspector Leonard Lewis on November 18th, to be declared inadmissible as no caution had been administered. For the time being the matter was left unresolved with the learned judge stating that the prosecution should not refer to the matter in their opening statements. The stream of witnesses then began to appear.

Perhaps the most macabre event of this first day was the evidence of Dr Raymond Evans, the house surgeon at Hove Hospital. He brought with him a human skull, although not that of Mr Bedford, to illustrate where the various wounds had been discovered. He also stated that Joseph Bedford had a rather thinner skull than he would normally have expected to find.

On the second day, Probert's disputed statement was brought into evidence. He, of course, still maintained that he was not present at the scene of the crime and at one stage, when outlining what he had claimed were his actual movements, he had said the words, "I can prove that I was there." In Inspector Lewis' notebook, though, there was a full stop after the word 'that' so the sentence now read, "I can prove that. I was there." It was perhaps a small matter of punctuation but according to the second reading, Probert was saying after all that he was present at the murder.

It was on this same day, March 15th, that the first of the accused men gave his evidence. Frederick Parker stated that on November 7th, he and Probert had been given a lift to Eastbourne by Charles Ralph Hall, a lorry driver of 1 Hartington Road, Brighton. They had gone to Eastbourne to see if they could commit any robberies there and in the course of their ride, Hall had given them the pistol and the tyre lever they used in the robbery on Mr Bedford's shop. Parker had taken the gun whilst Probert took the tyre lever.

Parker went on to say that they had chosen that particular shop to rob since Hall had told them that they might find money there. They had originally thought of robbing a jewellers but decided that such shops would be likely to have alarms. Parker was in the witness box for two and a quarter hours, during which time he collapsed once more. It was then Probert's turn to give his account of what had occurred.

Probert continued to say that he had not been at the scene of the crime. He admitted that the blue suit on which blood had been found did belong to him but said that Parker had borrowed this on the morning of the attack, stating that he was meeting someone from London who might give him some money and he wanted to look his best. The two men then split up and agreed to meet at Portslade station at some time between 8.30pm and 9.00pm.

Probert said he spent the day of November 13th in Brighton.

There he sold his overcoat to a man he met in a snooker hall before having lunch and then going for a walk on the Palace Pier. From there he visited the library. He wasn't sure exactly what time he left there but as he passed the Jubilee Clock Tower, he noticed that it was 6.00pm.

Walking slowly towards Hove, Probert had to shelter once or twice from the intermittent showers, finally arriving at Hove Town Hall at about 7.50pm. From there he later caught a bus to Portslade station, getting there at about 8.30pm. Parker turned up some 15 minutes later, said he had managed to get £3 10s, some of which he passed on to his friend. In effect, Probert was saying that although he wasn't in Joseph Bedford's shop, his clothes were.

The jury retired at 2.50pm on March 16th. They were out for 35 minutes before returning their verdict that both the accused were guilty as charged. Probert shouted, "I am innocent of the crime." Parker moved to speak but did not do so. As the judge pronounced the sentence of death, Probert's wife, sister and sister-in-law, who were all seated in the public gallery, began to moan loudly. Before the dread words of death had concluded, Mrs Parker collapsed and was taken to an ante-room from where her screams could still be heard.

On March 22nd, Probert announced that he would appeal. Four days later, on the 26th, Parker's solicitor made the same announcement. Those appeals were heard on April 17th before the Lord Chief Justice, Lord Hewart, and the Justices Avory and Humphreys. That appeal was to last two days.

For Probert, the defence continued to maintain that there was no real corroboration of Parker's statement incriminating him. They maintained that Parker was, by his own confession, guilty of taking part in the attack, but denied that Probert was involved. For Parker, the defence largely rested on the belief that he should have been found guilty of manslaughter instead. He had gone into the shop with the intention of taking part in a robbery but had wanted nothing to do with the attack on Bedford and indeed had tried to stop it. There was also the suggestion that Constable Peters, shining his torch into the shop, had startled Bedford, causing him to fall and crack his head. That might well have contributed to the poor man's death. The bench ruled, though, that there was ample evidence of the involvement of both men and the appeals were lost.

Last-minute attempts were made to save the condemned men. John Bosley, Probert's solicitor, drew the attention of the Home Secretary to the case of Donovan, Weaver and Taylor, three Brighton men sentenced to death for a very similar crime in 1928. In that case it was eventually decided that robbery and not murder was primarily in the minds of the condemned men. That appeal was successful and all three were subsequently reprieved. The Home Secretary was not moved and confirmed that the sentences would stand.

From prison, Parker wrote a last letter to his brother, Edward, explaining to him that he had gone along with the idea of robbery but he had never intended to harm the shopkeeper. He repeated that it had been Probert who struck the man a terrific blow which had ended in his death. Parker went on to say that the thought of what happened made him sick. Nevertheless, the law had decided that he was equally responsible and no matter who had actually struck the fatal blow, both men had to pay the penalty.

At 9.00am on Friday, May 4th, 1934, Albert Probert and Frederick William Parker were hanged together at Wandsworth jail. Thomas Pierrepoint was the executioner and he was assisted by his nephew, Albert and two other men: Stanley Cross and Thomas Phillips. It was the first double execution at that prison since that of Field and Gray, and they too had been hanged for a Sussex crime.

CHAPTER 11

GOSSAMER EVIDENCE

THE evening of Sunday, November 25th, 1934, was cold and crisp with a definite frost in the air. By 5.00pm it was, of course, already dark but Reginald Bertram Crane and his brother were enjoying a most pleasant stroll along the edge of the East Brighton golf course, close by the world famous Roedean School.

Reginald, a clerk from Hove, had met his brother at Black Rock around 3.00pm and from there, the Cranes had walked to Rottingdean where they had tea. Leaving Rottingdean at 4.30pm they strolled through Ovingdean, on to the Downs and finally on to the golf course. They were not very far from the clubhouse when Reginald heard what sounded like a scream. If that did not arouse their suspicions, the shots that followed certainly made them change their route and head in the direction the sounds had come from. They had walked perhaps quarter of a mile by the time the Cranes came to a small shed which had two concrete water tanks to one side of it. As they approached this scene, they spotted the figure of a man walking away, his features shaded by the darkness of the November night.

Thinking that this was a most curious incident, and one which ought perhaps to be brought to the attention of the police, the brothers walked down to the road in order to find a policeman and in due course, found Constable Hayes. He returned with the brothers to the water tanks, each of them 5ft square and some 2½ft deep.

Shining his torch into the gloom, Hayes discovered, in the furthest tank, the body of a young woman.

The body, was fully clothed, with a silk scarf tied tightly around her throat, floating, face up on top of the water. Constable Hayes, realising that he would probably need more help to remove the young lady and to search the immediate area, now took the Cranes back to the clubhouse where two members, Dr Robert Crothers, and Mr W. Barfoot, joined the party, all five returning to the tank.

Gently the young woman was removed but medical attention was not required as it was plain that life was extinct. Other officers soon arrived on the scene and at 6.30pm a methodical search of the immediate area by Detective Sergeant Walter Collyer and Police Constable Maskell, yielded a maroon hat and a lady's handbag. The contents of the handbag were inspected and this gave the police a name to go on. The dead woman was, apparently, 21-year-old Edith Constance Drew-Bear, who lived with her parents, Edith Emily and Thomas Emile Drew-Bear, at 8 Ship Street, Brighton, along with her brother Harold, who identified Edith's body at the mortuary at 11.20pm that same night.

The killer, whoever he was, must have made good his escape by one means or another and as a matter of routine, the crews of all the omnibuses which stopped anywhere near the murder scene were spoken to. One of these, Edward James Elliott, reported a curious incident which had taken place on his bus, the number 4, some time after the murder.

Elliott reported that at 7.00pm a man got on to his bus at Ovingdean Gap, and travelled towards Brighton. The man was very agitated and extremely wet. He wore no boots, jacket or waistcoat and the rest of his clothing was absolutely dripping with water. The only part of his clothing which appeared dry was his white mackintosh and even that was soaked around the bottom. Naturally Elliott asked the man why he was in such a condition and he replied that he had been walking by the sea at Rottingdean and had fallen in. This information was, in itself, very valuable, but he had an even more important contribution to make to the investigation. Elliott lived at 35 Lennox Street, and the soaking man who had travelled on his bus was a neighbour, living in that same thoroughfare, 20-year-old Percy Charles Anderson.

It was 9.10pm by the time Detective Sergeant William Clinch, and Detective Constable Victor Patching, knocked on the front door of Anderson's home. Invited in by Percy's mother, the two officers asked Anderson what he had been doing that afternoon. He replied, "I went to the front where I met my young lady." He was then asked if he knew where his young lady was at that precise moment, and said he did not know. At that point Anderson was cautioned and after further questioning, he admitted that he had indeed been with her at the point where her body had been found. Part of Anderson's statement read, "All right, we went for a walk to Roedean College and came to where there were two wells. We sat down and had a row. After that I had a pain in my head. The next thing I remember was when I was in the sea. I don't know where I left her."

Having received this admission, Sergeant Clinch informed Anderson that Edith had been found dead in one of those wells whereupon Anderson cried, "I took my pistol out to shoot rats. Murdered? Oh my God!" He was then taken to the police station where, at 9.40pm he was formally interviewed by Inspector Arthur Pelling. There, in the presence of Sergeant Clinch, Anderson made a full written statement.

According to that statement, Anderson had first been introduced to Edith at the fishmarket beach by a friend, Rene Parker, and on that first day, they had gone for a swim together in the sea. They had been keeping company with each other ever since then and he had often met her on the sea front opposite Ship Street where she lived, and indeed worked, in one of the restaurants.

On the day in question, Anderson had arranged to meet Edith at about 3.10pm but she had not turned up until just after 4.00pm. This agreed with Edith Drew-Bear's statement that her daughter had only returned from work that day at 3.35pm and left to meet Anderson soon after 3.45pm. They had then taken a slow leisurely walk to Castle Square and from there caught a bus to Arundel Road. Seeing that they were near the golf course, they decided to take a walk along the links and after some time, turned off the road which ran along the back of Roedean College and strolled down a path which led to a swing gate. Going through this gate they passed through a field close by the church at Ovingdean, walked back on to the links and came to the shed where there were two concrete wells, used to store water for the greens. Deciding to take a rest, they had sat together on the edge of the second well and after a few minutes, she brought up the subject of him having smiled at another girl. This led to an argument and they both lost their tempers until he suddenly felt a terrible pain in his head.

The next memory Anderson claimed to have was of being in the sea and swimming for his life. The water was bitterly cold and although he was a very strong swimmer, he found that the only way he could get back to shore was to kick off his shoes and his jacket. Finding himself on dry land again he managed to find his mackintosh which presumably he had removed before going into the water. This was at the edge of the water and had been lapped by the waves so that it too was soaking wet at the bottom.

Getting back on to the roadway, Anderson ran along to the nearest seat where a young couple were sitting together. By this time he needed a cigarette to steady his nerves and since his own were too wet to light, he asked the man if he could let him have one, which he was kind enough to do. From there, Anderson walked to the steps at Ovingdean Gap where he caught a bus to Arundel Road and from there, a second bus to Rock Place. Running up the street in order to get home, Anderson made one stop on the way and that was at Victor Charles Packer's tobacconists shop at the bottom of Lennox Street, where he bought some cigarettes. Here he was again questioned, by Mrs Packer, who served him, about his wet clothes and again said he had fallen into the sea. Arriving home he changed his clothes, sat down in front of the fire and had some tea, it now being around 7.30pm. The next thing he knew, the police were at the door.

By the time the statement had been taken down, by Detective Inspector Pelling, it was 10.20pm and Anderson was now charged with the murder of Edith Drew-Bear. It was then that Constable Patching noticed that Anderson's right hand was in his trouser pocket and he looked to be drawing something out. Instantly his arm was seized and upon examination, a bottle was found clenched in his fist. The bottle's contents were tested later and shown to be a mixture of zinc chloride and ammonium chloride, a combination which, if swallowed, might have proved fatal.

Anderson was then searched, as was his room at Lennox Street. On his person, officers found three bullets and three more were found at his home, as was the cardboard box which had once held a Walden safety revolver. The gun itself was never found and Anderson claimed that it must have fallen out of his pocket whilst he was swimming in the sea. The clothes Anderson had been wearing when he had come home were handed over to the police by his mother, Harriett Emma Anderson. They were still wet and tests showed that the water was saline. Meanwhile, other officers searched the foreshore where Anderson had said he had gone into the sea, in an attempt to find the gun he had used. Detective Constable William Lamming did find a jacket, a waistcoat and a trilby hat, but of the gun there was no sign.

The day after his arrest, Anderson made his first appearance before the magistrates, at Brighton Town Hall. Only evidence of arrest was given, by Inspector Pelling, though, already Anderson had managed to obtain representation in the form of Mr F.H. Carpenter. Anderson was remanded until December 4th.

On December 4th, a few more details about the victim were revealed. Edith, who had the nickname 'Dooly', had been born in Brixton but her family had come to Brighton whilst she was still a baby and she had recently worked as a cashier and bookkeeper at the Bodega public house in Ship Street. Her father was a retired engineer and the only other child of the family was their son, Harold Edwin. Details of the recovery of the body were also given and after this, Anderson was remanded again.

His third court appearance occurred on Tuesday, December 11th, when yet another remand was requested. This was granted and Anderson made his fourth appearance one week later, on December 18th. For the police, Inspector Pelling asked for another remand at which one of the magistrates, Mr Bally, demanded to know why. Inspector Pelling explained that the Director of Public Prosecutions was unable to proceed yet as certain reports from experts had not been completed. Somewhat reluctantly, the request for a remand was granted. In fact, there were three more magistrates' court appearances, one on December 27th, another on December 31st, and the final one on January 4th when Anderson was sent for trial at the next assizes, due to open in March.

Anderson's trial began on March 7th, 1935, at Lewes, before the Lord Chief Justice, Lord Hewart. Anderson, who had by now reached the age of 21, was defended by Mr Eric Neve, whilst the prosecution was led by Sir Henry Curtis Bennett, assisted by Mr Geoffrey Raphael. The jury consisted of 11 men and one woman. Anderson was smartly dressed in a dark suit with a stiff white collar and a black tie.

In addition to the witnesses already named, others were called to fill in some of the details of the night of November 25th. Albert Jesse Saunders had been the conductor on the second bus Anderson caught. He, too, noticed that the young man was wet and shivering and when he asked him what had happened, Anderson had told him that he had slipped on some seaweed and fallen into the water at Rottingdean. Saunders had then gone upstairs on the bus in order to collect some more fares and when he came back down, Anderson had gone. As the bus moved on, Saunders saw Anderson again, running up St James' Avenue.

Victor Charles Packer ran the tobacconist's at the junction of Lennox Street and Carlton Hill. He had known Anderson as a customer for perhaps seven years and confirmed that on November 25th, at around 7.30pm Anderson had come into his shop for some cigarettes. He was wet and again referred to having slipped on some seaweed.

The blue suit Anderson had been wearing, and which was handed over to the police by his mother, was identified by Ernest William Porter, the manager of Rego Clothing of 49 Vale Avenue, Patcham, as one he had sold to Anderson. The white scarf found around Edith's throat, was identified by her brother Harold as one that belonged to the accused man. As if further proof of this were needed, Reginald James Pratt, the landlord of the Miller's Arms, a public house which Anderson frequented, said he also recognised the scarf as one he had seen Anderson wearing.

Sir Bernard Spilsbury testified that he had conducted a post-mortem on November 27th. He had found that the dead girl was wearing two scarves. One, a red-spotted scarf, had been identified as her own and this was loosely fastened by means of a brooch. The other, which was wound twice around Edith's neck had been so tightly knotted around her throat, that it had to be cut off. This scarf was identified as one which belonged to Anderson.

There were five bullet wounds in the body. The first was a superficial wound, on the back, between the shoulders. The second was one behind the right ear, whilst the third was a similar wound on the left side of the head. The fourth was in the lower part of the back, to the right of the spine and the last was to the back of the left arm. None of these wounds would have proved fatal although the head injuries might have rendered the victim unconscious. There were no signs of drowning and the cause of death was asphyxia due to strangulation. Sir Bernard ended his evidence by saying that Edith would have been unconscious within half a minute of the ligature being applied and the bullet wounds had no relation to her death.

Dr Gerald Roche Lynch, a senior analyst to the Home Office, had examined Anderson's clothes. In addition to finding salt he found six bloodstains on the mackintosh, three of which were definitely human blood. The time now came for the defence to put its case.

Anderson went into the witness box to give evidence on his own behalf. He related his story much as he had done in his statement to the police but now explained that he had given Edith his scarf when they first began their walk and she complained of the cold. He had owned the gun for perhaps four or five years and it had really been nothing more than a toy. He was a mechanic by trade and so had bored out the barrel so that it could fire bullets of a larger calibre. As for the bottle found in his possession at the police station, it was a flux he used for soldering and he had no intention of using the substance to take his own life.

Relating some of his family history, Anderson said that he was the youngest child of a family of eight. He had suffered from blackouts and headaches ever since he was 12 years old when a golf ball had struck him with some force and he had fallen on to the back of his head.

Another defence witness was Anderson's mother, Harriett. She informed the court that whilst it was true that she had eight children living, Percy was actually the last child of 11. There was some evidence of mental instability in the family for one of Percy's siblings, a sister, had died at the age of seven whilst suffering from some kind of fit. She agreed that Percy had complained many times of severe headaches.

Finally there was the testimony of Herbert Southern, another neighbour, who lived at 19 Lennox Street. Although he had been called by the prosecution to confirm that the clothing shown in court was similar to that worn by Anderson, he had also related how the accused man had complained to him of head pains, and how he had been very depressed ever since he had lost his job in May. He also added that Anderson was in his opinion a decent and respectable young man who he had never known to be violent.

The defence were suggesting that Anderson had suffered from an attack of masked epilepsy at the time he attacked Edith and was not responsible for his actions. To counter this, the prosecution had called Dr Hugh Arrowsmith Grierson, the medical officer of Brixton prison and Dr Joseph Nicholl, his opposite number at Lewes prison. Both said that they had observed Anderson whilst he was in their care and had found no signs of insanity or mental disorder. Indeed, Nicholl said that in his opinion, Anderson had a very fair idea of right and wrong.

In his summing up, the judge made a number of telling observations. Anderson had been precise in his description of which of the wells he and Edith had sat upon, even though he claimed to have no memory of what had happened afterwards. The removal of his mackintosh before he went into the sea was a sensible thing to do and not the behaviour of someone whose mind was suffering from some kind of disorder and, of course, there had been an element of deliberation, for why had Anderson made no inquiries of a woman he professed to love and yet who he last recalled leaving on a cold and dark golf course?

The trial ended on March 9th, when Anderson was found guilty and sentenced to death. His execution was set for March 28th, but this was postponed when Anderson gave notice of appeal.

The appeal was heard on Friday, March 29th before Justices Avory, Hawke and Lawrence. There were two main grounds: first, the judge had referred in his summing up to the bottle found in Anderson's possession. During the trial the prosecution had first suggested that this was to be used by Anderson to destroy himself but they subsequently abandoned this premise. The judge, by referring to it again had prejudiced the jury.

The second approach was that the judge, again in his summing up, had referred to the evidence of insanity as 'gossamer'. There was, however, strong evidence that Anderson suffered from head pains and depression and this had not been properly dealt with. The judges, though, believed that neither of these points was valid and added that they thought it astonishing that Anderson had made no inquiries as to what might have happened to Edith. The appeal was dismissed.

A new execution date was set and, despite a petition organised by Anderson's brother-in-law, Edward Heather, which collected more than 10,000 signatures, and a second petition which attracted no fewer that 90,000 names, it was announced that there would be no reprieve.

The execution of Percy Charles Anderson took place at Wandsworth prison at 9.00am on Tuesday, April 16th, 1935. Thomas Pierrepoint officiated and he was assisted by Alfred Allen. The execution was not without incident, at least outside the prison walls. A crowd of several hundred people had gathered outside the gates and when, at precisely 8.00am, the campaigner Mrs Van Der Elst arrived, the police rushed to stop her car getting any closer. Leaflets were distributed, signatures were collected and Mrs Van Der Elst made a speech announcing that the authorities were hanging an innocent and insane man. She went on to guarantee that within six months, capital punishment would be stopped.

As the clock struck nine, the hour of the execution, someone shouted, "Will the gentlemen remove their hats?" All did so and a few seconds later many sang the hymn, *Abide With Me*. Still there was more controversy to come. The inquest on Percy Anderson was held by the coroner, Dr Edwin Smith, and the jury insisted on seeing Anderson's body and the scaffold where he had died. As the foreman said, "In any ordinary instance, instruments causing death — a revolver or a razor, are produced. We cannot fully inquire into this man's death if we do not see the instruments." After some discussion, the prison governor, Captain G.F. Clayton agreed to this request and the jury were taken to view the scaffold before they returned their verdict.

CHAPTER 12

A MATTER OF TIMING

KATHLEEN Lawrence, one of the chambermaids at the hotel situated at 22 York Road, London, was busying herself with her duties when she came to room 6 on the third floor. Kathleen knocked on the door but there was no reply from the couple who had checked in two nights before. After trying a couple of times, she called for the manager, Richard Vaughan Jones, who was attending to something in the very next room. He, too, tried to rouse the occupants of room 6, but when he failed to receive an answer, he walked down to reception and picked up his pass key.

Jones was soon inside the room. The light was still on and the male guest, Mr Armstrong, was nowhere to be seen. His wife, though, was in bed, apparently asleep. Richard Jones crossed the room and tried to gently wake Mrs Armstrong, but when he pulled back the sheets and blanket which covered most of her face, he froze. Part of the bedclothes were stuffed into the woman's mouth and she was quite obviously dead. Locking the room again, Jones ran back downstairs and summoned the police.

Detective Inspector William Fury was soon on the scene. Deciding not to move the body until the pathologist had arrived, Fury took a look around the room and noticed an empty half-bottle of sherry and a glass tumbler on the table. There were also two suitcases in the room and these were identified by Richard Jones as being the same ones carried by Mr and Mrs Armstrong when they had arrived at some time between 8.30pm and 9.00pm on New Year's Eve, Saturday, December 31st, 1938.

According to Jones, the couple had explained that they had married only recently and were at that time given room 8. They took their luggage up to the room, having signed the register as Mr and Mrs Armstrong of Seaford in Sussex, and then went out. By 10.00pm, though, the Armstrongs had returned and apparently retired for the night.

On New Year's Day, Jones saw Mr Armstrong at 9.55am and although he did not see the couple leave, they must have gone out together for they returned at 8.30pm when Jones asked Mr Armstrong what time he wanted to be called for breakfast the following morning, adding that he had moved their luggage into number 6, which was a better room. By now Mrs Armstrong had already started making her way upstairs and her husband asked Jones to wait whilst he went to check with his wife. Within minutes he had returned, paid the bill for the two nights and said that they wanted to be called at 8.30am in time for breakfast at 9.00am.

Mr Armstrong asked Richard Jones if he could borrow a corkscrew. Jones said that he did not approve of drinking in the hotel bedrooms but Armstrong told him that he and his wife had recently been beset by family problems. And, after all, they were celebrating the New Year. Jones finally demurred and handed over the corkscrew.

Just over an hour after this encounter, at some time between 9.30pm and 9.45pm Jones thought he saw Armstrong again. All he actually saw was the back of a man as he entered the lavatory on the ground floor, but he was sure from his build that the figure was that of Armstrong. If that was indeed Armstrong, it was the last time Jones saw him, although at 11.00pm Jones did hear the click of a door, almost certainly the front door. He presumed that someone had just left the hotel.

It transpired that the dead woman was not, as she had claimed to be, Mrs Armstrong. Items found amongst the couple's luggage identified her as 17-year-old Peggy Irene Violet Pentecost, who preferred to use her second name and lived at 148 Elm Grove, Brighton, with her mother and father. When Irene's father, Edwin Pentecost was contacted, he was able to put a name to the man who had been in the hotel room with his daughter: 38-year-old Harry Armstrong who worked as a houseman at the Downs School, and lodged at 12 Hindover Road, Seaford, just up the coast from Brighton.

Florence May Passingham was Armstrong's landlady and she confirmed that he had lodged with her since October 1937. She had last seen him at around 6.15pm on December 30th when he told her that he was going to spend the weekend with Irene in Brighton. Passingham later identified one of the suitcases and a pair of men's pyjamas found in the London hotel room as belonging to her guest.

Edwin Pentecost had confirmed that he and his wife approved of the relationship between Armstrong and his daughter and that it had been their intention to spend the weekend at Elm Grove. Armstrong arrived in Brighton on December 30th and slept at the house that night. The following day, Armstrong and Irene announced that they were engaged to be married but later Edwin Penetcost and his daughter had had a brief argument over some insignificant matter. By 6.30pm Irene and Armstrong declared that they were going away for the rest of the weekend instead and that was the last time he saw either of them.

The information from Edwin Pentecost and Florence Passingham meant that an excellent description of Harry Armstrong could be circulated. In fact, such methods were not to prove necessary for Armstrong had already been picked up for abusive behaviour. At 3.30pm on January 2nd, Police Sergeant Richard Ford had been on duty in London's Baker Street when he had seen a man, apparently the worse for drink, swearing and generally making a nuisance of himself. The man had identified himself as Thomas King of Bydown, Seaford, and was taken into custody and escorted to the Albany Street police station. Here King had been searched whereupon a postcard had been found. Addressed to Mrs Pentecost of 148 Elm Grove, Brighton, the card read, 'Dear Mother. This is the best way out. Love, Harry.' The card immediately linked Mr King with the Pentecost investigation and in due course, 'Thomas King' was shown to be none other than Harry Armstrong.

It was 9.00pm by the time Inspector Fury saw Armstrong. In

Above: The house at Bethune Avenue where Louisa Masset lived. See Chapter One.

Left: Manfred Masset. The picture carried around by Louisa Masset, the woman hanged for his murder. See Chapter One. *(Public Record Office)*

Mortuary photograph of Manfred Masset. See Chapter One. *(Public Record Office)*

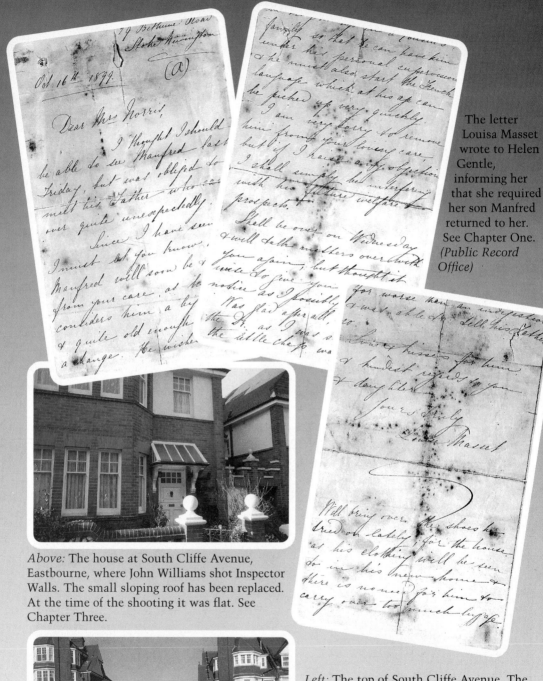

29 Bethune Road
Stoke Newington

Oct. 16th 1899   (a)

Dear Mrs Norris,

I thought I should be able to see Manfred last Friday, but was obliged to meet his Father who came over quite unexpectedly.

Since I have seen I must let you know, Manfred will soon be & from your care, as he considers him a big & quite old enough a change. He wishes

family so that he can have him under his personal supervision & he must also start the French language which at his age can be picked up very quickly.

I am very sorry to remove him from your loving care, but if I raise any objection I shall simply be interfering with his future welfare & prospects.

Shall be over on Wednesday & will talk matters over with you again, but thought it wise to give you notice as I possibly for worse than an indigestion Was glad after all, & was able to tell his Father the D. as I was so the little chap was

love & kisses for him & kindest regards to you & daughter

Yours truly

Louisa Masset

Will bring over their shoes he dried on lately for the house as his clothing will be seen so in his new home & there is no need for him to carry over too much luggage.

The letter Louisa Masset wrote to Helen Gentle, informing her that she required her son Manfred returned to her. See Chapter One. (Public Record Office)

Above: The house at South Cliffe Avenue, Eastbourne, where John Williams shot Inspector Walls. The small sloping roof has been replaced. At the time of the shooting it was flat. See Chapter Three.

Left: The top of South Cliffe Avenue. The murder house is at the far end of the street on the left hand side. The bench mentioned in the story has been replaced but was in the same position as the one in the photograph. See Chapter Three.

Patrick Mahon. This
picture was taken around
1920. See Chapter Seven.
(Hulton Getty)

Patrick Mahon leaving the
Officer's House at the
Crumbles after the first
inquest hearing. See Chapter
Seven. *(Popperfoto)*

Norman Thorne and Elsie Cameron. See Chapter Eight. *(Popperfoto)*

After his fiancée had disappeared, Norman Thorne was happy to pose for photographs. He is standing on the spot where Elsie's body is buried. See Chapter Eight. *(Hulton Getty)*

Above: Thorne being escorted back to prison after one of his appearances at the police court. See Chapter Eight. *(Hulton Getty)*

Left: The dying deposition of Annie Gillon. See Chapter Nine. *(Public Record Office)*

Left: The house at Mile Oak Road where Charles Gauthier shot his lover. See Chapter Fifteen. *(Public Record Office)*

Above: The house where Miss Drew-Bear lived prior to her death, now a solicitor's office. See Chapter Eleven.

Above: Annette Pepper lying dead at the foot of the stairs at 'Hillcrest'. See Chapter Fifteen. *(Public Record Office)*

Left: The basement where John Dorgan murdered his wife. Now a Brighton guest house. See Chapter Sixteen.

Left: The house in Portslade where Michal Niescior murdered his rival in love. Notice the low wall the struggling men fell over. See Chapter Eighteen.

Above: The house where John Whatman met his death. Inset:- Herbert Chapman, the man who found the body. See Chapter Nineteen. *(Beckett Newspapers)*

Right: The King's house in London where Arthur Boyce claimed his lover's life. See Chapter Twenty.

Above: Lewes Courthouse where so many of the cases in this book reached their conclusion. *(PA News)*

Left: John George Haigh, the Acid Bath Killer. See Chapter Twenty-one. *(Mirror Syndication)*

response to questioning, Armstrong would only reply, "I am saying nothing. I was not the last person with her. I can prove I was not in York Road last night after ten o'clock. I can prove where I was, but I am not going to say where I was now. I am saying nothing. I neither admit nor deny anything. I will tell the magistrate in the morning." Armstrong was then moved to Kennington Road police station where he was formally charged with murder.

There were a number of appearances at Tower Bridge court, the first on January 3rd. Other appearances took place on January 10th, January 16th and January 23rd, when Armstrong was finally sent for trial. During those days in court, the case for the prosecution was put by Mr Ernest Clayton whilst Armstrong was represented by Mr Cyril Samuel Brown. At one stage, Armstrong interrupted the evidence of Richard Jones, complaining to the magistrate, Mr Bernard Campion, that Mr Clayton was prompting the witness. The magistrate ruled that the questions had been properly put, but Armstrong made plain his displeasure.

The trial was set for February 13th but on that date an application was made to postpone matters so that Armstrong could undergo a medical examination. So it was that proceedings finally opened at the Old Bailey on March 1st, 1939, and lasted for two days. There were three women on the jury and the case was heard before Mr Justice Humphreys. Armstrong was defended by Mr J.F. Eastwood whilst the case for the prosecution was put by Mr L.I. Byrne.

Edwin Pentecost filled in some of the details of the relationship that had existed between Armstrong and Irene. She had once worked as a maid at a school in Seaford, which was how the couple had first met. Some two or three weeks before Christmas 1938, Irene had taken up a similar position at a school in Tonbridge. She had first brought Armstrong to the house in June 1938, and the couple appeared to be very much in love.

James Norris, who lived at 19 Brock Road, Walthamstow, was a friend of Irene's, having once lived in Brighton. He testified that at 1.00pm on January 1st, Irene had called at his home, and introduced Harry Armstrong as her fiancé. They stayed with him and his wife until about 5.30pm and during their time in the house were most affectionate towards each other, calling each other names such as 'dearest' and 'darling'. At one stage, Irene had sat upon Armstrong's knee.

Chief Inspector Frederick Cherrill was in charge of the fingerprint department at New Scotland Yard and he had examined the sherry bottle and the glass tumbler found in room 6 of the hotel. Both had carried prints and he was able to state that he had found a print on the bottle that matched Armstrong's right middle finger and one on the tumbler which matched his left thumb. There was, however, another print on the bottle which matched neither Armstrong nor Irene, although since it was somewhat obscured by a partial print of Armstrong's, it must have been on the bottle before, possibly when he purchased it.

The time came for Dr Keith Simpson, the pathologist, to give evidence. Simpson testified that there was bruising to Irene's lips, probably caused when material was stuffed into her mouth. When he examined the body, Irene's mouth was packed with part of the white coverlet and when this was removed, he found a man's white handkerchief had also been crammed tightly in. There were marks on Irene's throat consistent with a thumb and fingers of a man's left hand, although Armstrong was known to be right-handed. The cause of death was asphyxia due to the combined effects of strangulation and suffocation, and Simpson was also able to confirm that there was bruising around the vagina consistent with recent rough intercourse possibly at the time of death.

Simpson had examined the body at noon on January 2nd and he put the time of death at 13 hours before. This meant that Irene had died around 11.00pm on January 1st, which matched exactly with the time Richard Jones had heard someone leaving his hotel. The inference was clear, Armstrong had killed Irene at 11.00pm or just a few minutes before, and left the premises immediately afterwards. There was, however, one major problem with this scenario. Harry Armstrong had a cast iron alibi for 11.00pm.

Rose Kirby lived in St George's Road, London, and she had met Armstrong in a café in Westminster Bridge Road, at a few minutes after 10.00pm. Putting aside all considerations of Armstrong's morals, Rose testified that she and Armstrong had spent the entire night together in a hotel, he appearing to be perfectly normal and rational. At 11.00pm therefore, Armstrong was with Rose Kirby.

Upon hearing this evidence, the prosecution decided to move the goal-posts and offer evidence to change the time of death. Dr Simpson was recalled and asked if it were possible that Irene had died earlier, perhaps some time between 9.30pm and 11.00pm. Simpson agreed that it was and so the alibi which Armstrong had was rendered utterly useless. The picture now painted was that he could have killed Irene much earlier, left the hotel at perhaps 9.30pm or 9.45pm and still been in plenty of time to pick up Rose Kirby in the café at 10.00pm.

The defence were nothing if not thorough. A couple of days before the trial began they had employed two solicitor's clerks to enter the hotel at 22 York Road after midnight, and leave again a few minutes later. Richard Jones was forced to admit that he heard none of this and so it was shown that he would not necessarily have heard anyone enter or leave on the night of the murder.

When it came to Armstrong's turn to give evidence, he stated that he had left the hotel at 9.30pm, by which time Irene was already asleep in bed. Going to the café he met up with Rose and some of her friends at 10.00pm. Later he and Rose went to the hotel in Paddington which he only left at 9.30am. He felt very ashamed of what he had done and went into a pub where he had a few drinks. He then intended to return to Irene at the hotel and make his peace with her, but before he could do so he was picked up by the police. As for the postcard found upon his person, that merely meant that he thought it was better that they should leave Elm Grove that weekend, rather than have further trouble as the girl's father had been angry with her.

One of the final witnesses was Dr Hugh Grierson, the medical officer of Brixton prison where Armstrong had been held. He gave evidence that although there were no signs of mental disorder in his prisoner, there were indications that he was of uneven temper. This same witness, however, gave evidence of a series of mental problems with Armstrong's immediate family. A younger sister, who was feeble minded, had died at the age of 11. An elder brother committed suicide as did a great uncle. Another uncle had died in an asylum. As for Armstrong himself, he had very bad eyesight, being almost blind in the left eye and having only slightly better vision in the right. He had suffered from three separate memory losses, the third being in 1931, and in 1935 he had been charged with attempting suicide by taking aspirin tablets.

In his summing up, Mr Eastwood made much of the astounding way the prosecution had recalled a witness to change the suggested time of death in order to destroy Harry Armstrong's alibi. This was described as a most dramatic move, unprecedented in an English courtroom, but in the event, it did not sway the jury. They retired at 3.33pm and by 4.10pm had returned a guilty verdict. Asked if he had anything to say, Armstrong turned to the jury and said, "Ladies and gentlemen, I appreciate everything you have done. No doubt you have had a very difficult task. In spite of your verdict, I am not guilty of the murder of Irene Pentecost."

Surprisingly perhaps, Harry Armstrong did not appeal, preferring instead to rely on a petition for a reprieve on medical grounds. The plea did not succeed and in due course, the Home Secretary announced that the sentence of death would be carried out.

On Tuesday, March 21st, 1939, Harry Armstrong was hanged at Wandsworth prison by Thomas Phillips, who was assisted by Albert Pierrepoint.

CHAPTER 13

THE BODY
IN THE WOODS

VERY early on the morning of Wednesday, September 27th, 1939, 25-year-old William Hudson rose from his bed. Hudson was employed as a gamekeeper by Mr Duncan, who rented the shooting rights to some woodland from the Goring family, and had been asked to clear certain areas of rabbits. So, by 7.00am, he was strolling through the otherwise deserted woods around Hurstpier-point, setting his ferrets into rabbit holes and enjoying the crisp morning air.

It was 7.45am by the time Hudson stepped across a ditch in Shaves Wood and as he did so, he looked down and saw what appeared to be two wooden poles. Thinking that these were rather strange things for someone to dump in the woods, Hudson took a closer look only to discover that the poles were in fact legs. There was a body in the ditch, covered with brushwood and branches.

Dr J.M. Holmes of Burgess Hill was called by Superintendent Moss who was in charge of the investigation. Holmes made an examination at the scene but the body was so badly decomposed that when he tried to lift it by pulling at a belt around the waist, the head came away. About the only thing that was certain at this stage was that the body was that of a woman. The woman's skirt had been pulled high on to the thighs and her hands were stretched out over her head, indicating that she had been dragged to the spot. There were severe wounds in the skull, and this, together with the fact that the body had been covered, left little doubt that the police were dealing with a case of murder.

A number of clues were found in the wood. A brooch was discovered some yards away from the ditch, possibly indicating that the attack had taken place some distance away and the poor woman had then been dragged by the legs to the place where she had been found. A handbag was found, in which the police discovered the torn half of a cinema ticket, issued at the Princes in Brighton on August 19th, along with an entertainment guide to Brighton and Hove. Inside the handbag was also a handkerchief which had a laundry mark in yellow cotton, 'W/6' followed by the figures '11' picked out in red and blue, and a packet of De Reske cigarettes.

On the left wrist of the body was a wristwatch but the glass and the rim were missing. This was a highly significant fact for after the woods had been painstakingly searched, the small pieces of broken glass that made up the watch face were found, some 60ft from the ditch. Close by the watch glass the police found other shards, this time dark brown in colour and these pieces, when glued together, formed a beer bottle which might have been used as the murder weapon. Finally, close by this same spot, officers found a brown paper wrapper which they thought could have been used to carry the beer bottle. This wrapper bore an advertisement: "Tune in every Tuesday at 10.45am to Paris, 312 metres (Poste Parisien). Make a point of it. 2s a bottle. Point brand wines. Red Point (Rich Ruby) Amber Point (British Sherry) White Point (White Sweet)' The wrapper also bore a picture of the Eiffel Tower.

Despite the advanced decomposition, the body was identified almost immediately, by means of a letter found in the handbag, as that of 33-year-old Annie Farrow Cook. Annie, a slightly built woman, had been employed at an officers' convalescent hospital situated at 4 Percival Terrace, Brighton, and had been reported missing by the matron on the morning of August 22nd. The body fitted the general description and had, as mentioned, carried links with Brighton. The final proof came when one of Annie's fellow workers, Ruby Ethel Smith, a parlourmaid at the hospital, identified the items of clothing found on the body as the same as those Annie had been wearing when last seen at 6.00pm on Monday, August 21st.

The police already had a file on Annie Cook. On August 21st, she had been off work from 4.00pm but due back on duty at 10.00pm. At 6.00pm Annie had been in her room at the hospital and had asked Ruby Smith if she was going out for the night. Ruby had said she was and Annie left the house with her a few minutes later. They walked a few steps down the street before Annie headed off in a different direction. That was the last time anyone had seen her alive and when she did not return for her duty at 10.00pm, her fellow members of staff grew concerned and reported Annie's disappearance the next day. All the staff then made statements detailing what little they knew about the missing woman's movements.

One of those employees was 38-year-old William Charles Cowell. He was one of the night orderlies at the hospital and it seems that he had made arrangements to meet Annie on the night she vanished. On August 22nd, some time after 7.30pm Cowell walked into Brighton police station and made a voluntary statement saying that he had arranged to meet Annie at an area known as the Level, from where they would go to the circus together. Annie had turned up but seemed preoccupied and asked him for a loan of 15s, saying that something had come up and she needed to catch a train urgently. Cowell tried to find out what the trouble was, but Annie would say nothing more. As a friend, Cowell returned to the hospital, collected the money and handed it over to Annie. He last saw her heading off in the direction of the railway station. As for her ticket, he simply threw that away and went to the circus alone. However, when asked specifically what he had seen at the show, Cowell was vague, mumbling something about, "…horses and such."

Other people confirmed Cowell's arrangement to meet Annie on the Level. William Henry Edward Darling, a day orderly, said that Cowell had asked him to do a late shift for him as he was taking Annie to the circus. Margaret Marie Cotty, one of the two girls who shared a room with Annie, confirmed that Annie and Cowell had been out together a number of times and she, too, knew about the supposed date on the 21st. Indeed, the following morning, Margaret had asked Cowell if he had seen Annie home after the circus. Cowell told her that Annie had not turned up.

Emily Neale, Annie's other room-mate, had seen Annie change out of her uniform after coming off duty at 4.00pm. In fact, Annie had changed into a floral dress which Emily had given to her. When Annie did not return that night, it was Emily who reported the matter to the night sister, Audrey Mary Pike. She in turn on the morning of the 22nd, asked Cowell what he and Annie had done the night before. Cowell had repeated the story of the 15s loan but Audrey was far from satisfied and reported Annie's disappearance to the matron, Ethel Alexandra Curtis. After speaking to Cowell, Curtis contacted the police.

On the day after Annie's body had been found, Cowell returned to the police station, telling the officer on the desk that he thought he should make a further statement, clarifying what he had already said. That statement was taken down by Detective Constable Stacey to whom Cowell laughingly remarked, "I do hope you don't think I did it." In fact, that was exactly what the police were beginning to think, but proving it was an entirely different matter.

Investigations began into Cowell's history and it was soon discovered that in 1937, he had lived in a cottage in Muddleswood. This was situated just a few hundred yards from the wood where Annie had been found so it was reasonable to assume that the area in general would be one that Cowell knew quite well. The police decided to talk to Cowell for a third time and on October 3rd, Detective Inspector Manby called at the hospital to see him. By now Cowell had left his job at that establishment and was living at 18 New Steine. Here he was asked to make another statement. Cowell voluntarily accompanied Manby to the police station and made his statement which again went over the same ground as the previous two.

It was soon after this date that the publicity given to the case in the local newspapers brought forward a valuable witness. Percy Henry Richardson lived at Alexandra Terrace, Western Road, Hurstpierpoint, and was employed as a butcher's roundsman. Just after noon on August 22nd, he had been driving his van along the road that skirted the edge of Shaves Wood. At 12.15pm he noticed a man walking backwards out of the wood. The man took three steps, saw Richardson approaching and then stepped forward again, although he did not actually re-enter the wood. He then turned away from Richardson and walked off rapidly, glancing over his shoulder from time to time to see if Richardson was watching him. When shown a photograph of Cowell, Richardson said he was absolutely certain that this was the man he had seen. Cowell was now linked directly to the wood where Annie was killed.

It was October 20th by the time Inspector Manby returned to 18 New Steine to question Cowell yet again. To his dismay he found that Cowell was no longer living there, and had left no forwarding address. It took the police two more days to find out where Cowell was now living and it was there, at 1 Southover Street, that Manby once more saw his suspect, on Sunday, October 22nd.

Cowell again voluntarily accompanied Manby to the police station and made yet another statement repeating what he had already said. It was then that Manby told Cowell that he had a witness who would swear that Cowell had been seen coming out of Shaves Wood on the day after Annie disappeared. Cowell now claimed that he was there but was on his way to see a police sergeant he knew at Steyning. This sergeant had promised to give Cowell a mackintosh and some boots. Manby pointed out that the direct route from Brighton to Steyning showed that there was no need for Cowell, a man who knew the area well, to go into those woods.

Cowell thought for a time and then asked if some of the other officers present would leave the room. At Manby's instructions, these officers, including Constable Harman and Sergeant Buckland, did leave and it was then that Cowell made a contentious statement, "I went to see the body. I done it." Within 15 minutes, Cowell had started to make another statement in which he admitted his guilt. He was then charged with murder.

Cowell's first appearance was at the Haywards Heath police court, on October 23rd. Other appearances followed on October 30th, November 13th and November 29th, when he was finally sent for trial. It was during those dates that Cowell complained that his wife and child were now forced to live with his mother at Tunbridge Wells and all they had to live on was the old woman's pension of 10s a week. The court promised that they would see that someone would be sent to inquire into their circumstances and provide assistance if possible.

The final police court hearing, which started on November 29th, lasted for three days and a total of 25 witnesses were called for the prosecution. Here a number of letters Cowell had written to Annie were read out. In one he had said:

'My dear Annie, I want to say how happy you make me when I take you out and I want you to be happy too. You and I can be very happy together. You will have as good a friend in me as I have in you. I look upon you as true to me as I am to you ...I am always longing to see you alone. Without seeing you I feel myself sinking. I always want to be alone with you every night.' The letter was signed, 'Charlie'.

The trial of William Charles Cowell opened at Lewes on March 6th, 1940, before Mr Justice Humphreys. It lasted for three days and Cowell was defended by Mr Eric Neve and Mr Alban Gordon. The prosecution case was led by Mr John Flowers, assisted by Mr Gerald Thesiger. In addition to the witnesses already mentioned, the prosecution called Winifred Mary Travell, Annie's sister. Winifred lived at Hornsey and she testified that Annie had for some time been a professional dancer with a touring company but had forsaken this when the 'talking' pictures became popular. She was a quiet girl, and had been heard to remark that she disliked men. Winifred had visited Brighton with her two children, on August 16th, and said that this was the last time she had seen Annie alive.

Dr Leonard Robert Janes was the Brighton pathologist who had performed the autopsy on Annie's remains and he stated that the cause of death was a fracture to the skull. There were two injuries, one to each side of the head and this was consistent with a heavy blow being struck on the rear, left side. The injury on the right would have been caused when Annie struck the ground or possibly a branch, as she fell.

The most damning evidence, though, was Cowell's own state-ment. In this he confessed that he had visited the body for a number of days, from August 22nd to Saturday, August 26th, in order to make sure it was well hidden and no one had discovered it. Once he had visited the site for five consecutive days, he decided he did not need to bother anymore. The same statement went on to describe how Cowell had actually killed Annie by striking her with a large piece of wood after they had argued, although he never explained why or how they had travelled to the woods in the first place.

Cowell, though, claimed that this statement had been obtained under duress. At one stage, Sergeant Buckland had told him that if he ever wanted to see his wife and child again, he had better own up to what he had done. The police, of course, denied that any such pressure had been applied and notes made by Inspector Manby appeared to confirm that Cowell had admitted his guilt. After being charged, Cowell had been allowed to see his wife and Manby who was present made notes of their conversation. At one stage Cowell had said to his wife, "I don't know what made me do it. When you asked me a fortnight ago if I had done it I told you 'No.' I must have been mad. It's the rope for me now, or 'Majesty's Pleasure'. Look after him [*indicating his son*] because I can't help you now. I can't tell you how I done it and I am not going to. I shall soon meet the Almighty. That's all I've got now."

The jury retired at 2.53pm on March 8th, and were out considering their verdict for just 40 minutes. Asked if he had anything to say before the sentence of death was passed, Cowell replied, "All I can say is that I am not guilty."

Cowell's appeal was heard on April 8th, before Justices Hawke, Charles and Hilbery. The main grounds were that Cowell's statement which amounted to a confession to the crime was not a voluntary one. After examining the evidence, the judges announced that Cowell's conviction had followed because that confession was so clear and had contained details which only the killer could possibly have known. As a result, the appeal was lost.

On Wednesday, April 24th, 1940, William Charles Cowell was hanged at Wandsworth by Thomas Pierrepoint and Stanley Cross. There were only six people outside the prison gates at the time and four of those were road workers.

CHAPTER 14

❦

TWO LORRY DRIVERS

LEONARD George Bailey and George Tilbury were both dutiful members of the Home Guard. They took their duties seriously and rarely missed one of the regular drills at Halnaker, near Goodwood. So it was on Sunday, January 31st, 1943. The two men attended the drill and then began cycling home together.

It was 12.40pm when Bailey spotted something incongruous in one of the fields. There was a gap in the hedge and there, lying in the grass, was a figure in Air Force uniform. Bailey's first thought was that some serviceman, out on leave, had consumed rather more than one over the eight. Telling Tilbury what he had seen, he dismounted his cycle and went into the field to see if he could offer some assistance.

To his horror, the blue bundle turned out not to be a drunken airman but a young WAAF who had sustained extremely severe head injuries. Despite these, the woman was still alive, albeit barely, and Bailey covered her with his greatcoat whilst Tilbury dashed to the Richmond Arms at Waterbeach. A number of Army officers were billeted there, amongst them a doctor and a padre. They ran back with Tilbury to where the young woman lay.

When the group arrived back at the field, they saw that the woman was lying on her left side, with her head quite close to the hedge and her feet pointing towards the centre of the field. Her uniform was soaking wet, indicating that she had most probably been lying in the field all night. One stocking was pulled down over her shoe and some four and a half yards away lay her hat and what looked like a notebook but turned out to be a diary. These items were handed to the first police officer on the scene, Constable Thomas Hughes. Meanwhile the still unconscious woman was taken to the Royal West Sussex Hospital, in Chichester, where she arrived at 2.00pm. Here she was administered to by Dr Charles Kay Warwick, the house surgeon, but despite his care, his patient died during an operation at 8.30pm from an intra-cerebral injury. She had never regained consciousness.

With the diary and the fact that she was a WAAF, it was a simple matter to identify the dead woman as 22-year-old Marguerite Beatrice Burge, the adopted daughter of Ada Wellman of 51 New Road, Bedhampton. She had been in the WAAF for two years and had celebrated her birthday only the week before she had been attacked. Her family were devastated and none of them could bring themselves to view the body. Marguerite was formally identified by Louisa Nellie Allen, a neighbour, who lived at 49 New Road and had known her since Marguerite was two.

The initial inquiry was led by Superintendent Ernest Morris Savage of the Chichester Division, assisted by Detective Inspector John Reginald Widdicombe, but they realised that they would need the expertise of Scotland Yard and so Detective Chief Inspector Thomas Barratt and Detective Sergeant Charles Morris travelled down to Sussex from London. The Scotland Yard men soon turned up vital witnesses.

Frank Robert Gough and Leslie George Boxall were youths who lived next door to each other in a lane off the Waterbeach Road. On the afternoon of January 30th, they were watching a pheasant shoot when they saw an Army lorry pull up near a WAAF who was walking towards Waterbeach. Some sort of conversation followed, for Gough and Boxall saw the WAAF leaning into the doorway of the lorry. By then it was around 3.40pm and very soon afterwards, the same lorry passed the two youths, with the WAAF now sitting in the passenger seat. The vehicle had gone only 100 yards or so when it stopped again and remained there for perhaps 15 minutes before finally starting up again and vanishing from sight.

An Army lorry, presumably the same one seen by Gough and Boxall, was also spotted by Alfred Horner. By this time it was 4.15pm and the lorry was parked in the road very close to where Marguerite's body was later found. Horner saw a soldier standing near the cab and as he drew closer, the man ran around the back of the vehicle and reappeared a few moments later with some papers in his hand which he held up close to his face.

One other person had also seen this lorry. James Peter Glasspool was a shepherd, working in a field close to where Marguerite was discovered. He reported that he had seen the lorry stop at around 4.00pm. After 15 minutes or so, the lorry moved on a few yards and the driver got out and walked around the back. Within minutes, he was back in the cab and driving off again, only to stop again, close to the gap in the hedge. The soldier then got out of the cab again and walked through the gap, into the field. After being there for a couple of minutes or so, he got back into his lorry which then drove off at high speed, towards Goodwood. From all this, the police drew the not unreasonable assumption that a soldier, driving an Army lorry, had picked up Marguerite Burge at about 3.40pm and, having carried out a vicious assault upon her, dumped her in the field around 4.15pm.

Tracing Marguerite's movements was also a relatively simple affair. At 1.55pm on January 30th, she had been seen leaving the sergeants' mess at RAF Tangmere where she was based. Clare Berry, another WAAF, knew Marguerite well and waved her goodbye as she left the camp.

Sergeant Stanley Morris Clarke was an instructor in the Army Physical Training Corps. He had first met Marguerite on January 28th and after falling into conversation with her, had asked her out on a date in Bognor Regis on the 30th. Clarke had arranged to meet Marguerite at the Boxgrove corner and left his own billet at 2.00pm to catch a bus down there. He arrived at some time close to 2.35pm and waited for 15 minutes. When Marguerite did not turn up, Clarke thought he had simply been stood up and went into Bognor alone.

Marguerite had intended keeping that appointment, though, for George Hardwick, from the RAF Regiment, knew her well and he had seen her sitting on a fence near the Strettington crossroads. They chatted together before his bus arrived and by the time he left, it was perhaps 3.30pm. Marguerite had apparently missed Clarke and soon afterwards realised this and decided to head back to camp. She started to walk in the direction of Waterbeach and within ten minutes, someone had stopped and offered her a lift.

There were other clues. When the field had been searched, a grey balaclava and a glove had also been found. These items were handed over to Dr James Davidson, the director of the Metropolitan Police laboratory at Hendon. He found a hair inside the balaclava, but more importantly, found type 'A' bloodstains. These matched Marguerite's blood group and linked the balaclava to the murder. This in turn implied that the hair probably belonged to the killer and might well help to aid in his conviction. Finally, a screwdriver had been found, about 75 yards from the body. This bore traces of blood and was later shown to fit the wounds inflicted upon Marguerite's head.

On February 1st, the inquest was opened at the Royal West Sussex Hospital, before Mr Norman H. Hignett. Only evidence of identification was called and the proceedings were then adjourned. Meanwhile, the police inquiries moved on apace.

As a matter of course, the investigation concentrated on the various Army units in the area. There were many soldiers to interview and the Military Police assisted the operations. It was one of these MPs, Sergeant Joseph Raoul Rene Carrier of the Canadian Provost Corps, who provided the civil authorities with the information that would break the case.

On February 9th, one of the soldiers Carrier interviewed was a French Canadian from the Royal Canadian Army Service Corps. This man, 23-year-old Private Charles Arthur Raymond, number E22936, said that he had never seen the dead girl but did tell Carrier who he believed the killer was. In one part of his interview, Raymond said, "You had better make a close check up on Patry: he is a bad 'un, and he is always talking about the murder."

Thirty-one-year-old Arthur Patry was in the same unit as Raymond and drove a three-ton Chevrolet lorry, just as Raymond did, but routine checks showed that he could not possibly be the killer of Marguerite Burge. On January 29th, Patry had been in Scotland and only arrived back in camp at 11.00am on January 30th. Whilst it was true that he might conceivably have had the time to drive to the murder scene, he could not have done so for at 1.45pm he was allocated a new lorry and worked on it with two other soldiers, Private Donald Garfield Vikse and Private Glaser, until some time after 3.15pm. After this was over, Private Vikse went to work on another lorry and on a couple of occasions, saw Patry in the vicinity. Later still, at around 4.30pm, Patry was in the transport orderly room where he replaced the duty NCO, Corporal Morris Asch, who did not relieve Patry again until 7.00pm. There was no way that Patry could have left the camp.

On February 24th, Raymond was interviewed for a second time but on this occasion, besides Provost Sergeant Carrier, Chief Inspector Barrett was also present.

Raymond repeated his accusations against his compatriot but this time added the astounding information that he and Patry had seen the body of the girl on the morning of January 31st. They had been for a drink and on the way back to camp, he had seen something blue in a field. They came upon the body of Marguerite Burge but decided to do nothing in case they got into trouble with the police. Raymond was taken to Chichester police station where he made a written statement repeating all this information and adding that he had even heard Patry talking in his sleep 'about WAAFs and detectives'.

Patry was also interviewed for a second time. He agreed that he and Raymond had seen the body but had not reported it because they did not wish to get in trouble with the police. After seeing Marguerite, he and Raymond had gone to the Anglesea Arms for a drink, staying there for perhaps 20 minutes, before they returned to camp. During that time the two men spoke about what they had seen and came to the conclusion that she was already dead. And as she was beyond all help, there was no need to get involved. Patry had one other thing to add, though. The next morning, after church parade, Raymond had asked him if he thought that the police could trace fingerprints after it had been raining.

From the statements he had made it was obvious that Raymond knew a great deal about the murder. Since it was impossible for Patry to have committed the crime, the police felt that they had enough to arrest Raymond and he was taken into custody. He made his first court appearance on March 4th when matters were adjourned until March 24th. This time he was represented by Mr R.D. Bray of Bognor Regis and was remanded for six days. On March 30th he was committed for trial.

Raymond's trial took place at the Old Bailey and opened on May 10th, 1943, when there were three women on the jury. The trial was heard by Mr Justice Lawrence with the Crown's case being led by Mr Eric Neve, assisted by Mr John C. Maude. Raymond's defence was in the hands of Mr Thomas Carthew, assisted by Mr Harold Brown. Raymond pleaded not guilty and throughout the trial, all the testimony was translated into French for Raymond by Mr E.J. Carroll.

Marguerite Burge had, of course, arranged to meet Stanley Clarke on the day she was attacked and was picked up by someone at around 3.40pm. Raymond was known to be in the same location at the same time for he had dropped off Private Roger Alfred Joseph Dumas in Chichester at 3.10pm, telling him that he needed to fill up the lorry's tank. The petrol he used had to be signed for and the register showed that he had called at a garage near the murder spot at 3.30pm. In addition, Dumas stated that at the time, Raymond was wearing a grey balaclava, similar to the one found in the field near Marguerite's body.

Just ten minutes after Raymond had purchased the petrol, an Army lorry had been seen picking up a WAAF and the prosecution held that this WAAF was Marguerite Burge and the lorry was driven by Raymond. Testimony was given that on February 1st, Raymond had handed his tool kit over to another soldier and when it had been checked, a screwdriver was found to be missing.

Sir Bernard Spilsbury was called to give evidence. He testified that Marguerite had received four stab wounds to her head and three to the body, one of which had penetrated a lung. At one stage Sir Bernard produced a small glass case containing a piece of Marguerite's skull. He then showed that the screwdriver found in the field exactly fitted the wounds. There were no self-defence wounds on the body which implied that the stabs had been inflicted whilst the victim was unconscious. In all probability, Marguerite had received a violent blow to the chin which had caused her to fall backwards, striking the back of her head on some hard object, possibly within the lorry cab itself. It had been this blow which caused her to die but the overnight exposure and the stab wounds had also contributed. The only other marks on the body had been some bruises on the hands and lower limbs, consistent with a brief struggle before she was hit. Finally Sir Bernard was able to say that although Marguerite's clothing had been torn, she had not been sexually assaulted.

Dr James Davidson was able to provide more damning evidence for the prosecution. He had found bloodstains on Raymond's clothing which were type 'A' the same as Marguerite's. He had also found lipstick on Raymond's tunic which matched that worn by the dead girl and finally was able to say that the hair in the balaclava was similar to Raymond's but totally different from Patry's.

For his part Raymond continued to insist that Patry was the killer. He claimed that he had actually seen Patry's lorry stop in front of his and pick up Marguerite Burge. He had even seen Patry take the girl into the field, and strike her. He had rushed to help but Patry had told him to clear off or else. All this was despite the fact that witnesses had sworn that they saw only one lorry and the evidence that Patry had not left the camp. Raymond simply said that the witnesses were all mistaken and accounted for the blood on his clothing by saying that he must have picked this up when he and Patry viewed the body on January 31st. Patry, though, had already stated that although they looked at the body, they did not approach close enough to touch her. As for the lipstick, Raymond said he must have picked this up from another girl he knew.

The jury retired on May 14th and were out for only 20 minutes. Asked if he had anything to say, Raymond replied, in French, "I am not guilty." The sentence of death was also translated by Mr Carroll, who had to stop a number of times as he was visibly moved by what he was forced to intone.

The appeal was heard on June 22nd, but dismissed. On Saturday,

July 10th, 1943, Charles Arthur Raymond was hanged at Wandsworth by Thomas Pierrepoint and Stephen Wade. One cannot help but think that had either he or Patry contacted the authorities when they viewed the body of Marguerite Burge on January 31st, she might possibly have survived, and Raymond would not have lost his own life.

CHAPTER 15

THE GREEN EYED MONSTER

IN January 1943, Britain's fortunes looked brighter than at any time since the outbreak of war three and a half years earlier. The previous October, Axis forces had been removed from North Africa following the Battle of El Alamein, and after the Japanese attack on Pearl Harbor in December 1941, the United States was now deeply involved alongside Britain and her Commonwealth allies. Indeed, England was a mass of Army camps holding soldiers of all nationalities, including those from Canada.

Private Ronald Hill Webb was one of those Canadian soldiers and since Webb had his wife, Margaret Edith, with him in England, they had taken a lease on a private house, Hillcrest, 208 Mile Oak Road, Portslade, near Brighton. Also living at that address were 30-year-old Annette Elizabeth Frederika Christina Pepper and her eight-year-old daughter, Valerie, as sub-tenants. Annette's husband, Philip Leonard Pepper, was a prisoner-of-war, in Germany, and had been for some time. Annette, though, was not one to wait patiently at home for his return since, by her own admission, she was no longer in love with him.

It was on January 16th, 1943, that Annette Pepper met another Canadian soldier in a café. Charles Eugene Gauthier was a married man, 25 years old, although in a different unit to Ronald Webb,

Gauthier being in the Regiment De La Chaudiere. After enjoying a pleasant cup of coffee together, Annette invited Charles back to Hillcrest, and there she told him about her husband and the fact that she no longer cared for him. Nature took its course and the two soon started seeing each other on a regular basis, eventually falling in love. There was, however, one major problem with their relationship.

Annette, to coin a euphemism of the time, had a 'very healthy physical side' to her nature and this in turn led to her wishing to spend time with other men. On one occasion when she called at Gauthier's billet, only to be told that he was not there, she made love to one of the soldiers who was. Annette confessed this indiscretion to Gauthier when they next met and although he forgave her, and their relationship continued, he could never trust her again.

There was, however, more than one other soldier in Annette's life. Sergeant William Archibald Rendall, also a Canadian, was in the Edmonton Regiment, the same one as Ronald Webb. Rendall had first met Annette in November 1941 and he had certainly become involved with her at some level by early 1942, for from March to December of that year, he was based in Canada, yet kept up a string of correspondence with Annette. Once he had returned to England, their friendship was rekindled and he too became a regular visitor to Hillcrest.

Annette was certainly not one to hide her various friendships. Just as she had once confessed to making love to someone else, she also told Gauthier about her sergeant, although in this case she stressed that it was only a friendship, nothing more. Indeed, the same night that she told Gauthier about Rendall she added, "You know darling, we are very much in love with each other. I am married and you are married. We cannot get married, but shall we make a promise that no one will ever come between us? I will be like your wife and you will be like my husband." It was enough to satisfy Charles Gauthier's doubts. The relationship continued and by the early part of 1943, Annette Pepper was pregnant and she told Charles Gauthier that it was his child.

The fateful weekend began on Friday, March 12th, 1943, when

Gauthier heard that a Canadian sergeant was looking for him. That sergeant was, of course, Rendall, and he made a special trip to Portslade on the following day, Saturday, to try to trace Gauthier but without luck. The two men did not meet up until Monday, March 15th, and then it was by accident rather than design. On that day, Gauthier had returned to the café where he had first met Annette. The waitress there knew of the friendship and in the course of their conversation, she asked Gauthier if he had seen Annette. One of the other soldiers in the café at the same time was none other than Rendall and when Gauthier left the café, Rendall followed him out.

It was in High Street, Portslade that Rendall stopped Gauthier and asked if he was the soldier 'going about' with Mrs Pepper. Gauthier replied that he was and added that he was in love with Annette and she was in love with him. Rendell said that he knew differently and that he was the man she really wanted. A fight might well have broken out but both men saw that the only person who could really sort the matter out was Annette herself, and the only place she would certainly be found was back at her home. The two men agreed to meet at Hillcrest later that same day.

In fact, at this time, Annette was not at home. She and the Webbs had been to spend the day in London. Gauthier knew this and determined that he would meet them at the station so that Rendall would not be the one to see her first. He then walked down to Portslade station and waited for their train to pull into Portslade at 5.30pm. Ronald and Margaret Webb took Valerie on the bus back to Hillcrest with them leaving Annette and Gauthier to talk.

As they strolled, Charles Gauthier told Annette about his encounter with the sergeant and the discussion continued as they walked into a shop. As Annette made her purchases, Gauthier saw Rendall walk past the window and pointed him out to Annette with the words, "That's the one I told you about." Annette turned to Gauthier and pleaded, "Please darling, do me a favour: give me this evening with him. I have something very important to talk about with him."

Gauthier was taken aback and denied her request. Annette promised that all she would do with Rendall was talk, but again

Gauthier refused to leave them alone together for one evening. Finally, after much begging from Annette, Gauthier agreed to let her have her discussion with Rendall but still accompanied her home to Hillcrest.

By the time Gauthier and Annette reached Hillcrest, Rendall was already ensconced in the front room. For some minutes there was an uneasy atmosphere as Annette, Gauthier, Rendall and Valerie all sat together, with few words being spoken. Then, probably to escape the oppressive atmosphere more than anything else, Annette announced that she was going to make some tea and walked into the kitchen.

Within seconds, Gauthier had followed her. There he tried to put his arms around her but she pushed him away with a cry of, "No… no …" At this, Rendall, who had heard what was going on, also went into the kitchen but was told by both Gauthier and Annette to go back to the front room which he, albeit reluctantly, did. Once again Gauthier tried to put his arms around Annette's waist but she would have none of it. Instead she turned to face him and said, "I must tell you, I love Bill."

Gauthier was destroyed. "You don't love me?"

"No," replied Annette, "I never did." Gauthier lashed out, slapping Annette across the face, only for her to return the blow. Once again Rendall heard the commotion and stormed back into the kitchen. Harsh words followed and Annette repeated that she was in love with Rendall. Finally Gauthier saw that he was a beaten man. He went to leave the house but stopped in the kitchen doorway and half turned to say, "I go, but you know what is going to happen," and with that he walked out of Hillcrest.

Gauthier appeared to be in a daze. Walking to a nearby billet at the Old Brewery, Portslade, he asked the soldier on duty, Corporal Leon Wiggo, if there was any ammunition there, and was told that, of course, there was. It was by now 6.30pm and Gauthier left without further comment but less than an hour later he was back at the Old Brewery. He went on to the roof where he knew there was a Bren gun mounted, and removed it, together with its magazine. It was not until just after 8.30pm that Private Leopold Boudreax discovered that the gun had been stolen and reported the matter to his commanding officer. Gauthier, meanwhile, had returned to Hillcrest, hidden the weapon in the garden, knocked on the front door and had a long talk to Annette, but when it was clear that she would not change her mind, he left again. Within minutes, he had returned.

It was around 8.00pm when Charles Gauthier arrived back at 208 Mile Oak Road. Once more he knocked on the front door but this time there was no reply and the door remained firmly locked against him. It was the final straw and Gauthier began shouting, "Open the door," and kicking at it with all his strength. That was too much for Margaret Webb who finally opened the door, but as soon as she saw the Bren gun which Gauthier held, she slammed the door shut again and ran upstairs for safety.

Charles Gauthier fired three bullets through the front door and one of those hit Rendall just above his right ankle. Despite the wound, he managed to make good his escape through the back door and hobbled off to the rear of number 222 Mile Oak Road, to get help. Gauthier, meanwhile, had also gone to the back of the house and finding the door open, gained entry and positioned himself at the foot of the stairs, where he called for Annette to come down and talk to him.

Not unnaturally, Annette Pepper did not relish the thought of speaking to a man who was obviously extremely upset and who was armed with a Bren gun. She refused to go downstairs. Gauthier, who suddenly sounded much more controlled, once again called for her to show herself. "No." she replied, "If I come down you'll shoot me." Gauthier gave his word of honour that he would do her no harm and gingerly, she came to the top of the stairs.

Gauthier may have vowed to cause her no injury, but the very second he set eyes on her, he fired a bullet into her neck and she fell on to the stairs. Not content with that, he moved forward a little, aimed the gun at Annette's prone figure and put three more bullets into her stomach. She was dead by the time Gauthier threw down the gun and ran out of the house. He did not get very far. Attracted by the sound of gunfire, a Home Guard soldier, Roy Cecil Hotston, had run to his unit in the grounds of the nearby Industrial School and borrowed a rifle. This he aimed at Gauthier and told him to stand still, eventually positioning the fixed bayonet at Gauthier's back to emphasis that he should not think of running. Within seconds, other members of the Home Guard unit, Captain John William Claude Hadfield, and Private John Alban Doughty, joined Hotston, and assisted in holding Gauthier until the police arrived.

The inquest on Annette Pepper opened on March 16th before Dr E.F. Hoare, the coroner for East Sussex. Only the most basic evidence of identification was given and the proceedings were then adjourned. Two days later, on March 18th, Annette was buried at Portslade cemetery.

Legal proceedings began on April 2nd when Gauthier appeared before six magistrates of the Hove County bench. Here he was represented by Mr Henry Settegast whilst Mr Gerald Paling appeared to present the case for the Director of Public Prosecutions. A good deal of evidence was heard and it was not until April 3rd that matters were concluded. An application to expedite matters by sending Gauthier for trial at the Old Bailey was refused and he was committed to the Sussex assizes which were not due to begin until July.

Gauthier's trial took place at Lewes on July 12th, before Mr Justice Humphreys. The accused man was represented by Mr Eric Neve and Mr B. Dutton Briant whilst the Crown's case was led by Sir Charles Doughty, assisted by Mr H.J. Hannihen. There could be no doubt that Gauthier was responsible for Annette Pepper's death but the defence were claiming that it was a case of manslaughter, not murder. All the people involved thus far were called to give evidence, Sergeant Rendall had to be carried into court on a stretcher, due to the bullet wound in his ankle. In addition, Sergeant Cyril Gabbitas of the local police gave details of a long statement Gauthier had made once he had been arrested.

In this he claimed that he had been in some sort of trance for he had carried the gun quite a distance before he even realised he had it with him. He also submitted that when he arrived at the house, he had no intention of killing Annette. This did not, however, agree with statements made at the time of his arrest such as, "It was a Bren gun and I wanted to make sure I did not miss" Also, when held by the Home Guard he had shouted, "Don't take it rough. I have done what I wanted to do."

Evidence of Annette's injuries was given by Dr Frank Portas, who had been the first medical man on the scene, and Dr Leonard Robert Janes, the pathologist who had performed the post-mortem. One bullet had entered the neck two and a half inches below the level of Annette's lower jaw, passed through her windpipe and exited at the other side. That alone would have proved fatal but Gauthier had also fired a cluster of three bullets into Annette's stomach, three inches to the left of her naval and on a level with it. One of these had passed through the left kidney, one through the spleen and one through the large bowel. Finally, Dr Janes was able to confirm that Annette had been some six and a half weeks pregnant.

The jury retired to consider their verdict and after 45 minutes, returned to say that they were deadlocked. At the judge's request, they returned to the jury room but a further 15 minutes of discussion could not bring matters to a conclusion. As far as they were concerned there was absolutely no way they would ever agree and the judge had no option but to order that a second trial should take place.

Perhaps the most poignant occurrence at this time took place whilst Gauthier was held at Lewes prison. Annette had written him many letters at his camp and due to the war restrictions and the fact that his military duties could mean Gauthier was in different locations, these often took some time to arrive. Two such letters were delivered to the prison and in one, Annette had written, 'Charles dearest ...I am sitting at home by a lovely fire, and every now and again I look into the fire and see you there and I don't feel so lonely.' If things had continued in such a vein, none of the sad events involved in this case might have taken place.

The second trial took place, after all, at the Old Bailey, on July 25th, before Mr Justice Oliver. The same defence and prosecution teams were arraigned against each other and the same witnesses gave the same evidence.

The difference came in the judge's summing up. At one point Mr Justice Oliver said, "So far as provocation is concerned, I must tell the jury that there is no evidence upon which they could return a verdict of manslaughter." It therefore had to be either guilty, guilty but insane or not guilty. Under the circumstances, the jury did what they had to do and Gauthier was adjudged to be guilty of wilful murder.

Asked if he had anything to say before the sentence of death was passed, Gauthier replied, "I joined the Army to come over here to fight for my country. I never thought such a thing would happen. I am very sorry for what has happened. That is all."

Gauthier's appeal was heard on August 26th and the main grounds were the judge's comments ruling out all possibility of manslaughter. One of the three judges, Mr Justice Cassels, pointed out that the case clearly showed deliberation and preparation. Gauthier had deliberately armed himself and got ready to kill. He had said that he would kill Annette and did so and there was no evidence of provocation. The appeal was therefore dismissed.

Still there were attempts to save the life of Charles Gauthier. The Canadian Government made representations to have the case sent to the House of Lords. However, for that appeal to take place, Gauthier would need the fiat of the Attorney General, Sir Donald Somerville. He was in the United Sates at the time so, on September 13th, the request was instead sent to the Lord Chancellor, Viscount Simon. The matter was considered and when the Attorney General returned to England, he announced, on September 22nd, that permission would be refused.

At the same time, a petition was organised and this was forwarded to the Home Secretary but this last avenue also failed.

On Friday, September 24th, 1943, Charles Eugene Gauthier was hanged by Albert Pierrepoint, assisted by Alex Riley, at Wandsworth prison. Sentenced to death on July 25th, Gauthier had spent a record 60 days in the condemned cell.

CHAPTER 16

MONEY PROBLEMS

JOHN Joseph Dorgan was behaving somewhat strangely. It all began on Thursday, July 29th, 1943. On that day Dorgan, who was unemployed but had until recently worked at the Arlington Hotel, was on Brighton sea front with two of his friends, George 'Bones' Windsor and Percy White. Without warning, Dorgan took off his overcoat and sold it to a man he had never seen before, for £1.

Later that same day, this practice of selling items was continued in a local public house, the Queen's Head. Laura Emily Hobbs who worked at that hostelry, bought a clock from Dorgan for 25s. That evening Dorgan also offered a camp bed to Louisa Ayling, the wife of the licensee. Mrs Ayling, thought this was rather unusual and asked why the bed was for sale. Dorgan replied that there was some family trouble: his sister's husband had left her and he needed to raise some money to pay off some debts for her. Louisa bought the bed and later also took a suitcase full of lady's clothing for a total payment of £10. Louisa was careful enough to ask for a receipt as she said she wished to have nothing to do with stolen property. However, when she was later offered even more clothes, including a fox fur, her suspicions returned and she returned the items she had already purchased, even though Dorgan tried to explain by saying that he was now doing 'a bit of buying and selling' for a living.

The following day, the sale of goods continued. Returning to the Queen's Head, Dorgan, who was 47, managed to off-load some more clothes before returning home to the basement flat at 8a Madeira Place, which he shared with his 60-year-old wife, Florence Elizabeth Agnes.

A third person lived at the flat. Charlie Fyfe had lodged with the Dorgans for several years and slept in the front room of the flat. At 4.30pm on the 30th of July, Charlie left the flat to attend to his duties as a fire watcher at the Old Ship Hotel, where he was also employed as a waiter. The war was at its height and German bombers had already paid quite a few visits to the southern coastal towns. Charlie noticed that as he closed the door behind him, Florence Dorgan was in the kitchen, making herself a cup of tea. Her husband had already gone out, some 30 minutes earlier, so Florence was left alone at that time.

John Dorgan was still busily selling as many items as he could. At 6.55pm on the 30th, he walked into the Aquarium Inn, carrying a suitcase. Stepping inside the bar he noticed another friend, Ernest Beazley, known to all as Ernie. Dorgan offered Ernie a pair of earrings for £7, but Ernie was more interested in a radio he was told about. Dorgan wanted £9 and Ernie said he would buy it, providing, of course, it was in working order. Dorgan said that the best way to test whether it was or not was for Ernie to come back to the flat and hear it for himself.

Percy White, who was a furniture dealer by trade, was also in the bar and, not being one to miss a good business opportunity, he said he would go back to the flat too. Dorgan had made it plain that all he had was for sale and mention had been made of a wardrobe. The three men went back to the flat, Ernie agreed to buy the radio and Dorgan said he would have it delivered to the pub the following day. It was, however, whilst these three men were inspecting the various items that the first sign of trouble appeared.

Florence Dorgan had been married once before and had two grown-up children from that marriage. One of these, Beatrice Primrose Blaker, who lived at 72 Hollingdean Terrace, had called on her mother at 7.00pm. The flat appeared to be deserted and there was no answer to Beatrice's knocking. Determined to talk to her mother, Beatrice had returned at 8.00pm and again there was no reply.

At 9.20pm, Beatrice returned for a third time, now with her husband, Frederick. Looking through the basement window, Beatrice saw three men: her step-father, Beazley and White, who all seemed to be heavily involved in some form of business negotiations. Beatrice hammered on the front door which was eventually opened by John Dorgan.

Dorgan could see that Beatrice was angry about something and asked her if she had seen her mother, adding that Florence had left earlier to walk to Beatrice's house. Beatrice replied that she had not seen her mother and also that she did not believe what Dorgan had said. If Florence was on her way to Hollingdean Terrace, why had she not arrived?

Having seen her mother the day before, Beatrice knew that her stepfather had started selling property from the flat. What the purchasers had not known, however, was that all these goods actually belonged to Florence. As she spoke to Dorgan, Beatrice noticed that a clock was missing and asked what had happened to it. Dorgan admitted that he had sold it whereupon Beatrice suggested that he had better get it back if he knew what was good for him.

The three men left the basement flat and returned to the public house while Beatrice decided to wait to see if her mother returned. By then it was around 10.00pm. Soon after this, Alice Marion Cosham, who occupied 7 Madeira Place, came out to talk to Beatrice. She told her that she had seen Dorgan earlier that day, carrying out a suitcase full of goods. This confirmed Beatrice's worst fears. Her step-father was selling everything her mother owned.

It was 10.35pm when Dorgan finally returned home. He went into the flat only to come out a few minutes later when he announced to Mrs Cosham and Beatrice that his wife was not at home and he was going to bed. He went back inside, locked the door and turned out the lights. There seemed to be little that Beatrice could do so, somewhat reluctantly, she and her husband went home.

Dorgan was up very early on the morning of Saturday, July 31st. By 7.00am he was entering the Norfolk Arms, a public house that was allowed to open early for the sake of the nearby market traders. Half an hour later he was met there by Thomas Bates, a lorry driver's mate who was also a potman at the pub, and who happened to own a large barrow. Dorgan arranged with Bates that he should later go to the basement flat in order to load up some items he had sold, including the radio which Beazley had asked him to deliver. Whilst Dorgan was waiting in the pub, the landlord, Thomas Patrick Moore, saw him talking to two Canadian soldiers and it was Dorgan who was paying for all the drinks.

Dorgan left the Norfolk Arms at 8.30am. Almost exactly an hour later, Bates turned up at the flat with his barrow and the two men spent some time loading it up. Alice Cosham saw them finish putting suitcases and a radio on at 9.45am. This was the last time she saw Dorgan. The barrow was then pushed to the Queen's Head where Beazley was already waiting. He took delivery of his radio and one or two other items and handed the cash over to Dorgan.

At 10.10am, George Windsor arrived at the Queen's Head and he and Dorgan then spent much of the rest of the day together. In fact they drank together until 2.25pm and Dorgan insisted in paying for all the drinks they consumed. The two men met up again at 6.00pm in the Aquarium, and Dorgan was still spending freely. Indeed, at that time he bought drinks for everyone in the bar.

In the meantime, Charlie Fyfe had finished his stint at the Old Ship and at 2.15pm he returned to the basement flat. Almost immediately he noticed that the middle room, where Florence and her husband slept, was rather untidy, but this was nothing to do with him. Charlie returned to his own room in order to get undressed.

Sitting on the bed and bending down to put his boots underneath, he noticed that there seemed to be a bundle of clothes there. He reached in to pull out what he thought to be a rather bulky collection of garments. Then, to his horror, he realised that it was the body of Florence Dorgan. Charlie ran to fetch the police. The first to arrive was Detective Constable William Lamming, followed by Superintendent Arthur Pelling. Poor Florence Dorgan was eventually identified formally by her son, Sidney Ernest Pentecost.

John Dorgan was still enjoying his drinking spree and decided that it was time to return to his old haunts. At the time he was in Western Road, close to the Marks and Spencer store, and rather than walk he ordered himself a taxi-cab. The driver, Frederick Robert Taylor, was told to drive to the Aquarium Inn but as the car reached Steine Street, it was stopped by the police. As soon as the car came to a halt, three men stepped forward. Detective Superintendent Pelling identified himself and his two colleagues, Detectives Hill and Mannering, and took Dorgan into custody. On the way back to the station, Dorgan made a statement which was to prove most damning, "I have done the old woman in. I have done it properly this time." Back at the station Dorgan made a full written statement detailing what he had done.

According to that statement, Dorgan claimed that he and Florence, who, at 60, was 13 years his senior, hadn't been getting on well for some considerable time. They were always arguing and although he gave her £4 a week, she was always asking him for more. His step-children had also interfered a lot and this had not improved his health. After all, he had suffered from malaria and had once sustained bullet wounds to his head whilst fighting for his country. On July 29th, 1917, he had been classified as suffering from shell-shock and none of this was improved by the constant pressure he suffered from his wife and her family. On the day of Florence's death, Dorgan said he had asked her to be quiet but she persisted in her nagging so he grabbed her by the hair. The next thing he could remember was that he was dragging her into the front room and pushing her body under the bed.

The sad story began to be outlined at the various appearances at the police court, commencing on August 2nd, when the presiding magistrate was the Mayor, Councillor B. Dutton Briant. At this stage only evidence of arrest was given and the case was adjourned until August 16th, by which time counsel had been appointed. Mr Gerald Paling prosecuted for the Director of Public Prosecutions whilst Dorgan was represented by Mr J. Raymond Barry.

Dorgan, it seems, had served his country well during World War One and had been awarded several medals. He had joined up as soon as hostilities broke out in 1914, and had not been discharged until

1931. Four years before that, in 1927, he had married Florence, but the marriage had not been a happy one and there had been constant arguments.

To begin with, after his Army discharge, Dorgan had been employed as a waiter at a hotel on Brighton sea front. Later he had become a potman at a pub in Steine Street, but had lost this job in July. It was then that his financial problems had caused him to start selling Florence's goods.

For the past five and a half years Florence had been employed as a cleaner at Barclays Bank. Her immediate superiors were Lydia and William Thomas Souch, the bank's caretakers. They gave evidence that Florence often seemed worried and on the Friday she died, had brought into work a Westminster Chimes clock. This she had given to Ada, asking her to look after it as otherwise her husband might try to sell it.

Dr Leonard Robert Janes, the pathologist at the Royal Sussex County Hospital, first saw the body at 4.30pm at the scene of the crime and had later carried out a post-mortem on Florence at the mortuary. This had been performed at 8.30pm on July 31st and Dr Janes said that by that time she had been dead for 24 to 30 hours, and for perhaps two to four hours after her last meal. Florence's face was bloodstained and her tongue was protruding from her lips. A man's neck tie was fastened tightly around her throat and there was bruising around her mouth. All this was consistent with a hand being placed around her mouth to stifle her, she being manually strangled before the job was completed by use of the tie. Further, blood and urine stains on the settee in the middle room of the flat indicated that this was where Florence met her death. Her blood group had been AB, held by only three per-cent of the population and the same type had been found on Dorgan's trousers and shirt. Since his blood group was B, it linked Dorgan directly to the crime.

Dorgan's last police court appearance took place on August 31st, when he was committed for trial at the next Sussex assizes. These opened in late November and the trial of John Joseph Dorgan took place on December 2nd, before Mr Justice Charles. The accused man was defended by Mr Eric Neve.

There could be no denying that Dorgan had killed his wife but an attempt was made to show that he was insane at the time. Dr Alexander Wilson Watt, a physician to the Lady Chichester Hospital for Nervous Disorders, at Hove, had examined Dorgan for two hours and had also consulted past medical reports. In the opinion of that gentleman, Dorgan had been unstable ever since he had been a young man and this had not been helped by his experiences in the trenches in France. According to Dr Watt, Dorgan might well have been suffering from amnesia at the time of the attack upon his wife and this could be an after-effect from shell-shock he had suffered more than 20 years before. This did not sway the jury and after a short deliberation, Dorgan was adjudged to be guilty, and sentenced to death. There was to be no appeal and no reprieve. On Wednesday, December 22nd, 1943, 47-year-old John Joseph Dorgan was hanged at Wandsworth by Thomas Pierrepoint who was assisted by Henry Critchell.

CHAPTER 17

THE WOMAN WHO CRIED WOLF

BENJAMIN William Alderton lived at 39 Tarrant Street, Arundel, West Sussex, and believed himself to be a good neighbour. Yet in the small hours of Monday, September 18th, 1944, he and his wife had been woken by screams and shouts of "Murder!" and had taken no action. This wasn't because Benjamin, or his wife Esther, or any other of the occupants of Tarrant Street were unfeeling people, but because the screams had come from number 20, a house almost directly opposite to where the Aldertons lived.

Number 20 was occupied by 69-year-old Amelia Elizabeth Ann Knowles and she was well known in the locality as something of a character. Perhaps not the cleanest or most hygienic of people, Amelia could be seen most days, pushing an old perambulator loaded down with junk or perhaps full of firewood which she had collected from the woods. She invariably wore the same battered green woollen beret and an old black dress that had long ago seen its best days. And when she wasn't pushing her pram about the streets, she was behind the counter of the small shop she ran from number 20.

If anything, shop was rather too dignified a word for the business that Amelia conducted from her front room. The place was filled with useless odds and ends, from bits of broken crockery to ornaments, the business having been started many years before by Amelia's father, another local character known to all as 'Knocker'. He had died some ten years earlier and ever since, Amelia had lived alone in squalor. Rumour was, though, that she had money hidden somewhere in the house.

Amelia had one more eccentricity on top of all the rest. Nearly every night, her long-suffering neighbours heard the sounds of screams and heated arguments. In the early days they had tried to help but they had soon come to realise that these intruders and opponents were figments of Amelia's imagination and that the arguments and shouting were aimed at no one but herself. So when, in the early morning of that day in the autumn of 1944, there were more screams, the neighbours sighed heavily, waited for the noise to stop, and then returned to their slumbers.

Now, though, as Benjamin Alderton stood at his front door in the cold light of day, he could see immediately that something was different this time. There on the doorstep of number 20 stood a bottle of milk. Whatever else could be said about Amelia, she was a creature of habit and by now her milk was always taken in. Besides, the blackout curtains were still up and that was totally unlike Amelia. Benjamin knocked on Amelia's front door, but there was no reply. Thinking that the old woman might have been taken ill, he did the neighbourly thing and contacted the police.

It was 12.45pm by the time War Reserve Constable Dobbs and Sergeant Alfred George Pennicott arrived at Tarrant Street. They, too, knocked on the door and when they got no reply, Sergeant Pennicott turned the handle, only to find that the door was unlocked. The two officers entered and there found the dead body of Amelia Knowles, lying on her back in front of a settee. Her legs were wide apart and she was naked from the waist downwards. She had been raped and brutally beaten to death.

Detective Inspector John Reginald Widdicombe was called to the scene and made an examination of the premises. Near Amelia's right hand he found a small linen bag and he could see that some bank notes were protruding from it. Checking the contents he discovered a total of 63 10s notes. Once the body had been removed to the Royal Sussex County Hospital at Brighton, the clothing was removed by Detective Constable Arthur Wilkinson and he found a second linen bag, sewn in to Amelia's vest. This also contained money: a total of 37 10s notes.

On the day after Amelia's body was discovered, the West Sussex police called in the assistance of New Scotland Yard and that afternoon, Chief Inspector Thomas Barrett and Detective Sergeant Morris travelled down to Arundel. They searched the premises again and in yet another linen pocket sewn into a petticoat in a drawer they found more hidden cash. This time it was 88 £1 notes and a single 10s note. The rumours of cash at 20 Tarrant Street had certainly been well founded.

Two of the first people to be interviewed by Barrett and Morris were William and Esther Helen Alderton. They reported that they had gone to bed at 10.45pm on the night of Sunday, September 17th and were both asleep when screams from number 20 woke them. Glancing at the clock, Benjamin saw that it was half an hour after midnight. The screams were very clear and appeared to come from Amelia's front door and went on for about ten minutes, punctuated occasionally by cries such as, "Get out you pig!" After the screaming stopped, Benjamin and Esther heard a few low groans and then, at last, all was silent until, shortly afterwards they detected a door being opened and closed.

More interesting information was given by Dorothy Louise Dall, who lived a couple of doors away from Amelia at number 24. On the night of the 17th, she went to bed at 11.10pm and she, too, was woken by screaming and shouting. Dorothy also thought that the sounds were so clear that they must have come from very near to Amelia's front door.

In addition to hearing Amelia ordering someone out of her house, Dorothy also reported cries of "Murder!" and "Help!" Dorothy had found it very difficult to get back to sleep afterwards and estimated that she didn't finally drop off again until around 4.00am. She heard no other sounds that night.

Dorothy, however, did have more information to give to the police and most interesting it was too. A few days before the murder, she had been out exercising her small dog, a few minutes after 11.00pm. As she turned into Tarrant Street, almost at the end of her stroll, she saw an airman outside Amelia's door, crouching down as if looking through the letterbox.

Dorothy Dall shone her torch upon the man and demanded to know what he was doing. The airman replied that he owed Miss Knowles some money and wanted to repay the debt. At this, Dorothy pointed out that it was a rather strange time to pay money back and suggested that he return in the morning at a more civilised hour. The airman continued the interchange by asking if Dorothy thought that Miss Knowles would be open for business at 9.00am the next day. Dorothy, by now highly suspicious, thought she would, in all probability, and again suggested that he go away. It was then that another man's voice came from the darkness on the other side of the street. Dorothy could not recall if he shouted, "Come on Paddy," or "Come on Pat ...let's get going." At that the airman outside Amelia's bade Mrs Dall goodnight, crossed the road and walked off with his companion.

It seemed reasonable to assume that there might well be a connection between a mysterious airman trying to get into Amelia's shop at 11.00pm one night, and her murder just a few days later. The police inquiries concentrated on servicemen stationed in the area. Meanwhile, on September 21st, the inquest opened at Arundel Town Hall, in front of the Horsham District coroner, Mr F.W. Butler. After evidence of identification was given, the proceedings were adjourned until October 23rd.

As a result of his inquiries at surrounding RAF camps, Chief Inspector Barrett soon believed that he had a first-class suspect in the shape of 26-year-old Andrew Brown. The evidence was merely circumstantial but Brown did seem to fit the known facts. To begin with, he was the only Irishman on his base and the only one known by the nickname 'Paddy'. Better than that, though, it could be shown that he was the man seen crouching down near Amelia Knowles's door, by Dorothy Dall.

Leading Aircraftman Archibald Nicholson Brown, who was no relation to the suspect, was stationed at the same camp and he told the officers that on the night of either September 11th or 12th, he and Andrew Brown had gone together to the pictures in Arundel.

After the show they went to a pub where they stayed until 10.30pm. Both Browns left the pub at the same time but Archibald needed to urinate and went to the back of the premises to do so with some degree of privacy. When he returned to where his friend had been waiting, he found that Andrew had left.

Archibald walked on towards camp, assuming that Andrew had tired of waiting and just gone on ahead. As he drew close to the Eagle pub, he noticed Andrew on the opposite side of the road, apparently in conversation with a woman. Archibald had then called out, "Is that you Paddy?" Andrew had answered in the affirmative whereupon Archibald had suggested they get a move on. As they walked back to camp together, Archibald had asked Andrew what he was doing in Tarrant Street and he had replied that he had just been seeing a young lady home. The problem was, could Andrew Brown be placed back in Arundel on the night of the murder? Other RAF men gave statements which showed that he could.

Corporal James Alfred Arthur Grundy had gone into Arundel with Brown and another airman named Illsley, on the evening of September 17th. Grundy said that the three of them arrived in Arundel a little after 7.30pm where they visited three different pubs, the last one being the Eagle which they left together at about 10.00pm. By Grundy's estimation, Brown had consumed five or six pints of beer and a whisky by the time they decided they had to get back to camp. The three men started to walk home but suddenly, without warning, Brown turned and walked in the opposite direction. Neither he nor Illsley saw Brown again that night.

Aircraftman Harry Sidney Birdwood had also been in Arundel on that same evening but he had been with friends in the St Mary's Gate pub. Birdwood left the St Mary's Gate a few minutes after 10.00pm and very soon after, he saw Brown in King Street.

Thinking that Brown might be in trouble for getting back to camp late, Birdwood asked him if he was 'out of bounds'. Brown did say something but Birdwood was unable to distinguish what it was. At that time another RAF man by the name of Jameson came along and asked Brown if he was heading back to camp. The reply, heard by both Birdwood and Jameson was, "Not yet awhile." Birdwood and

Jameson then walked off together leaving Brown alone on King Street.

Brown was first interviewed by the police on September 26th, when he was seen by Detective Sergeant Alan Hoare and Detective Sergeant Abbott. Brown admitted that he had been in Arundel on the night of the 17th, but had returned to camp around 11.00pm. He had been with other airmen including Grundy and Illsley all evening and though he had briefly spilt from those two on his way back to camp, he had followed them almost immediately and could hear them talking, all the way back to camp. Later that same day, Brown was seen again and agreed to go to the police station to clear things up.

Andrew Brown was interviewed by Chief Inspector Barrett on September 27th. He gave a written account of his movements on the night in question but these did not tie in with what Barrett had already been told by other witnesses and Barrett told Brown that he was not satisfied that he was telling the truth.

Brown thought for a few moments and then made a fresh statement admitting that he had not gone straight back to camp as he first claimed, but had wandered around the streets of Arundel to see if he could find a woman. Still not satisfied, Barrett left Brown for a short time, whilst Sergeant Morris finished taking down this second statement.

At 1.40pm on September 27th, Chief Inspector Barrett returned to the interview room and read over this second statement. Seeing that one particular point still required clearing up, Barrett then asked, "Did you turn right into Tarrant Street, or did you turn left towards the Square?" Brown hesitated and then admitted that he was the man they were looking for.

Brown made a third statement outlining what he claimed had happened in 20 Tarrant Street in the early hours of September 18th. Then Brown directed Chief Inspector Barrett, Detective Inspector Widdicombe and other officers to a bridge on the Chichester to Arundel road. The bridge spanned a small stream and Brown pointed to a piece of cloth lying amongst the reeds. This was part of the clothing he had torn from Amelia as he attacked her. The car was then driven further along the Chichester road until Brown directed that they stop near a gateway leading into the woods. Here he indicated a small heap of stones and there officers found ten 10s notes folded together.

Andrew Brown's trial for murder took place at Lewes on December 7th before Mr Justice Humphreys. The counsel for the defence were Mr Eric Neve and Mr Harold Brown with the prosecution being led by Mr Cecil R. Havers assisted by Mr R.H. Blundell. In answer to the charge, Brown replied in a firm voice, "Not guilty of murder, sir. Guilty of manslaughter."

In addition to the witnesses already mentioned, the prosecution called Mrs Ivy Alice Curtiss, who lived in Walberton, a few miles from Arundel. On September 18th, she had been outside the cinema, waiting for it to open, it then being about 4.40pm. She was acquainted with Brown and when he saw her he came over to her and said, "Hello, fancy seeing you." He then asked her if she was going in to see the show. She said that she was but couldn't afford to go in the good seats upstairs. Brown flashed a wad of 10s notes which he said had been sent over by his family in Belfast. Not only did he treat Ivy to the best seats but later he took her to the Royal Oak Inn at Walberton and paid for four drinks for them.

Then came medical evidence. Dr Alexander Baldy, a physician at the Institute for the Treatment of Delinquency, had examined Brown at Lewes prison on November 25th. He had come to the conclusion that Brown was not quite normal and believed he suffered from *petit mal*, a form of epilepsy which could be aggravated by the intake of alcohol. Dr Baldy had read a report from a Dr Sprool in Ireland that Brown had always behaved abnormally. Dr Baldy also claimed that Brown was abnormally over-sexed and surmised that Brown had forced his way into the house, Amelia had resisted him and this had brought on an attack of *petit mal* during which Brown was not responsible for his actions. This testimony was largely countered by Dr J.W. McNicol, the medical officer at Lewes prison, who believed that Brown was sane, and Dr Harvey Snell, who had examined Brown on November 30th and said he had found no signs of epilepsy.

Brown's final statement was then read out in court. In this he said that he had walked in the direction of her house and when outside he heard her making strange noises from behind the door. Concerned that she might be ill, Brown knocked on Amelia's door and after five minutes she opened it part way. Brown forced his way in and Amelia immediately attacked him and tried to push him back out, screaming and shouting at him as she did. Brown pushed Amelia and she fell back on to the settee. He fell upon her and they struggled. Suddenly Amelia fell quiet and he realised she was dead.

In the struggle, Brown had felt something which he thought might be money. He found a pocket containing lots of 10s notes and helped himself to some, leaving the rest behind. The next day he returned to Arundel and in a pub, heard people talking about the murder which had taken place the previous night. He then went to the cinema where he saw Ivy Curtiss and later walked about, trying to forget what had happened. He hid the money under the pile of stones, intending to retrieve it when all the fuss died down.

The jury took only 11 minutes to return the guilty verdict and Brown was sentenced to death. He appealed against that sentence on January 12th, when his defence claimed that the trial judge had misdirected the jury when dealing with the defence of insanity. The three judges, Lord Caldicote, the Lord Chief Justice, and Justices Singleton and Croom-Johnson, rejected that plea and the sentence was confirmed.

On Tuesday, January 30th, 1945, Andrew Brown was hanged at Wandsworth by Albert Pierrepoint who was assisted by Stephen Wade.

CHAPTER 18

THE ETERNAL TRIANGLE

JESSIE Eileen Elphick had seen her husband Charles go off to war in 1942. Charles was a signalman in the Royal Corps of Signals and although he had been called to the colours at the outbreak of hostilities, he was not sent abroad until three years later. And he was not to set foot on English soil again for another three, long, years. Jessie waited at home but as the months turned into years, she sought solace in the arms of another man.

Michal Niescior was a 29-year-old chef at the Royal Crescent Nursing Home in Brighton, although he too had once been in the forces having served his native Poland as a sailor. Once Niescior was invalided out, he had taken up his present position and when off duty, enjoyed nothing more than visiting local dance halls. It was at one such establishment, in May 1944, that he first encountered the lonely Jessie Elphick.

The two seemed to get on famously from the very beginning and started to meet up on a regular basis. Things developed so much, that less than a year later, in April 1945, Niescior was invited to move in to Jessie's home at 69 Abinger Road, Portslade, near Brighton. For a time at least, Jessie was content.

To be fair to Jessie, she had written to Charles to tell him what was going on, for it was in late 1944 that he had suddenly decided to cut off the allowance he had been making to her from his Army pay.

Jessie, though, did not inform her husband that her lover had actually moved in with her.

In August 1945, Charles Elphick returned to England and was granted 96 days' leave, prior to being demobbed. On the 10th of that month he arrived back at Abinger Road but as he entered his home for the first time in more than three years, he was to find something he had not bargained for. Jessie was in the bath and Michal Niescior was sitting up in Charles' bed. Not surprisingly, harsh words were spoken and Elphick, not unreasonably many would think, ordered Niescior from his bed and his house. Jessie's reaction was straightforward enough: if Niescior were to leave, then she would too. That night, the players involved in this particular dramatic triangle slept under the same roof and the following morning, true to her word, Jessie left the house with Niescior and took lodgings in Gardner Street.

The next few weeks saw a rather strange situation continuing. Charles Elphick lived alone at Abinger Road, Jessie and Niescior shared rooms in Gardner Street, and each day Jessie would return to Abinger Road to cook her estranged husband's meals for him. It may well have been this which caused a strain in Jessie's relationship with Niescior for there was a series of rows between them and after two weeks, Jessie announced that she was returning to the marital home.

Just two weeks after walking out, Jessie returned to Abinger Road and swore to Charles that she would give up Niescior for ever. Shortly after this, in early September, Jessie and Charles decided to take a short holiday together in Hastings, in order to further sort out their recent problems. When they returned, they were dismayed to discover that someone had smashed a few of the windows in their home and Jessie, thinking that there was only one likely candidate, went to see Niescior. He denied any responsibility but, of course, the important thing was that contact had been re-established between him and Jessie. Within a very short time, the affair was rekindled and Jessie once again had two men in her life. For more than a month this situation continued, until, on the night of Monday, October 22nd, things came to a head.

It was around 11.20pm when Jessie and Charles Elphick were

woken by a loud and constant hammering on their front door and someone shouting, "Open this door!" Both the Elphicks were certain of the caller's identity, but it was Charles who went downstairs to confirm it. The front door had a clear glass panel and Charles looked through to see that the visitor was indeed Michal Niescior. He had a bicycle with him, but more importantly, he was holding a knife. Charles dashed into the kitchen to collect a large scaffolding hammer with which to defend himself. Meanwhile, Jessie had made her own way downstairs. Before Charles could return with the hammer, Jessie had opened the front door. As Niescior stepped forward to enter, Charles reappeared from the kitchen and Jessie found herself trapped between the two armed men.

Jessie could not be sure what precisely Niescior shouted but it was either, "This is for you," or "I'll finish you." With that he lunged out with the knife, trying desperately to strike over Jessie's shoulder. At the same time, Charles was trying to strike Niescior with the hammer, also lunging over the top of Jessie. For a few moments the three were tangled together, with Jessie trying to push both men away from each other. The struggle moved on to the pathway outside the house and at one stage, Jessie tried to take the knife from Niescior, suffering a cut hand in the process.

The small garden had a low wall, no more than a couple of bricks high, and the group fell over this, into Abinger Road itself. Charles continued to wield the hammer and Niescior, for his part, aimed half a dozen slashing blows with the knife. As the fight continued, Jessie went to get her bicycle, intending to ride to the police station for assistance but then she felt a hand restraining her. Niescior would not allow her to leave and by now Charles was lying in the road, bleeding profusely from a number of stab wounds.

"You killed my husband." cried Jessie, to which Niescior replied, "And I will kill you too." In the event, he made no attempt to injure Jessie but in order to get him away from the scene and a possible further attack on Charles, Jessie walked off into the night with the man who had stabbed her husband.

Charles Elphick, though, was not dead. He pulled himself to his feet and began to follow Jessie but had not gone very far when he collapsed again. Neighbours had heard all this commotion and some of them dashed out to offer assistance. Charles was helped back inside his house from where one of the neighbours telephoned for a doctor and the police. Charles was taken to Southlands Hospital at Shoreham where he arrived at 12.30am on October 23rd. Despite the efforts of Dr Kenneth William Oldham, the assistant medical officer, Charles Elphick died from his injuries at 9.40am. There were numerous stab wounds on the head, arms and trunk and the cause of death was given as shock.

After the attack, Jessie and Niescior had simply walked the darkened streets together, talking about what had happened. Niescior was still very excitable and Jessie did her best to calm him down. At first, Jessie said that she had to go back to Charles to see how bad his injuries were, but Niescior said he would kill her if she did. Soon afterwards she tried a different approach and announced that she thought she should go to see the police. At this Niescior took the knife out again, held it close to Jessie and threatened, "If you go to police, I put this through you here."

Eventually Jessie and Niescior found themselves back at the top of Abinger Road. Number 69 was brightly lit and Jessie saw her chance to get away from Niescior by suggesting that the police must already be there. He did not need warning twice and hurried away, leaving Jessie to return home. Niescior returned briefly to his place of work, washed the knife he had used on Charles Elphick, replaced it in the kitchen and then walked to the police station and gave himself up saying that he had a wound on his hand which needed attention.

On October 23rd, Michal Niescior made his first appearance at the Hove County magistrates' court. All the testimony was translated into Polish for him by Marceli Reimus, a chief petty officer of the Polish Navy, but only evidence of arrest was given. Two further appearances took place, on November 5th and November 20th, by which time Niescior was defended by Mr Stanley Cushman. After hearing all the evidence, during part of which Jessie Elphick broke down in tears, Niescior was sent for trial.

That trial opened at Lewes on December 10th, 1945, before Mr Justice Wrottesley, Niescior being defended by Mr Eric Neve and Mr

Harold Brown. The Crown's case was led by Mr Tristram Beresford and Mr Granville Sharpe. There was one woman on the jury and the proceedings lasted for two days.

Michal Niescior did not deny being responsible for Charles Elphick's death but claimed that it was a case of self defence. He said that some weeks before, in one of his meetings with Jessie, she had told him that Charles kept a knife with him in bed. That was why he had taken a weapon, in order to defend himself in case things got out of hand. He had not taken the knife out before Charles attacked him and when he finally did start to defend himself, he hit out blindly and if Elphick was hit, it must have been by accident. As for the reason for his visit, Niescior said that this was merely to return Jessie's bicycle, although he could offer no explanation as to why this he had decided to do this at such a late hour.

Jessie Elphick was called to give evidence and she admitted that when Charles had first arrived home on August 10th, she had greeted him with, "What are you doing here? I have finished with you long ago. Now you can meet the boyfriend." She also admitted that since she had returned to her husband she had written three very affectionate letters to Niescior, despite having told Charles that she had given him up. At least one of these letters had been posted in Hastings whilst Jessie was on holiday with her husband.

Inspector William Hunt testified that Niescior was charged with wounding at 6.15am on October 23rd and replied, "I went to the place: Mr Elphick hit me first." Seen again five hours later and told he would now be charged with murder, Niescior had said, "Let them take me from here and shoot me right away."

Michal Niescior's statement was then read out, "Last night I went to Mrs Elphick's with the bicycle to return it to her …I knocked on the door, Mr Elphick came downstairs and looked through the window. When he saw me he quickly ran upstairs and returned with a small axe. Mr Elphick tried to hit me with the axe and as he came towards me I raised my right arm to defend myself, and I received a cut on the wrist. We all fell down in the yard, and I hit Mr Elphick with his own axe …Mr Elphick ran after me and I ran away to the police to report the matter."

This statement made no mention of the fact that Niescior had armed himself with a knife, or that he had used it to stab the dead man and later threaten Jessie. When the police had mentioned this, Niescior apparently recalled that he did have this weapon with him but he had not used it in the fracas though he did take it out later when he saw that Elphick had picked up the axe and was following him. Niescior had then briefly fought with Elphick again and stabbed him in order to protect himself.

As a result of this evidence, it took the jury only 65 minutes to decide that Niescior was guilty as charged, although they did add a strong recommendation to mercy on account of his being provoked. As the verdict was announced, Jessie Elphick broke down in court.

The appeal was heard on January 14th, 1946, before Justices Humphreys, Lewis and Collins, but dismissed as being groundless. Seventeen days later, on Thursday, January 31st, 1946, Michal Niescior was executed at Wandsworth by Albert Pierrepoint, assisted by Stephen Wade.

CHAPTER 19

MURDER IN THE SNOW

AT 9.30am on the morning of Sunday, March 3rd, 1946, Herbert Chapman, a horse-slaughterer who lived at 7 Cornfield Terrace, St Leonards, called at the house owned by his employer, 72-year-old John Whatman.

Mr Whatman lived alone at an isolated detached house known as 'The Choice' which was situated in Blackpath Lane, Hollington, Hastings, and had employed Chapman for some ten years by this time. By all accounts, Whatman was a successful man and was known to keep a fair amount of money at the house which served not only as his home, but also his business premises.

Herbert Chapman found that the front door of 'The Choice' was locked and there was no answer to his knocking. There was nothing unusual in this. Whatman often worked in some of the storerooms and outhouses at the back of the property so it was to the back door that Chapman now strolled. The door was not only unlocked, but swinging open, as was the door to an outhouse where some of the horse meat was kept. Chapman knocked on the back door and shouted inside for his employer but when again he received no reply, he gingerly entered the house. He had not gone very far when he realised that something was very wrong. There, on the scullery floor, lay a box which had been broken open and in the front room was a safe which had been forced open, papers being strewn about the room. Someone had obviously robbed John Whatman. Chapman wasted no time in telephoning the police.

Whilst waiting for the officers to arrive, Chapman trudged around the outside of the house, looking for any signs of what might have happened to his employer. It was when he reached the front door of the house once more that Chapman noticed some bloodstains in the thin layer of snow that had fallen over the past few days. Following this trail to a recess by a coachhouse, Chapman saw what he first took to be some old sailcloth thrown into a shallow ditch. Satisfied that Whatman was not on the premises, Chapman walked up the lane in order to meet the policemen who would surely be on their way.

It was 9.45am by the time Detective Sergeant Pike and Detective Constable Longhurst turned their car into the lane that led to John Whatman's property. They had not driven very far when they spotted Herbert Chapman walking towards them. After a brief conversation, Chapman climbed into the back of the police car and travelled back to his employer's house. Once again a search of the premises was begun and it was only now that Chapman took a closer look at the old piece of sailcloth.

In fact, the sailcloth turned out to be a man's coat and this had been neatly tucked around the body of John Whatman. He was dressed in ordinary indoor clothing, and was wearing only slippers on his feet. There were two bullet wounds in the body and a murder investigation was now under way. Upon checking the property, Pike and Longhurst noted that all the drawers in the house had been ransacked. The safe, which Chapman had already noticed, had a bent poker and a broken spanner lying on top of it, tools obviously used to force it open. A second safe was found and it was plain that an attempt had been made to force this open too, since the handle had been broken off. On a table in the front room, Sergeant Pike found a copy of a newspaper dated Saturday, March 2nd, on top of which rested a pair of spectacles. It looked as if Whatman had been enjoying a quiet read when someone had knocked on his door, engaged him in conversation, shot him and then ransacked his house, stealing whatever they could find. By 2.00pm on March 3rd, the scene was being examined by Detective Superintendent Arthur Pelling of the Sussex CID. In those days provincial police forces did not always possess the resources to conduct a murder enquiry, so Pelling realised that his men would almost certainly need the expertise of Scotland Yard and, Detective Chief Inspector Somerset and Detective Sergeant Walter Monk, travelled down to Sussex from London on that same afternoon.

It was a relatively simple matter to determine an approximate time of death. John Whatman was certainly alive some time between 5.30pm and 5.45pm, for it was then that Mark Spice, a deliveryman, called at 'The Choice' and dropped off some bread. In fact, Spice delivered bread three times a week but on the Saturday, Whatman paid his weekly bill in cash.

It was what started as a fairly routine inquiry, miles away in Hertfordshire, which led to the arrest of a suspect for the murder of John Whatman. A young man had been seen in the public houses of Markyate, trying to sell gold and silver watches. This information had found its way to the police and believing that the watches might well have been the proceeds of a robbery, Sergeant Alfred Charles King together with Constables Gray and Harris, decided to call on the young man at his lodgings, 51 High Street, Markyate.

It was 6.00pm on March 6th, when Sergeant King and his colleagues arrived at number 51 to interview 22-year-old Sydney John Smith. At the time, Smith was not at home but he turned up 45 minutes later, whereupon Sergeant King identified himself and asked to see a gold watch and chain which Smith had been showing off to some friends of his. Smith happily produced a silver hunter watch but Sergeant King insisted that the watch he had heard about was a gold one. Smith then produced not only a gold watch, but announced that he had some more besides that and then proceeded to hand over four others.

Looking at a couple of the watches, Sergeant King could not fail to see that two of them carried engravings. On the inside of the silver hunter he read, "Whatman, John" and inside another he noticed, "John Whatman, Hollington, Hastings." Smith was searched and Sergeant King found that he was carrying £29 in cash. Only a few days before Smith had been borrowing money but now appeared to be flush with cash and carrying property linked directly to the scene of a shooting in Sussex.

Sergeant King asked Smith to account for his movements on the weekend of March 2nd and 3rd, 1946. Smith replied that he had been down to visit his parents who lived in Potman's Lane, Bexhill. He had travelled down on the Saturday, leaving Markyate at around 11.30am. He had bought the watches from a soldier on the train from Brighton on the Sunday, paying the man £9 in cash. As for the money he had, Smith claimed that he had been saving up for some time. As he travelled down to Sussex he had a large quantity of cash on him and explained the fact that he had borrowed money by the unlikely story that he didn't want to break into this store of cash if he could possibly avoid doing so. Far from satisfied with these answers, Sergeant King took Smith in to Hemel Hempstead police station for further questioning. Meanwhile Constable John Henry Harris began a search of Smith's rooms and in a vase on the mantelpiece, he found three revolver bullets and four empty cases.

Late that same evening, the two Scotland Yard detectives, Chief Inspector Somerset and Sergeant Monk, together with Superintendent Pelling, travelled up to Hemel Hempstead from Sussex. It was not the most pleasant of journeys since a blizzard raged across the whole of the south of England, and it was late by the time the three officers arrived. As a result it was decided that they would leave questioning Smith until the following day.

On March 7th, Smith was interviewed about the shooting of John Whatman. He denied that he had been anywhere near Whatman's house, saying that on the night the shooting took place, he had been at the house of a friend of his, Frank George Fish, of 77 Buxton Drive, Bexhill. Smith had stayed there until about 8.00pm and had then walked back to his parent's house, arriving at about 9.30pm. He had stayed in the rest of the night, finally going to bed at 11.00pm, although since his family was out at the time, there was no one to verify his story. Smith repeated the story of buying the watches from a soldier on the return train journey on Sunday and explained away a 4s piece found in his rooms as a coin he had been given in his change at a St Albans cinema. John Whatman was known to also keep a small collection of coins which included crowns (worth 5s) and double florins, or 4s pieces, coins minted in the latter part of the

19th century. On the strength of the connections between Smith and the crime in Sussex, it was decided to escort him back to Hastings.

It was March 8th, at Hastings police station, that Smith made his second statement. After lengthy questioning from Superintendent Pelling, Smith was left alone in an interview room with Sergeant Monk. The two men were alone from around 3.45pm to 5.30pm when Pelling returned. Almost immediately Smith said that he wished to make a second statement. This was a complete admission of guilt and read, "I went down to see Mr Whatman, knocked at his door. He came out. I asked him to lend me some money. He said 'No.' so out I pulled the revolver from me inside pocket and shot him through the back. With that I went to his side pocket and took the wallet, went to the safe inside the door, broke it open, when it was open there weren't any money in there, just these watches, so I took those. After that I got the watches in me pocket. I came out. All the stuff you have got came out of the house. The large silver coins were in the safe. I had the revolver in me hand. I got over the bridge and tossed it in the hedge. I caught a train to Bexhill. That's about the lot now I think."

Later that day, Sergeant Pike went to the spot described by Smith and there he found a .45 revolver, hanging in the bushes, some 72 yards from the house. This gun was handed to the firearms expert Robert Churchill and he was able to show that it was indeed the weapon used to kill John Whatman.

Sydney John Smith made his first court appearance at Hastings on March 8th. Further appearances followed on March 14th, March 21st and April 10th, when, after a two-day hearing, Smith was sent for trial. That trial lasted only one day and took place at Lewes on July 18th, 1946, before Mr Justice Singleton. The case for the prosecution was led by Mr Anthony Marlowe, assisted by Mr T. Southall. Smith's defence rested in the hands of Mr Aiken Watson, who was assisted by Mr B. Dutton Briant.

The early evidence showed that Smith had direct links with the dead man. William Percival Felling had employed Smith as a cattle drover some two years before. In the course of his duties, Smith had paid visits to John Whatman's house. Felling was also able to testify that on the day after the death of Whatman, Smith and his brother Victor, who went by the nickname of 'Mic', had visited his yard. After a brief chat, Felling said he needed to go to his uncle's house, and Smith accompanied him, arriving there at about 9.15pm. They stayed for perhaps ten minutes and then Felling drove Smith to Bexhill station where he bought a ticket to take him back home. He last saw Smith on the platform, waiting for the train to Brighton, which was the first leg of his journey home.

Edward George Ward, who also lived in High Street, Markyate, was friendly with Smith. In January 1946, he had travelled down to Sussex with Smith and visited the family house in Bexhill. Whilst he was there, Smith's father handed a revolver across the table and asked Ward if he wished to buy it. He turned down the offer but Smith then picked it up and said he would take it. Since that time he had seen the gun again, in Smith's lodgings in Markyate and testified that it looked like the same one now produced in court.

Smith's own father, also called Sydney John, agreed that the revolver found by the police was one he had sold to his son for £2, in January. He went on to confirm that his son had visited him on the weekend in question and before he returned to Hertfordshire, Sydney had shown him a gold watch, saying that he had bought it off 'a Yankee soldier'.

Rose Diana Johnson was a waitress at Joe's Café in Silverhill. On the evening of March 2nd, at some time between 7.30pm and 8.00pm a man came in who ordered a cup of tea and then said he was the brother of a man she knew as Mic.

The Mic she knew was Victor Smith, who had more than one brother, but Rose later identified Sydney John Smith as the man she had spoken to that evening. The café was not far from where Whatman lived and this testimony put Smith close to the scene of the shooting on the night it took place.

Frank George Fish, had been a sergeant signaller in the Home Guard during the war and for some time, Smith had served under him. Fish had discovered that Smith could neither read nor write and taking pity on the boy, had tried to teach him the rudiments of both. Although Smith had left the area about a year before, they had kept in touch and Smith had visited him three times since, the last occasion being March 2nd, the night of the shooting. Whilst Smith was at his house, Fish saw him take a revolver out of his overcoat pocket, explaining that he had it with him to shoot rabbits and birds. However, Smith did not leave Fish's house at 8.00pm as he claimed, but at some time closer to 5.00pm, saying that he was going to see a lady with whom he had been staying.

Evidence was given that before he left Hertfordshire, Smith had been very short of money but upon his return he appeared to have cash to spare. Leonard Norman Sewell ran an off-licence at 100 High Street, Markyate, and he testified that on the evening of Sunday, March 3rd, Smith had been in his shop where he bought some bottled beer and some cigarettes, spending about 25s and paying with a £5 note.

The final link was supplied by forensic evidence that some of the banknotes found on Smith when he was taken into custody, were found to be stained with red. When these stains were tested, they showed a positive reaction for human blood.

All this, of course, merely confirmed what Smith had already admitted, that he was responsible for the death of John Whatman. It was now that his second statement, the one in which he confessed to murdering Whatman before robbing him, proved to be highly contentious.

Whilst Superintendent Pelling was giving his evidence, the subject of this second statement came up and immediately Smith's defence team objected to it being read out in court. At the judge's orders, the jury were escorted from the court whilst the matter was discussed. Smith was now claiming that he had been induced to make this statement by Sergeant Monk.

According to Smith, once they were left alone at Hastings police station, Monk had said to him something like, "You know you are telling a blasted lot of lies. I should come clean and tell them the whole truth. Then Mr Pelling will help you." For his part, Sergeant Monk denied using anything like that phrase. There had been a brief conversation whilst the two men were having a cup of tea. Smith had said that he did not know what to do. Monk had asked him what he meant by that, to which Smith had replied, "If I tell the truth, they will charge me and they will charge me if I don't." Monk reminded Smith that he had been cautioned and stated that he must please himself about what course of action he took. At no stage had he promised that Superintendent Pelling would help Smith in any way. In the event, Mr Justice Singleton ruled that the second statement was admissible and recalled the jury to hear it.

The time came for Smith to tell his own story in the witness box. He began by outlining his early life. He was born at Chatham in Kent on January 17th, 1924. Much of his childhood had been spent travelling about with his parents and as a result, he had received no schooling. Finally the family had settled down in Potman's Lane but by then it was too late for him to attend school and so he could neither read nor write.

Smith said that as a young man he had suffered an injury to his ankle due to a horse kicking him. This injury had affected his mobility and had left him unable to run. Neither could he lift heavy weights. The significance of this would become clear when Smith described the events of the evening of March 2nd.

According to this third version of events, Smith had gone to see Whatman in order to sell him the revolver and to pick up a 12-bore shotgun he had lent the man a couple of years before. The gun he carried was in an inside pocket and was not loaded as he knocked on Whatman's door at around 7.50pm.

Whatman came to the door and after discussing the gun, asked Smith if it would be any good for shooting cattle. Smith replied that it probably would be and at that Whatman asked him to wait for a few minutes and went back inside his house. He was away for about three minutes and when he returned, asked Smith how much he wanted for the gun. Smith replied that he wanted £10 but whilst giving his evidence, immediately corrected himself and said that he had asked for just £5. Whatman asked Smith to wait and when he finally returned, announced that he had decided that he did not want the gun.

Smith asked Whatman for the return of his 12-bore but What-man told him that he could not have that either. Feeling that he had been badly done by, Smith told Whatman that he was going to fetch the police and tell them about the various illegal deals he had done over the past two and a half years. At that Whatman swore at Smith and dug his knee into Smith's stomach. Smith fell to the ground and only now saw that Whatman had a gun in his hand.

Unable to fight due to his weakened constitution as a result of his ankle injury, Smith rolled on to his stomach and took his revolver out of his pocket. He then loaded it with two bullets and fired twice at Whatman. Only now did he decide to rob the place, having first removed Whatman's gun and put it underneath a pillow in the front room. Later he put a coat over the body before leaving for home. He had thrown the gun away simply because it was no further use to him.

What might have been a plausible story was rather negated by the testimony of the pathologist, Dr Keith Simpson. He testified that whilst Whatman had indeed been shot twice, both bullets had been fired at his back. One had entered the back of the victim's left shoulder and had emerged from his chest. The second had entered the left side of the back of his neck, just above the collar line and emerged from his left cheek, just below the eye. Although the upward path of the bullets might have suggested that Smith was telling the truth about loading his gun whilst lying on the floor, photographs of the crime scene showed that 'The Choice' had doors which were reached by means of a short series of steps. The trajectory of the bullets could also be explained by Whatman standing in his doorway, or on the steps, and his killer standing at the foot of those steps.

Now it was for the jury to decide. Mr Marlowe had asked for a verdict of guilty of manslaughter but in his summing up, Mr Justice Singleton made three telling points. In the first place, if Smith had so much wanted the return of his 12-bore, why had he not taken it with him and how come he could not state the name of the manufacturer which was plainly emblazoned upon it. Secondly, could the jury accept that an elderly man of more than 70 had offered violence to the much younger Smith and had then calmly waited to be shot whilst Smith loaded his gun in full view of Whatman whilst he apparently had a gun trained on the young man. Finally, if Smith had really been in terror of his life, why had he not fled the spot as soon as he had shot Whatman, instead of spending what must have been a good deal of time forcing open the safe, attempting to open another, and ransacking the entire house?

The jury were out for just 30 minutes and decided that Smith was indeed guilty of murder. Almost immediately the defence team announced that there would be an appeal and this was heard on August 20th, before Justices Charles, Cassels and Lewis. There were three main grounds: first, that the second statement to the police was improperly admitted; second, that the judge had misdirected the jury by inviting them to say that Smith was not telling the truth about the 12-bore; third, that the literacy of Smith was such that he might not recognise his own gun by the name of the manufacturer, since he could not read it.

After due deliberation, the judges announced that the medical evidence plainly showed that the story Smith had told in the courtroom at Lewes was untrue. Whatman had been shot in the back, not as Smith had described, and it was highly unlikely that he could have loaded his own revolver under the circumstances described by him. The appeal was dismissed.

At 9.00am on Friday, September 6th, 1946, Sydney John Smith was hanged at Wandsworth by Albert Pierrepoint. There were two assistants, Henry Critchell and Harry Allen since at the same time, another killer, David Baillie Mason, who had murdered in Wallington, Surrey, was also hanged.

It was a bad day all around for the Smith family. Shortly before Sydney was executed, another of his brothers, Alfred, was found lying injured beside his damaged cycle near St Mary's Lane, Ninfield. He was later detained in Bexhill Hospital where he eventually made a full recovery from his injuries.

CHAPTER 20

MURDER IN THE KING'S HOUSE

THE case of Arthur Boyce was unique in that it was the only one which involved, albeit indirectly, a European monarch, in the form of the King of Greece.

In 1946, the king had purchased a rather imposing London residence at 45 Chester Square, Belgravia. The premises were intended as a home for his daughter, Princess Catherine, but before she could move in, the house would need to be redecorated. Painters would need constant admittance so the king, through his secretary, Sophocles Papanikoladu, arranged for a housekeeper to live in and keep the place tidy.

So it was that in late May, 41-year-old Elizabeth McLindon was appointed. She was a strikingly good looking woman who had, until fairly recently, served as housekeeper for a doctor in Brighton. Some two months before, in March, Elizabeth had moved to London and just two weeks after that move, was given this new and prestigious position. She occupied a number of rooms on the ground floor and seemed quite happy in her work.

On the evening of Sunday, June 9th, the King of Greece, who was staying in a West End hotel, paid a brief visit to the house. There was no sign of his new housekeeper and the king's chauffeur noticed that a bottle of milk had not been taken in from the front door. After a brief stay, the king was driven back to his hotel.

Two days later, on June 11th, Mrs Wilton, a cleaner, called at Chester Square to help Elizabeth with the tidying up. There was no reply to her knocking. It seemed that neither Elizabeth nor the young man who had moved in with her were at home. This was most inconvenient because, up until June 7th, Mrs Wilton had had her own key but at Elizabeth's request, had given it to her male friend.

The next visit took place on June 12th when Mr Papanikoladu called. Once again his visit was fairly brief but he did notice that the downstairs rooms were locked and that there was still no sign of Elizabeth McLindon. Whilst the secretary was at Chester Square, the telephone rang. The caller, who gave his name as Boyce, asked to speak to the housekeeper but was told that there was no sign of her. Boyce said he was becoming most anxious about Elizabeth as he had not heard from her for some days. He added that he had also written to Elizabeth but still had not heard from her.

The letter in question lay on the mat behind the front door. Dated June 11th, it read in part, "My dear Elizabeth — Just a few lines to let you know I phoned you but got no answer, nor when I phoned on Sunday ...Now, Elizabeth dear, let me know where you have been ... For your future sake play the game." It was signed, "All my love is yours for ever. Arthur, xxx"

On June 13th the secretary visited again and found yet another letter waiting for Elizabeth. This one was dated June 12th and was also signed by Arthur. It read, "My dear Elizabeth. Will you please let me know what is the trouble? I phoned you but got no reply. If you have finished with me, let me know as you promised you would as we have lived together as man and wife for three months. Have you gone back to live with the other man? If I don't get into touch with you I am going to get into touch with the king's secretary ...I am getting fed up with the way you are treating me. All my love, from your loving and true hubby."

The housekeeper had not been seen for some days, someone was worried about her apparent disappearance and no one seemed to know where she was. It was time to call in the police. So it was that on June 14th, two Detective Inspectors, Ball and Hearn, forced the locked downstairs door at Chester Square. There, sitting in a chair near the telephone table was the body of Elizabeth McLindon. She had been shot through the back of the neck and the position of a bullet mark on the far wall showed that she had been in this position when she was shot. There was no sign of a struggle and no property had been removed. On the floor, close by the body, lay a cartridge case, presumably from the murder weapon and on the hearth rug in front of her body, the officers found the spent bullet.

A full-scale search of the premises was organised. By this time, of course, the police had spoken to the king's secretary and his statement, together with the two letters sent to Elizabeth, implied that she had been involved with someone named Arthur Boyce. The careful search revealed, in a front bedroom at the top of the house, an identity card in the name of Arthur R. Boyce. The last address recorded on it, shown at June 7th, was 42 Chester Square, suggesting that Boyce had been living with Elizabeth until very recently. Two ration books were also found, in the name of A.R. Boyce but the address on these was 40 Park Crescent, Brighton. Ball and Hearn contacted their colleagues in the south coast resort.

The house at Park Crescent was owned by Mrs Rose Rix. She confirmed that she had once had a lodger named Boyce but she had given him notice to quit in late May. His girlfriend, a woman named Liz, had come to believe that Rose was interested in having Boyce for herself and had insulted her over the telephone. Mrs Rix wasn't the slightest bit interested in her tenant, she said, but she wanted no trouble so told him to find new lodgings. She was, however, able to tell the police that Boyce had been a painter on the Palace Pier and that he now rented rooms at an address in Elder Street.

The house at Elder Street was owned by Esther Florence Fryer. She confirmed that Boyce had taken rooms on June 1st. Almost immediately he left for London and she did not see him again until June 6th. This stay was itself very brief and Boyce announced that he had to return to London almost immediately. He came back at 10.40pm on June 8th but only to say that he was going to let the rooms go and was going to live in London permanently. However, he was back at Elder Street on June 11th and had remained there ever since.

189

That same evening, Detective Sergeant Taylor of the Brighton police, spoke to Boyce at Elder Street and asked him to accompany him to the Town Hall as an officer from London wished to speak to him. Immediately Boyce said, "Is it about my fiancée? She works at the Greek Embassy. She has been missing for a week and my mother and I have been trying to find her."

Detective Inspector John Ball had travelled down from London and he saw Boyce at Brighton Central police station at 2.30am on June 15th. Boyce made a lengthy statement which included, "I have known her for about three months and lived with her at Chester Square for a week. We were going to be married on 16th July. Her brother, who is a priest, was going to marry us. The last I saw of her was on Victory night [*the anniversary of which was celebrated in the immediate post-war years*] when I left her at about 7.30pm at Chester Square and kissed her goodnight on the doorstep. I have not seen or heard of her since. When I left her I came straight to Brighton."

Up to this point, no mention was made of Elizabeth's death but now Inspector Ball informed Boyce that she had been found dead in the house, and that the cause of death was a bullet wound. Boyce seemed only too eager to help catch the possible killer and asked, "Have you seen the fellow Matlow? He has been knocking about with her, and she was friendly with a man named George. He works in the ironmongery at Selfridges." He went on to say that he could prove someone had called at the house after he had left and claimed that he had never owned a gun of the same calibre as the murder weapon, a .32. He did admit, however, that he had once owned a .45 Colt which was useless so he had thrown it off the pier seven weeks before.

The police were sure that they already had the killer in their hands but, first, they had to build a solid case against him. Luckily for them, Boyce had recently forged a cheque so that same June 15th, he appeared in court charged with having, "...with intent to defraud, forged a certain document purporting to be a cheque drawn on the Midland Bank, Fulham Road, Waltham Green, London, for £20 on 7th June, 1946," and was held in custody, pending further inquiries. Slowly the police began to build their murder case.

Boyce had mentioned two men: Matlow and George. These two were soon identified as William Matlow, who lived at Walgrave Avenue, Tottenham, and George Moore, who did indeed work at Selfridges. When Matlow was interviewed, he admitted that he had known Elizabeth for about 15 years. His sister lived in Brighton and Elizabeth had stayed with her. That was where they first met and in due course they became lovers, living together from 1934 to 1939. Matlow said he had first met Boyce in April and from the first, had objected to his relationship with Elizabeth.

She had recently written to Matlow, telling him that she was to marry Boyce and that he had given her a diamond ring worth £150. Matlow thought this most curious. He knew that Boyce was a painter and at best earned £8 per week. How could he possibly afford such a gift? Determined to sort things out, William Matlow went to see Elizabeth at Chester Square, on June 7th.

He did not beat about the bush and asked Elizabeth where Boyce was getting all his money from. She said that Arthur had told her he knew a princess who was financing him. Matlow said that was nonsense and when Elizabeth added that Boyce was going to start up a business and had put £500 into a bank account in her name, he lost his temper. It was all too fishy, he said. Elizabeth, hurt by criticism, told him that if this was how he felt, it would be better if he did not call on her again.

On June 18th, the police spoke to other members of staff on the Palace Pier at Brighton. One of those was a fellow painter, Richard Frederick Goble. He stated that at the end of May, he had seen Boyce brandishing a small gun. Goble had served in the Royal Navy and was quite used to handling weapons. In his opinion, the gun was a .32.

Inquiries into Boyce's past movements showed that he had once lodged at a house in Dawes Road, Fulham. About six men had lodged there at any one time and one of those who had shared with Boyce was John Rowlands. Rowlands was now a signalman in the Royal Signals, based in Caernarfon, and when he was interviewed he told the police a most interesting story.

At the time, Rowlands had owned a .32 pistol and Boyce had sought to purchase the gun from him. Rowlands had told him that it wasn't for sale and when the time came for Rowlands to leave Fulham and travel up to Wales, he remembered carefully packing the pistol in his belongings. For a time the various cases were left unlocked but when eventually Rowlands came to unpack his things, in Wales, he found that the gun was missing. Realising what had happened, he wrote a polite letter to Boyce, asking for his gun to be returned. He never received a reply. The very next day, Boyce gained a new roommate, Arthur Frederick Bucknell, and when he was traced, he confirmed that Boyce told him he had the gun but that he had every intention of sending it back in due course.

In fact, John Rowlands was to provide much more evidence than mere suspicion. He had owned the .32 for some time and amongst his belongings was a spent cartridge which he had fired from the weapon. This cartridge was handed over to Robert Churchill, the firearms expert, and after comparing it with the one found at the murder scene, Mr Churchill stated that both had been fired from the same gun. On July 1st, Arthur Robert Boyce was charged at Marlborough Street, with the murder of Elizabeth McLindon.

There were a number of appearances at the magistrates' court. Remanded until July 15th, Boyce also appeared at Marlborough Street on July 26th, when he was defended by Mr J.T. Halsall, the prosecution case being handled by Mr Maurice Crump. Finally, Boyce was sent for trial at the Central Criminal Court. The original cheque forgery case had, of course, long since been put on hold as the authorities now looked for a conviction on a charge of murder.

The trial opened before Mr Justice Morris on September 16th, 1946. The prosecution was now in the hands of Mr E. Anthony Hawke and Mr Henry Elam whilst Boyce was defended by Mr Derek Curtis-Bennett and Mr R.E. Seaton. The prosecution were to claim that Boyce murdered Elizabeth on the evening of Saturday, June 8th, the same day that London, and indeed the rest of the country, had celebrated Victory Day, the first anniversary of the end of World War Two.

It was shown that Elizabeth McLindon had last been seen alive on that day, at around 11.00am. A housekeeper at another address, opposite number 42, had seen her leaving the house at that time. She

The yard of Haigh's 'factory' at Crawley. Note the boxes of soil ready to be taken away for analysis. See Chapter Twenty-one. *(Popperfoto)*

Right: Mrs Olive Durand-Deacon, the last victim of John George Haigh. See Chapter Twenty-one. *(Popperfoto)*

Below: Haigh leaving the Police Court. See Chapter Twenty-one. *(Popperfoto)*

Left: Mrs Constance Lane, the woman who reported Olive Durand-Deacon missing and consequently broke the Haigh case. See Chapter Twenty-one. *(PA News)*

Above: The house in Gloucester Road where Haigh claimed his early victims. See Chapter Twenty-one. *(Mirror Syndication)*

The first victim attributed to John George Haigh; William Donald McSwann. See Chapter Twenty-one. *(Mirror Syndication)*

Another of Haigh's early victims; Mrs McSwann. See Chapter Twenty-one. *(Popperfoto)*

Mrs and Mrs Henderson who died in Haigh's workroom at Crawley. See Chapter Twenty-one. *(Popperfoto)*

Inside the workroom at Crawley. Three people met their deaths in this room. See Chapter Twenty-one. *(Mirror Syndication)*

Above: Police searching the yard at Crawley. See Chapter Twenty-one. *(Popperfoto)*

Left: A police officer carrying the acid drum into court. See Chapter Twenty-one. *(PA News)*

Above: William Sanchez de Pina Hepper showing his paintings at an exhibition on Hove seafront. See Chapter Twenty-five. *(PA News)*

Above: The house at Worthing where James Virrels murdered his landlady. See Chapter Twenty-four.

Right: Margaret Spevick, who died at the hands of Hepper. See Chapter Twenty-five. *(Mirror Syndication)*

⟨ E. DALY?

Above: Hepper under arrest in Spain. See Chapter Twenty-five. *(Mirror Syndication)*

Right: The house in Hove where Hepper's studio was located on the top floor and where Margaret Spevick died. See Chapter Twenty-five. *(Mirror Syndication)*

Right: Police in an unmarked car watch Terry's house in Chiswick. See Chapter Twenty-six. *(Popperfoto)*

Below: Terry under arrest after being flown back to London. See Chapter Twenty-six. *(Popperfoto)*

slammed the door shut and walked around the corner, out of the square. Almost immediately, Boyce appeared from the other side of the square and rushed after her. According to the witness, Boyce appeared to be very angry.

Arthur Edward Standing gave evidence. He lived in Coronation Street, Brighton, and testified that on May 25th, Boyce and Elizabeth had stayed at his house, as man and wife. Towards the end of the evening, Standing had taken them supper, finding the pair of them sitting up in bed. As he placed the tray on a table, Elizabeth asked him if he knew whether Boyce had a gun or not. Puzzled, Standing asked her why she wanted to know. Elizabeth replied that Boyce had threatened to shoot her. Throughout all this, Boyce was sitting next to her, grinning broadly.

Scientific evidence was given by Dr Keith Simpson, who stated that the cause of death was haemorrhage and shock from a bullet wound in the head. The bullet had entered Elizabeth's neck at the back, just about at her hair margin, one inch above her collar. The exit wound was one inch to the right of her right nostril. There was no other injury on the body.

Witnesses were called to suggest that after killing Elizabeth, Boyce was purposefully creating an alibi by painting a picture of himself as the caring lover trying to find out what had happened. Elizabeth's sister, Veronica, who lived in Moscow Drive, Liverpool, stated that she had spoken to Boyce several times on the telephone. In early June these calls were all about the engagement but on June 12th, and again on the 13th, he rang to ask if she had heard from Elizabeth as he had not heard from her.

Mary Schofield, who worked at the house next door to number 42, testified that on the evening of June 10th, Boyce had called at her house and asked if she had seen 'Liz' during the weekend. Added to this there were his letters to the house, his telephone conversation with the king's secretary and his initial statement to the police when he was interviewed. There was, the prosecution declared, one major problem with this picture of the caring fiancé. Boyce was already married. He had claimed that Elizabeth knew that he was not free to marry her but none of her friends had received this impression and letters she had written to Boyce gave the inference that she believed him to be free. The time came for Boyce to tell his story. He entered the witness box towards the end of the second day of the trial.

Boyce said that he had first met Elizabeth in Brighton, in April. He now agreed that he had owned two guns, a .45 and the .32 which had belonged to Rowlands. He had not stolen this gun. Rowlands had merely left it behind when he went to Wales. The .45 was, as he had said, largely useless, so he threw it into the sea at Brighton.

Once Elizabeth had moved into Chester Square, she began to receive a large number of visitors, many asking if the king was there. These were troubled times in Greece and not all the king's subjects were loyal to him. Some of these callers might well have wished harm upon the Greek royal family, and Elizabeth needed to protect herself. She knew that Boyce had a .32, and on June 1st, when he went to stay with her at Chester Square, he had this gun in his coat pocket. Elizabeth found it there and said it was just what she needed in order to feel safe. After some discussion he had reluctantly agreed to give her the weapon, which she then put away in her rooms.

Boyce agreed that he had been the man seen rushing after Elizabeth on the day she was last seen alive, but there was nothing sinister in this. They had agreed to meet for lunch and he was a little late. As he walked into the square he saw her leaving and merely ran after her to catch up with her. They then watched a Victory parade together, had something to eat and returned to the king's house where they went to bed.

It was whilst they were in bed that the doorbell rang. Elizabeth pulled on a robe and went downstairs. When she returned she told Boyce that a message had arrived from the king saying that he was calling at the house that night. Obviously Boyce was not supposed to be there so at her request, he said he would return to Brighton until the following day. He left the house that night and never saw Elizabeth again. He could only suggest that someone else had either been admitted to the house or had forced their way in, possibly looking for the king and had shot Elizabeth with her own gun. As for his apparent wealth, whilst being only a poorly-paid painter, Boyce explained that as a sideline he also acted as a bookmaker from time to time and this brought in the extra cash he was able to lavish on Elizabeth.

The jury retired on the fourth day of the trial, September 19th, and after a deliberation lasting 75 minutes, returned their guilty verdict. Before he was sentenced, Boyce thanked the judge for giving him a fair trial and expressed sorrow for the family of the victim. He again proclaimed his innocence and was then sentenced to death. Boyce's appeal was heard on October 17th. It was dismissed and the death sentence confirmed. There was, however, a most interesting postscript to the case.

On July 3rd 1946, a man named Arthur Clegg was arrested in Kent on a relatively minor charge. When he was searched, the name and address of Elizabeth McLindon was found on him. Further, on August 30th, Clegg was due to appear at Maidstone assizes and on that day, beneath the windows of the cells there, a note was found. Written in block capitals the note read in part, "The man Clegg is mixed up in a case of murder. He says they can't touch him now as they have a man named Boyce in Brixton prison for the job ..." The police investigated but came to the conclusion that Clegg had nothing to do with the murder of Miss McLindon and in all probability had written the note himself. Clegg had been unbalanced for some time. No further action was taken against him.

There was to be no reprieve for the convicted man. On Friday November 1st, 1946, 45-year-old Arthur Robert Boyce was hanged on the scaffold at Pentonville prison. Albert Pierrepoint officiated and he was assisted by Henry Critchell.

CHAPTER 21

THE GUEST IN ROOM 404

CONSTANCE Lane simply could not understand it. One of her closest friends had apparently vanished from the face of the earth. For nine years, Miss Lane had been a resident of the Onslow Court Hotel, South Kensington, London. Another guest went by the rather grand name of Olive Henrietta Helen Olivia Robarts Durand-Deacon and the two ladies had grown rather close over the last few years.

Olive Durand-Deacon had not appeared for dinner on the night of Friday, February 18th, 1949. That might not have seemed to be a cause for undue concern but Mrs Durand-Deacon was a creature of habit and it was most certainly not like her to be absent without giving any explanation. The following morning, Constance saw that Olive's table was again empty. It also seemed that she was not the only one who thought there might be something amiss. Sometime between 9.00am and 10.00am, whilst Constance was eating breakfast, that nice Mr Haigh had come over to asked if there had been any sign of Mrs Durand-Deacon. Constance had to admit that she had not seen her and was growing quite worried.

John George Haigh had also been a guest at the hotel for some time, his room number being 404. He was a company director and by all accounts, something of an entrepreneur. Constance knew that Olive was interested in a business venture producing false fingernails and had spoken to Haigh about the idea. Haigh had said he was sure that he could come up with something at his factory and a day or so later, had spoken again to Mrs Durand-Deacon, saying that he thought he had found a method of manufacture. He then invited his possible business partner to his factory which Constance thought might be somewhere in Croydon. The arrangements had been made and coincidentally, the visit was supposed to take place on the very day that Olive disappeared.

When Constance Lane first questioned Haigh about this, he agreed that he was supposed to take Mrs Durand-Deacon down to his factory but she had said that she wanted to make a purchase at the Army and Navy Stores in Victoria Street first, and would meet him there later. Haigh had reached the Stores at 2.35pm and waited there until 3.00pm. When Mrs Durand-Deacon still hadn't arrived he assumed she must have changed her plans and drove on to his factory alone. For the time being, the matter was allowed to rest there.

By the following morning, February 20th, Olive Durand-Deacon had still not put in an appearance and John Haigh again approached Constance Lane to see if she had any news of her friend. Not only had Constance not heard but she had by now grown so concerned, she told Haigh, that she must go to the police and report her friend's disappearance. Haigh appeared concerned at that, but a couple of hours later, at 11.30am he returned to Constance and said that he would go with her to the police. After all, the appointment Olive had made had been with him. That same day, Olive Durand-Deacon was reported as a missing person at Chelsea police station.

On Monday, February 21st, Divisional Detective Inspector Shelley-Symes, called at the Onslow Court Hotel as a matter of routine, to interview John George Haigh. Shelley-Symes asked for further details about the appointment Olive Durand-Deacon had failed to keep and Haigh was more than happy to assist. He pointed out that the last time he had actually seen the missing woman was at 1.50pm on the 18th, when she had told him she was going to the Army and Navy Stores. He waited, as he had already stated, and then went down alone to his workshop at Leopold Road, which was in Crawley, and not as Miss Lane had thought, at Croydon. After doing some business there he had a meal in a local hostelry before leaving at around 7.00pm.

Police inquiries soon showed that there was something very strange about the entire affair. Acting on a hunch, Inspector Shelley-Symes ran a check on John Haigh's police record. It turned out that Haigh had seen the inside of a prison a number of times. At the age of 25, he had received a 15-month sentence for selling cars he didn't own, and in 1937, when he was 27, he got four years for fraud. His third and final sentence, for looting from bombed-out houses, was handed out within a year of Haigh being released from his second. The whole thing made such interesting reading that Inspector Shelley-Symes decided to dig a little deeper into the man's affairs.

A talk to Mrs Hilda Kirkwood, the book-keeper at the Onslow Court revealed that until fairly recently, Haigh had had financial problems and had had some difficulty when it came to paying his bill. A cheque for £32 5s 5d had been returned unpaid and Haigh had been pressed for a cash payment to cover this amount. On February 16th, two days before Olive Durand-Deacon had vanished, Haigh had paid his bill in full, a total of £49 18s.

The time came to look at the workshop in Crawley. The premises actually belonged to a company called Hurstlea Products who had once operated from Leopold Road but had moved to larger premises in West Street, in early February, 1947. The managing director of the company, Edward Charles Jones, said that he knew Haigh well and had first met him in early 1935. There had been suggestions of a business partnership between the two men but nothing had come of this. Haigh, though, had accepted an unpaid position as the London representative of the company. It was a fairly informal relationship and Jones allowed Haigh to use the storeroom to conduct occasional experiments.

Jones confirmed that Haigh had visited him on February 15th and asked him for a loan. Jones had handed over £50 in cash but explained that he needed this back to pay an insurance premium. The loan had to be paid back by the weekend at the very latest. Haigh had told him that this would not be a problem. It seems that this at least explained where Haigh had found the money to pay his hotel bill but he had only done so by becoming indebted to someone else. That debt in turn had to be repaid and Haigh it seemed was running out of time.

On February 17th, Haigh was back at Crawley and asked Jones to take the leg off a stirrup pump for him. Jones did as he had been asked, simply assuming that the pump was needed for one of Haigh's experiments. At the same time Haigh had mentioned that he was bringing someone down from London to look at an idea he had had for producing false fingernails. Jones held the keys to the Leopold Road storeroom and Haigh had to ask him for them whenever he needed them. Arrangements were made to pick the keys up the next morning.

On the morning of February 18th, Haigh arrived at Crawley early. Edward Jones needed to collect some steel from Leopold Road and Haigh took him down there in his car. The steel was loaded and it was Haigh who locked the doors and pocketed the keys. Late that afternoon, Jones saw Haigh again and was told that the prospective business partner had not turned up. As for the debt, £36 of it had been repaid but Jones was still waiting for the rest.

Where had Haigh obtained that £36? He had been so short of cash that he needed to borrow from a friend to pay his hotel bill, but now he suddenly appeared to be in possession of a good deal of cash. So it was that on February 26th, Detective Sergeant Patrick Heslin, entered the storeroom and began a search of the premises.

There were a number of interesting items in the storeroom. Heslin noticed three large carboys containing acid, standing in the centre of the floor. On a bench lay a rubber apron and a pair of gauntlet gloves, as well as an Army-type respirator. The stirrup pump Edward Jones had referred to was propped against the wall and on another bench, in the far corner of the room, was a square, leather hat box which was locked.

A number of papers were also found and taken away, along with the hat box. One of these papers appeared to be a receipt from a cleaners in High Street, Reigate. The receipt was for a fur coat and when officers visited the premises and spoke to Miss Mabel Marriott, she said that the coat had been brought in by a well-dressed gentleman. She would be unable to positively identify him but she did produce the garment. It turned out to be a Persian lamb coat of the type Mrs Durand-Deacon had been wearing when she disappeared.

On February 28th, 1949, Detective Inspector Shelley-Symes, along with Detective Inspector Albert Webb, called once more at the Onslow Court Hotel and asked to speak to John Haigh. Taken into Chelsea police station, Haigh was again questioned about Olive Durand-Deacon's disappearance. He initially gave much the same story as before, but he was then confronted with the evidence of the fur coat and told that his story simply did not fit the facts.

After some time in custody, Haigh was left alone with Inspector Webb. For a few minutes silence reigned and then suddenly Haigh asked, "Tell me frankly, what are the chances of anybody being released from Broadmoor?" The remark took Webb aback somewhat and he simply replied, "I cannot discuss that sort of thing with you."

Haigh was not to be stopped now, though, and continued, "Well, if I tell you the truth you would not believe me. It sounds too fantastic for belief." He fell silent again for a few minutes and then announced, "Mrs Durand-Deacon no longer exists, she has disappeared completely and no trace of her can ever be found again. I have destroyed her with acid. You will find the sludge that remains at Leopold Road. Every trace has gone. How can you prove murder if there is no body?" When Inspector Shelley-Symes returned, Haigh made a full statement describing how he had killed and disposed of Olive Durand-Deacon.

Despite the fact that they had a full written confession the police needed much more if they were going to prove that a murder had been committed. According to Haigh, the missing woman had been dissolved in acid and the remains dumped on the soil at Leopold Road. To make sure of their case they had to prove first that a murder had indeed taken place, second that the murdered person was Olive Durand-Deacon and third that the person responsible was John George Haigh. With that in mind, on March 1st, Dr Keith Simpson, the pathologist, visited the alleged murder scene.

One of the first things Simpson noticed was that on the whitewashed walls, between the two windows, was a group of what appeared to be blood spatters. Scrapings of those stains were taken for further analysis. Outside, some 475lbs of dirt, all the top soil to a depth of three or four inches, was loaded into wooden boxes and taken back to Scotland Yard. Meanwhile the leather hat box had been opened and found to contain a revolver which had recently been fired.

Back in London, Simpson carefully sieved and separated the soil, a painstaking task which revealed a number of items. First there was the handle of a red plastic handbag. Such a bag, missing its handle, had been found in the yard dumped behind a pile of bricks. Tests would show that the handle fitted that bag and Olive Durand-Deacon had been seen with a bag just like this on the day she vanished.

Other items found included a full set of upper and lower dentures. In due course these were examined by Lily Patricia Mayo, a dental surgeon of New Cavendish Street, London. Mrs Durand-Deacon had been a patient of hers for more than 20 years. During that time Miss Mayo had made her at least five sets of dentures and was able to confirm that she made this set for her in 1947.

Continuing his search, Dr Simpson found 28lbs of a highly greasy substance which he identified as some form of animal fat. There were also three gallstones and 18 fragments of human bone. Not only was Simpson able to piece together some of the bones to show that they were female but was also able to say that the presence of arthritis in some of them indicated a woman in late adult age. Olive Durand-Deacon would have been 69 on February 28th.

Other scientific minds were also brought to bear on the case. Dr George Turfitt, the deputy director of the Metropolitan Police laboratory, examined the inside of a large green metal drum that had been found in the workshop. He found a considerable quantity of what proved to be animal fat and also substantial traces of sulphuric acid. Dr Henry Smith Holden, the director of the same laboratory, made an examination of the Persian lamb fur coat. The bottom of the coat and one of the sleeves had been patched and he found that portions of fabric inside the red plastic handbag matched the material exactly. He also found traces of blood on the respirator case, human blood on the rubber apron and also amongst the whitewash scrapings from the storeroom wall.

On March 2nd, Haigh made his first appearance at a court held in Horsham Town Hall. The proceedings lasted only five minutes and he was remanded until March 11th. The police meanwhile were making inquiries into other missing persons with whom Haigh claimed to have been involved. So it was that the next day, March 3rd, officers visited the back room of premises at 79 Gloucester Road, South Kensington, and dug a large hole. Samples of soil were removed as was part of the drainage system. Other officers were needed to keep the large crowd under control. By March 4th, it was common knowledge amongst journalists involved in the case that there might well be more than one murder placed at the door of John Haigh, but thinking that and saying it was another matter. One newspaper, though, went too far and published the speculation.

There had been three editions of the *Daily Mirror* printed on March 4th and each one carried banner headlines about John George Haigh. At this time of course, Haigh had been charged with one murder and in all probability he would face a trial for that one crime, as is common in British courts. The *Daily Mirror,* though, had published articles naming other missing people and had also given details of Haigh's alleged practices, stating plainly that he was a vampire. This was prejudicial to the case and as a result, on March 8th, Haigh's legal representatives made an application to the King's Bench Division Court for leave to apply for a writ of attachment against Mr Silvester Bolam, the editor of the *Daily Mirror*. The case would eventually be heard on March 25th, before the Lord Chief Justice, Lord Goddard, and Justices Humphreys and Birkett. So seriously did they view the articles that they fined the newspaper's proprietors £10,000 and jailed Mr Bolam for three months. On the same day, Haigh, who had also been remanded on March 11th, and March 18th, was further remanded until April 1st.

It was on April 1st that the case finally opened at Horsham. The prosecution was handled by Mr E.G. Robey, with Haigh being defended by Mr G.R.F. Morris. This initial case would last two days, evidence only being given on the single crime with which Haigh had been charged.

It was shown that Haigh had lived at the hotel since 1945. Over that period he had taken his meals at the table next to that of Olive Durand-Deacon, so it was quite natural that they should become acquainted. Evidence was given that on February 7th, Haigh's account at the Gloucester Road branch of the Westminster Bank had been overdrawn by the sum of £83 5s 10d. By February 23rd, only £5 had been paid in, reducing the overdraft to £78 5s 10d. He had obviously not been able to obtain money from this source and so had resorted to murder to clear his debts. Haigh's statements had given detailed accounts of his movements over the period in question.

On February 17th, he purchased the large 45-gallon drum he would need in order to dispose of his victim's body. The following day he and Mrs Durand-Deacon left for Crawley in his motor car at around 2.00pm. When they arrived at Crawley they first went to the George Hotel for tea. The couple were seen here at some time after 4.00pm by the hotel's book-keeper, Hannah Caplin. She knew Haigh and was able to identify Mrs Durand-Deacon from a photograph shown to her by the police.

Going down to the workshop, Mrs Durand-Deacon was shown some papers which Haigh said he could use to manufacture fingernails. As the poor woman turned towards the windows in order to see things better, Haigh stood behind her, levelled his revolver at her head and put a single bullet into her brain. He then removed her fur coat and jewellery and put the body, along with the rest of her belongings, into the 45-gallon drum.

Deciding he needed a break, Haigh returned to Crawley town centre where he entered The Ancient Priors, a restaurant, and enjoyed a cup of tea and some poached eggs. He then returned to Leopold Road where he filled the drum with acid. He then went back to the George where he had dinner, finally leaving Crawley at about 9.00pm.

On February 19th, Haigh returned to Crawley via Putney. On the way he stopped at a jewellers, Barrett & Sons Ltd, in the High Street. Here Haigh spoke to Herbert Louis Richmond to whom he offered for sale an 18-carat diamond and ruby wrist watch. Haigh, who gave the name F. Miller, asked for £15 but finally accepted £10.

Arriving back at Crawley he inspected the large tank and found that the reaction was not yet complete. Picking up the fur coat which had thus far been lying on a bench in the workshop, he travelled to Horsham where he had the rest of the jewellery valued. On the way he stopped off at Reigate and handed in the coat for cleaning. On Monday, Haigh was back at Crawley. The chemical reaction was almost complete now but there was a good deal of sludge floating on top of the tank. Haigh emptied this off with a bucket, topped the tank up with fresh acid and returned to London.

On the Tuesday, Haigh sold the rest of the jewellery for £100. In fact, he only picked up £60 on that day as the jeweller did not have enough cash on the premises. Haigh picked up the balance the next day. Meanwhile he had returned yet again to Crawley where he emptied the tank of its macabre contents. He also visited Edward Jones and paid him back some of the money he had borrowed. On the strength of that evidence, Haigh was committed for trial at the next sessions at the Old Bailey, which were due to commence on April 26th.

The case duly came up for trial on April 27th, the second day of the new sessions, before Mr Justice Humphreys. The defence claimed that they were not ready and made an application to defer the case to the next sessions. Justice Humphreys made plain his displeasure that the case had ever been sent to London. He stated that this was obviously a Sussex case. The murder which Haigh had been charged with had taken place at Crawley, in Sussex, and should be tried by a Sussex jury. Not only did he refuse permission for the case to be heard at the next Central Criminal Court sessions, but sent the case back to Sussex, to be heard at the next sessions at Lewes. These were due to open on July 11th.

Haigh's trial itself opened on Monday, July 18th and lasted for just two days. Although it had been Mr Justice Humphreys who transferred the case from London, it was that same learned gentleman who presided over the Sussex assizes and so heard the evidence against Haigh. A good deal of eminent legal talent were arranged against each other in court. For the prosecution, Sir Hartley Shawcross led and he was assisted by Mr Gerard Hayward and Mr Eric Neve. The defence lay in the hands of Sir David Maxwell Fyfe, assisted by Mr G.R.F. Morris and Mr David Neve, the son of Eric. The revelations in the courtroom were nothing short of astounding.

Although charged with only one murder, Haigh had in fact confessed to no fewer than nine. In addition to Olive Durand-Deacon, his final victim, Haigh also claimed to have killed three members of the McSwann family, Archibald and Rosalie Henderson, a woman he met in Hammersmith, a young man he met the same year and a woman named Mary who he had killed at Crawley after he had met her at Eastbourne. Little credence would be given to these last three but the other six victims were discussed in detail when Haigh's long confession was examined in court.

Haigh had once worked as a repairman for William Donald McSwann, who operated a number of amusement arcades in London. In the summer of 1944, Haigh happened to bump into McSwann who mentioned that he was rather concerned about being called-up since the war was still raging in Europe and the Far East. Haigh suggested that he might well be able to help McSwann out on that score and also mentioned that he had taken a basement store at 79 Gloucester Road, where he was working on a new pin-ball machine. McSwann said he was extremely interested in seeing this, with a view to putting it into his arcades, and agreed to accompany Haigh to the address.

The two men met by arrangement at the Goat public house in Kensington High Street, some time in September 1944. From there they travelled on to the basement of 79 Gloucester Road where Haigh coshed the young man over the head. Once he was sure that William Donald McSwann was dead, Haigh said he made a small incision in McSwann's chest and took a glass of blood from the body. Having drunk this down with relish, Haigh then placed the body into a 40-gallon tank which he then topped up with acid. Once the reaction was complete, the sludge that remained was poured down a manhole in the basement, from where it continued into the drainage system.

Haigh's next task was to keep McSwann's parents happy. One of his many talents was forgery and he now produced a number of letters, ostensibly from the missing man, which Haigh posted to the McSwanns. These letters stated that he had gone into hiding in order to avoid his call-up. If anything, the McSwanns were most grateful that Haigh had been able to help!

Less than a year later, in July 1945, both parents, William McSwann and his wife, Amy, had been lured separately to Gloucester Road by Haigh, bludgeoned to death and their bodies dissolved in acid. Haigh then used his forgery skills to obtain the title to the property which the McSwann family had owned. He also sold their furniture and some shares, in all making around £4,000. It was time for him to move on.

It was 1945, when Haigh ran into an old friend, Edward Jones of Hurstlea Products. The two men had first met in 1935, and Jones was well aware of Haigh's talented, creative and inventive mind. It was at this time that Haigh was given the unpaid position of salesman and told he could use the premises at Leopold Road whenever he wished.

Dr Archibald Henderson was a successful man, a man of property and position. He and his attractive wife, Rose, lived in a large house at Dawes Road, in Fulham, by coincidence, the same road in which Arthur Robert Boyce from the previous chapter, had taken lodgings. This house had now been converted to flats and Dr Henderson wished to sell them. One of the prospective buyers who saw the advertisement which offered the flats for sale, was John George Haigh.

Haigh viewed the flats and made an offer on them. Even when this offer did not turn into anything more substantial, the Hendersons, who had been charmed by the professional and plausible Haigh, decided to keep in touch with him. So it was that when they said they were going down to Brighton for a holiday, Haigh booked into a room in the same hotel, the Metropole.

On February 16th, 1948, Dr Henderson and his wife vanished. In fact, Haigh had lured Dr Henderson to Leopold Road where he shot him dead with the man's own gun which Haigh had earlier stolen from the address at Dawes Road. Returning to Brighton, Haigh then told Rose that her husband had been taken ill and offered to drive her to Crawley so that she could be by his side. Once at the storeroom she, too, was shot, both bodies then being dissolved in acid. Before this, as with the McSwanns, Haigh had taken his glass of blood from the corpses, and drunk it down.

This was to be Haigh's most successful killing to date. Using his talent for forgery, he managed to convince the Henderson's family and servants that they had gone to South Africa. Further, he then went on to appropriate their not inconsiderable property, and sell the lot. It was not until 1949, that Dr Henderson's brother became unduly concerned about Archibald. In that year he asked the BBC to appeal for his brother to return home as their mother was seriously ill. Haigh had been so convincing that even now, the doctor's brother believed that if anything had happened to Archibald and Rose, it had taken place in South Africa.

With such a long and detailed confession there could be no doubt that Haigh was guilty of murder, but was he a sane man? The defence called Dr Henry Yellowlees, a psychiatrist who had examined Haigh on four occasions in Brixton prison.

Yellowlees detailed something of the history of John Haigh. He was born on July 24th, 1909 and his parents were Plymouth Bretheren who had brought up their son in a strict religious household where both newspapers and radio were forbidden. As a child, Haigh was always alone and had no friends. This lonely child grew into an inadequate man who married on July 6th, 1934. The marriage did not last for very long and Haigh once more led a life of solitude. There was, however, something else in his emotional background.

Ever since he had been a young child, Haigh had been fascinated by blood. He had once accidentally hurt himself with a hairbrush, drawn blood, licked it and found the taste agreeable. From that time on he had taken to hurting himself deliberately in order to taste the blood. Haigh also told Dr Yellowlees of two recurring dreams. The first of these was a dream of Christ on the cross, blood pouring from his wounds. The second, which Haigh called the 'tree dream', was more sinister. In this, a forest of crucifixes slowly turned into trees from which rain appeared to be dripping. A figure collected this liquid in a chalice and it soon became clear that the rain was actually blood. The dream would end where the figure offered the chalice up to Haigh with an invitation for him to drink it.

For some years these dreams and the urges they produced in

Haigh were surpressed by him until one day in 1944, when he was involved in a serious car accident near Three Bridges, in Sussex. Haigh's head was cut and the blood ran down into his mouth. This had rekindled his desires and led to him drinking the blood of the people he killed. Dr Yellowlees stated under oath that in his opinion Haigh was a lunatic and although he might not have quaffed the blood, which is after all an emetic, he almost certainly had carried out his ritual as described and at the very least, tasted some from each victim.

The jury retired on the second day and took only 17 minutes to decide that Haigh was sane, and guilty of murder. It was announced that there would be no appeal, Haigh's defence instead relying on the medical evidence to obtain a reprieve for him.

The Home Secretary of the day, Mr Chuter Ede, immediately set up a panel of medical experts to examine all the evidence in great detail. Eventually they presented their conclusion: they agreed with the jury that Haigh was perfectly sane.

On Wednesday, August 10th, a crowd of 500 people gathered in the bright sunshine outside Wandsworth jail. At 8.30am a telegram for Haigh was delivered to the prison although the Home Office would never reveal what message it contained. At 9.00am, John George Haigh was hanged by Albert Pierrepoint, assisted by Harry Kirk. Pierrepoint used a calf-leather wrist strap which he reserved for special occasions.

The execution set another precedent. It was the first time in history that a man had been hanged whilst the judge who sentenced him to death was still presiding over the same assizes. Mr Justice Humphreys was still busy at Lewes, dealing with an action involving the Hastings speedway.

CHAPTER 22

A FATAL SUSPICION

WILLIAM John Davies had been having some trouble with the woman in his life, Lucy Wilson. Although Lucy was a married woman, she had last lived with her husband in 1942. Three years later, she moved in with Davies and they lived at various addresses, finally arriving at a lodging house at 34 Terminus Place, Eastbourne.

For some time the couple appeared to be happy enough together but then Lucy managed to convince herself that Davies was rather too friendly with the woman who lived in the next room, Mrs Monaghan. Davies denied that there was anything going on, told Lucy not to be so silly and hoped that there the matter would end. Lucy, though, persisted in her allegations, and after she had threatened to beat up the other woman Davies decided that he had had enough and ordered Lucy from the house. She took him at his word and, on Saturday, March 8th, 1949, walked out.

Both Lucy and Davies had been working in the hospitality industry of late. Lucy was employed as counter hand at Campbell's Restaurant, also situated on Terminus Place, at number 186. This establishment was on two floors with a café on the street level and a full restaurant upstairs. For his part, Davies had worked as a kitchen porter at the Grand Hotel where he had been since October 18th, 1948. However, he had left this position on March 5th and so officially, at the moment, was unemployed.

One might have thought that when Lucy Wilson left Davies, that would have been the end of the entire affair, but Davies appeared to take extreme exception to what he claimed was a totally unfounded accusation and determined that Lucy should withdraw her words. He saw her again on March 6th, but not only did she refuse to retract her former statements she added that she was going to look for another man. The very next night, as Lucy finished work, Davies was waiting outside the restaurant. He saw her come out of Campbell's on her own but then walk off with another man. Had Lucy been true to her word? It was time to sort matters out once and for all.

Campbell's opened as usual on the morning of Tuesday, March 8th. At around 11.00am, Davies entered the premises, sat himself at a table and ordered a cup of coffee and a roll. Although Lucy was not a waitress, she was the only person available that day so she served Davies and took the money from him. For the next few minutes, Lucy went about her duties whilst Davies sat in silence, sipping at his drink and occasionally taking a bite from his roll.

It was approximately 11.10am when Lucy turned to the cook, Jean Grant Copeland, and said she was going upstairs to lay the tables in the restaurant area. Thinking that Davies might be leaving soon, she then told Jean that she had already taken the money for his order.

Almost as soon as Lucy had gone, Davies rose from his seat and made to follow her. As he passed Jean Copeland he remarked, "It is all right: I am just going to see the waitress." Lucy was not employed as a waitress and so Jean thought he might be talking about the regular waitress and pointed out that she was off duty. Davies, though, ignored these words and carried on up the stairs.

Seconds later Jean Copeland heard a terrible scream from upstairs. She ran to see what the problem was and saw Davies and Lucy struggling on the half-landing where the stairs turned. Davies had his right arm around Lucy's throat and a bloody knife in his left hand. Lucy had her arms up to her face and there was blood everywhere. Seeing that she could offer no immediate assistance, Jean ran back downstairs to fetch the chef. Oscar Mench was not only the chef, but also a director of the company which owned the restaurant. He was in the kitchen, which was in the basement, but heard Jean Copeland shouting for help. He and Jean dashed back upstairs only to see Lucy staggering down from the top floor, her face a mass of blood and her injuries so appalling that her left eye was hanging out of its socket and resting on her cheek. A few steps behind her came Davies, who no longer carried the knife.

Mench took hold of Lucy and laid her down upon the floor. She soon slipped into merciful unconsciousness and, after making sure that she was as comfortable as he could make her, Mench telephoned for the police and medical assistance. He then turned his attention to Davies who throughout this period had simply stood off to one side, watching what was going on with apparent disinterest. Taking charge of the situation, Mench ordered Davies to sit down at one of the tables, which he did without resistance. Then, just in case Davies should try to make a run for it, the chef locked the doors and waited for the police and an ambulance to arrive.

Detective Sergeant Ralph Haddon arrived at Campbell's at 11.20am. He made notes on what he found and later reported that there was a large pool of blood on the floor of the café and further splashes on the counter. A trail of blood led from the ground floor up to the half-landing and it was in a passage near that landing that he found the knife. So much force had apparently been used to inflict Lucy's wounds that the blade of the knife was badly bent. Here there were more pools of blood and foot marks could be clearly seen in the crimson liquid.

Davies was still seated at the table and when Haddon identified himself, Davies who spoke with a stutter, replied, "I did it sir. I lost my head. I will tell you why I did it." Later he made a full written statement, admitting once again that he was responsible. Lucy, meanwhile, had been rushed to the Princess Alice Hospital in East-bourne. She was suffering from severe facial injuries and the optic nerve of the left eye was severed. On the right side of her face there was a hideous star-shaped wound close to her upper lip. Another wound was seen on her left upper lip and there were also two small wounds on her right hand. There was no way the left eye could be saved and she was rushed to the operating theatre where it was removed by Dr Rose, assisted by Dr Wilson Hall.

The day after the terrible attack on Lucy Wilson, Davies appeared in court where he was charged with feloniously wounding her with intent to murder her. He was remanded until March 18th. On that date a second remand was agreed but just a few days later, on Wednesday, March 23rd, Lucy Wilson died. On March 25th, William John Davies was remanded on a charge of murder. On the same day, the inquest opened before Dr A.C. Somerville at the Eastbourne Town Hall. Only evidence of identification was given, Lucy's estranged husband explaining that she had been born on March 17th, 1912. They had married and lived at addresses in Brighton, St Leonards and Hastings before he had joined the Army in 1942. He did not return to England until 1946, and she announced the same day that she was leaving him. The inquest was adjourned until April 8th.

Three further court appearances followed before Davies was sent for trial. That trial opened at Lewes on July 14th, before Mr Justice Humphreys. The prosecution was led by Mr Theodore Turner, assisted by Mr Geoffrey Lawrence, whilst Davies was defended by Mr John Flowers and Mr C.J.T. Pensotti. The jury consisted of 11 men and one woman and the entire proceedings would last only three and a half hours.

Charles Edward Aldred, a kitchen clerk at the Grand Hotel, identified the knife used to kill Lucy as one that had been taken from the hotel. The knife clearly carried the name of the establishment and this showed that Davies had taken the weapon with him on March 8th, and not, as he had first claimed, picked it up in the restaurant.

Clifford Henry Lawrence, of Patcham in Brighton, was a sales supervisor and in the course of his business, he had called at Campbell's Restaurant on the morning of the attack. He had been present when Davies attacked Lucy and had accompanied the poor woman to hospital in the ambulance.

Jean Grant Copeland repeated the evidence she had given at the inquest but added that after Lucy had collapsed at the foot of the stairs, she heard Davies cry, "What have I done to you, Luce?"

Dr Walter Montgomery, the senior scientific officer of the police laboratory at New Scotland Yard, had received a sample of blood on March 14th. This blood, taken from Lucy whilst she was still alive, had been delivered to the laboratory by Sergeant Haddon. He had determined that this blood matched stains on a silk scarf and overcoat belonging to Davies and on the knife recovered from the restaurant.

Dr Geoffrey Knight, a surgeon at the Joyce Green Hospital, Dartford, in Kent, testified that he had seen Lucy at the Princess Alice Hospital on March 14th. He performed an operation to see if the wounds inflicted on her had caused any clotting to the brain. He found no evidence of this but as her condition did not improve, she was moved to the Joyce Green Hospital on March 17th, because the facilities there were much better. Here an X-ray of her skull was taken and it clearly showed the path the knife had taken, passing through the left orb towards the temporal lobe of the brain. It was at Joyce Green that Lucy Wilson died on March 23rd.

Dr Francis Camps was the pathologist who had performed a post-mortem on Lucy at the Joyce Green Hospital. He gave details of all the wounds inflicted but stated that although there were three stab wounds to the head, only one was serious enough to cause death. This was a cut running from the left side of the nose towards and into the left eye. This wound penetrated at least two and three quarters of an inch into Lucy's brain and the actual cause of death was hypostatic pneumonia due to the cerebral lacerations and haemorrhage occasioned by the wound through the eye. Camps also testified that the wounds were probably caused by a left-handed stab inflicted by a backwards movement. Davies was right-handed but he had injured his right hand in a fall from a window a few days before and it was heavily plastered at the time of the attack.

Davies's statement was then read in court. He had given a few details of the early relationship with Lucy and pointed out that the trouble between them all began when she accused him of having an affair with the woman in the next room. Davies went on to explain how he followed Lucy to the upper floor of the restaurant on March 8th and once more demanded that she take back what she had said. Lucy had replied, "No, I mean it." Davies then claimed that he must have lost his head and he picked up a knife and attacked her with it. Told that the knife he had used did not belong on the premises and that he must have taken it with him, Davies admitted that it must have been in his pocket, although he couldn't recall taking it from his home. Whatever the truth of that, he had just struck out blindly. He ended by saying that when he went to Campbell's he had no intention of using the knife but had taken it just to frighten her. He remembered nothing of the attack itself and did not even realise that Lucy was injured until he saw her lying on the floor.

Davies's defence asked that the jury should return a verdict of manslaughter due to the provocation he had received at the hands of a woman he cared about deeply. The jury took just 18 minutes to decide that the only correct verdict could be guilty of wilful murder. As the verdict was announced a woman at the back of the court screamed out, "Oh Lord! Oh Lord!" and had to be escorted out. She could still be heard sobbing and shouting as the death sentence was intoned.

Davies's appeal was heard on July 28th before the Lord Chief Justice, Lord Goddard and Justices Oliver and Stable. Here the defence complained that the trial judge had refused to allow the jury to consider the alternative charge of manslaughter. The appeal court judges, however, ruled that Mr Justice Humphreys had been quite correct in that direction and the appeal was dismissed, Lord Goddard describing the crime as cruel and shocking..

On Tuesday, August 16th, 1949, William John Davies was hanged at Wandsworth by Albert Pierrepoint and Harry Kirk. At the time, only 13 people waited outside the prison.

CHAPTER 23

THE FINAL STRAW

IT was thirsty work, doing the alterations to Silverston Cottage, and having cleared things with his boss, Walter Laurence Blunden was granted permission to take a well earned break.

There were three men working on the cottage in Fish Lane, Bognor Regis, on the afternoon of Wednesday, June 7th, 1950: Blunden; his boss, Alfred Woodland; and another labourer, Sid Court. Since all three now fancied a nice refreshing drink, Blunden was asked to go across to a café and get each of them a cup of tea.

The nearest café was close to the west car park, and this was reached from Fish Lane by walking across a piece of waste ground. To the sides of this land were tall grasses and bushes and as he strolled across, Blunden noticed a handle of some kind protruding from the grass. At that time he made no further investigation but on his way back to the cottage, he decided to see what exactly the silver glinting handle was, so walked over to it and pulled.

The handle turned out to be that of a maroon coloured pushchair and on closer inspection, Blunden discovered that inside that push chair were two small children, who appeared to be asleep. Shocked by the fact that someone could abandon two children in such a fashion, Blunden ran over to his workmates and told them what he had seen. Alfred Woodland told him that they had better not interfere with someone else's children but Blunden was so insistent that eventually all three men walked back across the waste land, and inspected the contents of the pushchair.

There were indeed two children in the chair but when Woodland gave the handle a sharp tap, they did not waken from their slumbers. The children were not in fact asleep, but were both dead.

Sid Court ran to fetch the police whilst Woodland and Blunden stood guard over their terrible discovery. Very soon afterwards, Constable Joseph Ainsley arrived on the scene, to be followed minutes later by Dr Ramsden. At 4.30pm the doctor pronounced life extinct and stated that in all probability, the cause of death was asphyxiation. The authorities were looking at a double murder.

Whilst this drama was being acted out in Bognor Regis, another was about to unfold in New Malden, Surrey. Joan Edith Doe lived with her husband, Leonard George Doe, at 7 Oakfield Close, New Malden. Not far from Joan's house lived her cousin, Albert Price, his wife Doris Maude and their two young daughters. The families were quite friendly and Joan often called on Doris to see how she was getting on. Of late, the Price family had had financial problems and these had caused Doris to suffer rather badly from nerves.

Joan called at Doris' home, 20 Grange Close, on Saturday, June 3rd but it was clear that the family were not at home. In the front window someone had propped a hastily scribbled note reading, "No bread or milk till Monday." Without even bothering to knock, Joan returned home but she called again on Tuesday, June 6th. The note was still there but by now the milk and bread had been delivered and stood uncollected on the doorstep. Joan knocked on the door, but since there was no reply, she once again went home.

On Wednesday, June 7th, she was back again. Now there were three days' worth of milk and bread on the doorstep but the note was still in the window and once again she received no reply to her insistent knocking. This time Joan, by now very worried about what might have happened, walked around the house and looked into a bedroom window. Although she couldn't see very clearly, there in the bed was the unmistakable shape of a human body. She now returned home and told her husband what she had seen. By 5.45pm the couple were back at Price's house and the police were on their way.

Once the police had climbed into the house, through a kitchen window, it was clear why Joan Doe had received no reply to her knocks and shouts. In the bed lay the body of Doris Price, a pillow covering her head. When this was removed it was seen that she had been battered to death by means of a sharp instrument. Detective Inspector Whitfield organised a search of the premises and in due course found a sharp axe near the coal shed in the garden. This was heavily bloodstained and proved to be the murder weapon. Doris Price's body was examined by Dr Haler, who said that death was due to shock from the multiple head injuries. Around nine blows had rained down upon her head and since there were only minor defence wounds, it was probable that she was asleep when the first blow hit her, stirred slightly and was then finished off by further blows.

The finding of the two children's bodies in Bognor and the discovery of Doris Price's body in New Malden an hour or so afterwards, might have been thought to be two separate incidents but it very soon became clear that the crimes were related. The two girls were identified as three-year-old Jennifer Valerie Price and her sister, 18-month-old Maureen Ann Price. These girls were the children of Doris and it now became imperative to find the man of the house: 32-year-old Albert Price.

On the same day that all three bodies were found, the police issued a description of the man they wanted to interview. According to this, Price was, "A painter of around 40 years of age, 5ft 6ins in height, of slim build with brown hair which was thinning on top. He had a sallow complexion and what appeared to be a sullen manner. When last seen he was wearing a grey jacket, grey trousers with either a white or cream open-necked shirt."

In fact, there were a large number of witnesses who could give some details of the movements of Albert Price. Although two police forces were involved in the investigations, they pooled their information and this produced a rather comprehensive timetable of events.

Eileen Elsie Fleming was the Prices' next-door neighbour, living at number 18. She had last seen Doris on the evening of June 2nd. None of the Price family were seen again until the following morning when, at about 7.30am, the postman, a gentleman named McLean, had delivered a registered letter for which Albert Price had signed.

Shortly after this, at 8.00am, Mrs Fisher, who was the caretaker of a school some 40 yards away from the Price home, saw Albert and the two children crossing her school playground.

The next certain sighting of Price had been at 11.45pm on that same night of June 3rd. Edith Peskett lived at 28 Claremont Avenue, New Malden, and she had known the Price family for a number of years. It was just before midnight when Albert called and asked her if she would put him and the children up for the night. Edith asked Price what had become of his wife and he replied that she had left him. Not wanting to become involved in some sort of family dispute, Edith turned down Price's request and suggested that he go home.

It was the evening of Sunday, June 4th before Price was seen again and by this time he was in Pagham, close to Bognor, enjoying himself on the beach with his two children. It was there that he met Alfred West, a brickyard worker, and told him that he had missed his last train home and had nowhere to stay. A kind soul, West took Price back to his home at 8 Ockley Road, Bognor, and introduced him to his wife, Nellie, who gave the children some milk, bread and butter.

Although Nellie West could not give Price a bed for the night, she did go to her neighbour at number 10, Rosina Ide, who did agree to put him and the children up. She could not provide them with food but would let them have the room for 2s 6d per night. Price told her that he would need the room for only the one night, but in the event, he returned on the Monday evening and asked to stay again. He finally left on the morning of Tuesday, June 6th, and Rosina never saw him or the children again.

Mr Cooper was the attendant of the west car park in Bognor and it was late in the morning of June 6th when a man, pushing two children in a pram, came up to him and asked where he could put the youngsters so that they would be in the shade whilst he had a cup of tea in the café nearby. Cooper pointed out a quiet spot in the far corner, just on to some waste land and the last he saw of the man, he was steering the maroon coloured pushchair in that direction. The spot Cooper indicated was exactly where the two children were subsequently discovered, hidden amongst the long grass.

The two inquests were both opened and adjourned, only

evidence of identification being given. The one on the children was held at Bognor Regis Town Hall by the Chichester coroner, Mr G.F.L. Bridgeman and here it was also revealed that a post-mortem had been carried out by Dr Keith Simpson. The cause of death was indeed asphyxiation but the bodies also contained large quantities of a sleeping pill called Carbromal, available without prescription. It appeared that Price had drugged the children and then smothered them whilst they were asleep. Perhaps the saddest part of the evidence was testimony that Maureen had been found with her thumb in her mouth whilst Jennifer had a protective arm around her sister.

The search for Price spread across Sussex and Surrey and into London but it was a fortunate observation by two probationary police officers which led to his capture. At 4.30am on June 13th, Constables Adams and Fisher were patrolling their beat which included Green Park in London. It was there that they saw a man sleeping in a deck chair and upon rousing him, realised that he fitted the description of the wanted man. Faced with the accusation that he was Albert Price the man merely replied, "I know what you want me for. It had to come sooner or later." He was then taken to Cannon Row police station and later moved to Wimbledon where he made a full statement and was then charged with the murder of his wife.

Price appeared at the Kingston magistrates' court, on the day of his arrest, June 13th. He was remanded for eight days and made his final appearance before the magistrate on June 26th when he was committed for trial. There was some debate over where the trial should take place. The magistrate wished to send the case to the Old Bailey but the prosecution solicitor, Mr Maurice Crump, asked that the trial take place at the Surrey assizes. At this, Price's solicitor pointed out that since these assizes opened the following Tuesday, they would not have time to properly prepare their case. In the event, purely so that the case could be heard at the Central Criminal Court, there was a further hearing at Kingston on July 4th where no evidence was offered but the case transferred to London.

Price's trial took place at the Old Bailey on July 12th before Mr Justice Parker with a jury of nine men and three women. The prosecution case was handled by Mr Christmas Humphreys with Price's defence being handled by Mr C.G.L. Du Cann and Mr Alan Garfitt. The proceedings lasted only one day with the defence relying on a plea of insanity.

In addition to the witnesses already mentioned, the prosecution called Frank Saunders, a dispenser at Boots the Chemist in Esher. He testified that on June 3rd, Price had come into the shop and said that he had pains in the head and could not sleep since he had suffered from anxiety of late. Saunders sold Price a box of 25 Carbromal tablets, warning him to keep them away from the children.

Detective Inspector Whitfield told the court how he had seen Price at Wimbledon police station and charged him with the murder of his wife. Price then made a long and detailed statement and it was perhaps that document which was to prove the most damning witness of all.

Price's statement detailed how he had incurred a gambling debt in May 1948. This, added to other regular payments such as the rent and furniture meant that he was now constantly getting into arrears with all sorts of people and companies. For a short while, around the time of Maureen's birth on January 5th, 1949, things improved but Maureen had been premature and Doris had fallen ill after the birth. All this added more pressure to Price's finances and he ended up borrowing money from a bookmaker he knew. It was that debt which took him to court in Kingston in February 1949, when the company, Langley Brothers, sued him for the debt. As a result he had to pay them £2 per month.

All these extra payments meant that Price now began to get into arrears with his rent and in December 1949, a second appearance in Kingston court added further payments to his long list of debts. In order to try to extricate himself from this predicament, Price took to gambling on the horses and dogs, staking larger and larger amounts. Of course, few of these brought any dividends and he only found himself even deeper in debt. In April 1950, he heard that the bailiffs were about to be sent in and this caused his wife to become ill again through worry.

Price's own words tell of the straw that finally broke his back, "On

Saturday, June 3rd, I received a registered letter from the Malden Council Offices giving me notice to give up possession of the house. This was the final blow. The wife was asleep when I received the letter. I thought we were in a hopeless situation as, if we were turned out of the house, we would have nowhere to go, so, I decided to put an end to it all. I got the axe and hit her on the head. She was asleep at the time. I hit her several times. I waited for a time to make sure she was not suffering in any way."

Price went on to say how he had taken the two children downstairs intending to kill them and himself there and then but his nerve failed him. Instead he took the girls to Kingston where they walked down by the river, ending at Hampton Court where he bought them lemonade and ice cream. After wandering about until it was quite late, he tried to get lodgings at Edith Peskett's house. When she turned him away he returned home and made up the children's beds in the kitchen. He got no sleep that night and the following morning decided that he would go down to the seaside and kill the three of them there.

Arriving in Bognor, his original idea was to give the children sleeping pills and then take some himself. They would be lying on the beach and the incoming tide would do the rest but there were too many people about and the girls were enjoying themselves so much. In the event he did decide that the time had come to end it all and after giving his daughters the sleeping pills in their milk, he smothered them. However, once he had done this he found that his nerve failed him again and he could not take his own life.

From Bognor, Price travelled to Brighton, sleeping that first night on the racecourse there. The following day, he introduced himself to a man who ran a travelling coffee shop and worked with him for a day. On the Friday, though, he read in the newspapers about the finding of the bodies and decided to return to London and give himself up.

Arriving in London late on Friday he took lodgings for one night in Praed Street and on Saturday, walked to Scotland Yard intending to give himself up but found that he simply couldn't do so. That night he started sleeping in Green Park. On the Sunday, he attended three services in Westminster Abbey and on Monday made three more attempts to give himself up, all abortive. Finally, he was picked up in Green Park, much to his own relief. His poignant statement ended with, "Knowing what I had done is wrong, I did not want them to suffer for my misdoings. I know they are better off in the next world, where I hope to join them. I did love them. Everybody knows that."

In the event, the defence called no evidence and asked for a verdict of guilty but insane at the time of the events. Mr Du Cann pointed out that if Price had succeeded in killing himself there would probably have been a verdict of suicide whilst the balance of his mind was disturbed. If that was right, then the jury had to now come to a similar conclusion about the state of his mind in this trial. The jury, though, took only 40 minutes to decide that Albert Price was simply guilty of murder, Although they did add a strong recommendation to mercy. Price's defence team announced that it was their intention to appeal.

That appeal, heard on July 31st, was on the grounds that Price was insane at the time he had committed the crime. After all, he had killed his wife and then spent some days playing with his children before killing them. Surely this was hardly the actions of a sane man? Giving his judgement, the Lord Chief Justice, Lord Goddard, said that there was no medical evidence of insanity and Price had described in great detail exactly what he had done. The appeal was dismissed.

The defence now appealed to the Attorney General, Sir Hartley Shawcross, asking for his fiat to stay the execution and grant leave to appeal to the House of Lords. That too was refused and in due course, the Home Secretary, Chuter Ede, announced that there would be no reprieve.

On Wednesday, August 16th, 1950, Price was hanged at Wandsworth by Albert Pierrepoint who was assisted by Harry Allen. At long last, Albert Price's troubles were over.

CHAPTER 24

JAM SANDWICHES

BRIAN Roy Roberts saw nothing unusual when he first walked into the hallway of his home at 56 Kingsland Road, Broadwater, Worthing, on Monday, January 29th, 1951. It was lunchtime and Brian had come home from school, as he did every day, to have something to eat with his mother. There was no immediate sign of 40-year-old Alice Kate Roberts, so Brian, thinking she might be doing some housework upstairs, called out to her. There was no reply.

Deciding that she might be in the yard at the back, Brian walked through to the scullery and there saw a sight that shook him with fear. His mother lay on the scullery floor, a mass of wounds and blood. Brian ran to the house of one of his aunts who lived close by and she returned with him. They had not been back inside number 56 for very long when the police arrived in the shape of Detective Inspector Alan Hoare and Detective Sergeant Lester. The detectives examined the scene and confirmed for themselves that a murder had taken place. They did not, however, have to organise a major search to find the culprit, though, for he was already in custody.

In fact, there were eight people living in the house at 56 Kingsland Road at the time of the attack upon Alice Roberts. In addition to Alice and her eldest son, Brian, there were four other children and two lodgers. It was one of those lodgers, 56-year-old James Virrels, a man who had been engaged to Alice, who was now admitting that he was responsible for her death.

Back at the police station, James Virrels had made a full statement revealing what had happened. On the morning in question, he had risen for work as normal and had left the house before Brian Roberts had even gone to school. He did not, however, stay long at his job for, as he said, "I did not feel very grand this morning and I came back from work about a quarter to ten." In fact, Virrels had also explained that he had been off work ill recently and was still not fully recovered.

Having arrived back home, Virrels sat himself down very close to the fire at which point Alice came in and swore at him, asking why he didn't 'get on top of the fire'. Virrels made no reply and Alice left the room and returned to the scullery where she was busy doing the weekly wash. Virrels continued, "I went out into the scullery to get to the sink to clean my teeth when she said 'Have you looked for a place?' It was only yesterday when she told me to go and find fresh lodgings."

Virrels was later to add that he and Mrs Roberts had been involved in a relationship for some time and the subject of marriage had been raised but of late things had cooled considerably between them, culminating in a request from Alice for him to get out of her house. The statement went on, "We had a few words and she walked back into the sitting room and then came back to the scullery. She said something to me and I swore back at her"

"I turned round and she had a dagger in her hand. She made for me with the dagger and I put my hand up..." Virrels then told the officers how his hand had been cut in the ensuing struggle but eventually he managed to wrestle the knife from Alice and stabbed her with it. He went on to describe, in quite matter of fact terms, what had happened next, "She pleaded. I picked up the chopper and I hit her with it several times. Afterwards I went and had a tot of rum at the Wigmore and afterwards I went to my brother's place and told him to ring for the police. She had been tantalising me for weeks and she has put the children up to tantalising me. What I have said is the truth, that is always the best."

James Virrels may well have told the truth but his statement did not give the entire picture of the wounds he had inflicted upon Alice Roberts. In all, she had been stabbed 40 times. As if this was not enough, Virrels had also struck her, with some force, five times with a small hatchet. The scullery floor had been awash with blood, mingled with water from an upset tub that Alice had been using for her washing.

Even with a full confession, the police still had to build a complete case and a number of witnesses were interviewed. Brian Roberts, the boy who found his mother's body, told the police that the knife used was a sheath knife belonging to him. The last time he had seen it the weapon was where he habitually kept it, on a shelf in the living room. Further, the hatchet used was usually kept on top of the roof of a low shed out in the yard. He had never known it brought into the house, implying that if Virrels used it in the scullery, he must have gone outside to retrieve it.

Henry Rodger Wiltshire, was a bus conductor who lived next door to Alice at number 58. He said that on January 29th, some time around 11.45am or perhaps a little later, he had heard screams coming from number 56. The first scream was a long one and this was followed by a number of shorter ones. At the time he had put this down to one or more of the children larking about.

Mrs Diana Margaret Mary Seymour was the daughter of Mr Wiltshire, and lived with him at number 58. She had spoken to Alice earlier in the day, having seen her in the yard at the back as Alice hung out some washing. This was around 11.20am. 20 minutes after this, at 11.40am Virrels was in the Wigmore Arms public house where he was served with a double rum by the manager, John Alfred Turrell. He knew Virrels very well and noticed that he seemed pale and sick. Turrell invited him to come over and sit by the fire but Virrels remained at the bar, drank his rum very quickly and then walked out without saying a word. In all, Virrels was there no more than two minutes.

Linda Clara Virrels lived at 9 Downlands Avenue, a few minutes walk from Kingsland Road. She was Virrels' sister-in-law and it was to her house that Virrels went after he had left the Wigmore. It was some time before noon that he had knocked at her back door. Linda said Virrels was white, very shaky and his overcoat was wet. Inviting him in, Linda was shocked to hear Virrels confess that he had just committed a murder. He was babbling rather and added something about 'her' coming at him with a dagger.

Virrels never actually told Linda who this 'her' was but it was perhaps logical to assume that Linda was aware that Virrels was talking of Alice. At the end of his diatribe, Linda asked Virrels why he had done this thing and he replied, "I have been going to work with only bread and jam to take with me." After she had made Virrels a cup of strong sweet tea, she telephoned for the police and that was where Inspector Hoare and Sergeant Lester came into the picture.

James Virrels made his initial appearance in court on January 30th where he was represented by Mr C.H. Homan. As was usual, only evidence of arrest was given and Virrels was remanded until February 7th. One further remand followed and it was not until February 14th that Virrels was sent for trial.

The trial opened at Lewes on March 12th, before Mr Justice Parker. Virrels was defended by Mr Derek Curtis Bennett and Mr Stanley Rees whilst the case for the Crown was put by Mr Anthony Marlowe and Mr Malcolm Morris.

There could, of course, be no doubt that Virrels was responsible for the death of Alice Roberts, but was it possible that it was not actually murder? He had said that Alice had been the one to get the knife and that she had used it on him first. Evidence was now given of the injuries he had actually sustained.

Dr Henry Rosenberg was the deputy police surgeon at Worthing and he had examined Virrels after his arrest. Dr Rosenberg said that there was a laceration on Virrels' right ring finger. There were three further lacerations over the back of his right hand and a small one on his left ear. His left wrist bore three superficial scratches, and there were three more such scratches on the left of his neck. As a matter of fact, Virrels was a patient of Rosenberg's and the doctor was able to add that he had always found him to be particularly quiet and even tempered.

Other witnesses were called to show that Virrels might have had mental and other health problems. Theodore Arsenault was a foreman for Worthing Rural Council and he had worked with Virrels, who was a gardener. Arsenault, too, described Virrels as a man of even temper and confirmed that he had recently been off work due to ill health. James Brown, who lived at 6 West Street, was a fellow gardener and he had worked with Virrels for some time. He was able to testify that, especially of late, Virrels had often complained of very severe headaches and had sometimes had to go home early.

The time had now come for Virrels to take the stand for himself and according to him, the marriage between him and Alice was supposed to take place in April but towards the end of January, her attitude towards him had changed. On January 28th, for instance, she had criticised his family and claimed that his sister had given birth to a child out of wedlock. The argument ended with Alice telling him to get out of the house and find new lodgings. The very next day, the day of Alice's death, he had seen yet again that all there was for him to take to work was bread, margarine and jam, and this led to a new argument.

Virrels now expanded his statement on the attack itself. The very start of the trouble had been when he went to clean his teeth. Alice had lashed out with some wet clothes she was holding and had caught him across the face. She had followed this attack by taking her son's knife with which she now made a lunge at him. Virrels grabbed at her wrist and got his finger cut in the process. He claimed that this seemed to make his mind go blank and he did not to know precisely what happened then until he managed to get the knife and stab Alice with it. She fell to the floor but within seconds had started to get up again. By now he had dropped the knife so, fearful that she might have found it and be about to use it on him, he lashed out with the hatchet, which he claimed he had found against the wall near the back door.

The time came when Alice finally lay still and Virrels seemed to regain his senses at this point for he knelt down and felt for a pulse. Having found none, he went to the Wigmore and then on to his brothers. He denied that he had told Linda he had committed a murder, saying only that he had had a row.

One of the final witnesses was Dr J.M. Matheson, the medical officer of Brixton prison. He had been observing Virrels ever since his reception at the jail, on January 30th. He stated that the prisoner had complained of blackouts and said that when he suffered from these he got vivid flashed of red light before his eyes. However, Matheson added that in his opinion, Virrels was perfectly sane and fully aware of his actions when he struck out with the knife and hatchet.

Faced with this mountain of evidence, the jury had no qualms in returning a guilty verdict. Virrels immediately announced that he would appeal. That appeal was heard on April 9th when the defence again argued that there should have been a verdict of manslaughter. Dismissing the appeal, one of the judges, Mr Justice Oliver, suggested that the ferocity of the attack was such that Alice Roberts was murdered over and over again.

In fact, this entire period was a very sad time for the resort of Worthing. As Virrels' trial ended, another one began. Twenty-three-year-old Brian Moore had been charged with murdering his girlfriend, Jacqueline Aldhouse, on November 13th, 1950. Jacqueline had been found strangled at Moore's home, 2 Beaumont Road. Moore's trial ended on March 16th and he was found to be guilty but insane. Suffering from schizophrenia, Moore was sent to Broadmoor.

There was to be no such escape for Worthing's other killer. On Thursday, April 26th, 1951, less than three months after Alice Roberts had been killed, James Virrels was hanged at Wandsworth by Albert Pierrepoint, assisted by Syd Dernley.

CHAPTER 25

AN ARTIST OF SOME REPUTE

CHRISTMAS 1953, was not a particularly happy time for 11-year-old Margaret Rose Louise Spevick, for it was at that time that she fell at her home, 12 Embankment Gardens, Chelsea, and broke her wrist. Still, she had plenty of friends to keep her company as she recuperated, and one of the closest of those friends was Pearl Hepper.

Pearl lived just ten minutes away, at 7 Ormonde Gate. One of five children, Pearl now lived with her mother. Her father, an artist who suffered badly from asthma, had taken a studio on the south coast at Hove, near Brighton, where the sea air would hopefully improve his health. Pearl still saw her father, of course, as he made regular visits to London and on occasion had even taken her and Margaret to tea. It did not come as any surprise, therefore, when Pearl's father, William Sanchez de Pina Hepper, took an active interest in Margaret Spevick's recovery.

On January 17th, 1954, Hepper wrote to Margaret's mother, from Brighton.

The letter in part read, "Dear Mr and Mrs Spevick. I have been wondering whether you would like Margaret to spend a fortnight's convalescence with us here. I have had for some time special interest to paint an oil portrait of your daughter for an exhibition to take place here, and I think this an excellent opportunity when she can't go to school for some weeks yet ..." Margaret's mother and father,

Elizabeth and Louis, talked the matter over and wrote back on January 23rd.

"Dear Mr Hepper. Please forgive the delay in answering your very kind letter. We had to wait and see what the doctor had to say. The arm is out of plaster but Margaret has to attend for exercises every day so it would be the end of February before she would be discharged from the hospital ..."

Hepper, though, was not to be dissuaded and wrote again on January 27th.

"...Thank you for your letter of the 23rd. I was so glad Margaret has got her arm out of plaster. With reference to her holiday here, I explained the position to the nurse sharing the flat and she has told me that she could arrange with the Alexandra Hospital to continue her daily exercises if you would get a letter from her doctor, describing the exercises needed."

If there had been any doubts in Elizabeth Spevick's mind, that letter seemed to settle them. Mr Hepper had made a kind invitation, he had space at his Brighton flat, and even had a resident nurse who took care of him and who could therefore take care of Margaret. However, to settle the issue once and for all, Hepper took matters into his own hands and on February 2nd, turned up at Elizabeth's home, saying that he had to return to Hove the next day and this would be a perfect time for Margaret to come with him. Finally, Elizabeth demurred and permission was given.

On Wednesday, February 3rd, 1954, William Hepper called for Margaret and they were then accompanied to Victoria Station by Elizabeth Spevick. She saw her daughter off on the train, having first made arrangements to visit Hove on the Sunday. Hepper agreed a time when he and Margaret would meet Elizabeth at Brighton station and then took Margaret, her arm still in a sling, off to Sussex.

Two days later, on Friday morning, Elizabeth received a postcard from Hepper on which he had written the previous day, "Dear friend. We are writing sitting on a deck chair at the West Pier head. It is like a summer's day. Margaret is happy. I took her to a cinema and to the skating theatre to see the girls doing their exercises. I am going home tomorrow for three hours and she will be busy at the skating rink. We went in a taxi to the hospital this morning and got an appointment for Wednesday ..."

Sunday, 7th February finally arrived and Elizabeth Spevick caught the train down to Brighton. Although Elizabeth arrived on time, at 12.25pm, and waited around for two hours, there was no sign of Hepper or Margaret. Under normal circumstances, Mrs Spevick would simply have caught a bus or a taxi to the flat but unfortunately she had not brought the address with her. There was nothing for it but to return to London, pick up the address and then travel all the way back to Sussex. By the time this round trip was finally over, and Elizabeth arrived at the address, it was very late in the day.

The first disappointment came when Mrs Spevick got to Hepper's studio. He did not, after all, reside in a large spacious flat but occupied room 14 at 112 Western Road, Hove, a block situated over Felicity's Hairdresser's and converted into small flatlets. Hepper occupied one room at the back of the fourth floor and since there was no answer to Elizabeth's insistent knocking, he was not apparently at home.

Mary Holly lived in room 12, and hearing Elizabeth rapping on Hepper's door, came to see what the problem was. The two women talked briefly and Mary remarked that she had indeed seen Margaret a couple of times, but not since the Thursday. Taking Elizabeth into her room so that she could warm herself by the fire, Mary Holly now walked down to the caretaker's flat and left a note asking him to call upon her when he got in.

David Bishop, the caretaker, lived in the basement flat and it was around 10.00pm when he read Mary Holly's note. Immediately he went upstairs and listened as Elizabeth Spevick told him about her daughter and Mr Hepper. By now it was too late for her to travel back to London and since Hepper was not around, it seemed that the best idea was to let Elizabeth use his room, at least for the one night. Bishop unlocked the door and Mary Holly went inside to put the fire on in order to take the chill off the room.

It was only later, just as Elizabeth was due to retire for the night, that the dreadful discovery was made. Mary went into the room first, in order to pull down the bedclothes and then she saw it — a human foot. She called out to Bishop and it was he who pulled back the blankets and found the body of Margaret Spevick.

Margaret was naked from the waist down, apart from a pair of grey socks, and there were bruises all over her flesh. Near the body lay a pillow case and the sling the child had been wearing and both these were bloodstained. To one side of the bed, a half-finished portrait of Margaret lay on an easel. Ensuring that neither of the two ladies could enter the room and see that awful scene, Bishop ran into the street where he found two policemen, Sergeant Kyrke and a constable, and told them what he had found. They later stated that their arrival at the murder scene was at 10.50pm.

M. Prior

The officer in charge of the inquiry was Superintendent H.J. Nicholson, the chief of the Hove Police, Although the actual day-to-day running of that investigation lay in the hands of Detective Inspector Reginald Bidgood. The most important thing, of course, was to find Hepper. Descriptions were widely circulated, as were photographs of the wanted man. Even chemists and doctors were specially warned as Hepper took sodium amytal to help him sleep and his supply had been left behind at Hove. There were reported sightings from as far as Hastings and Birmingham but all these amounted to nothing and Hepper's whereabouts remained a mystery.

In fact Hepper had gone to Spain from where he wrote to a number of relatives and friends, asking them for financial assistance. One of those relatives, living in Gibraltar and having read reports of the crime, contacted the authorities and finally, on Wednesday, February 10th, Hepper was arrested in the border town of Irun by the local police commissioner, Don Frederico Pita Iglesias. The Spanish police contacted their British counterparts and immediately the wheels of extradition were put into motion.

The very next day, February 11th, the body of Margaret Spevick was laid to rest in the Hove Borough Cemetery. On the same day, Hepper was moved to San Sebastian prison where he would await the results of the behind-the-scenes moves to get him back to Britain. Hepper, of course, did his best to avoid this fate by claiming that he was a Spanish national but the fact that he had travelled to Spain on a British passport issued on July 14th, 1949, counted heavily against him.

232

On February 15th, Inspector Bidgood flew to Madrid with Detective Sergeant Lane, an officer from Scotland Yard's Special Branch who spoke Spanish and would act as interpreter. They had to stay in Spain for some time, mostly conferring with the Spanish authorities in order to expedite the request for extradition that would soon arrive from Britain. Meanwhile Hepper was visited on two occasions by the British Vice Consul, Wing Commander Adrian Nicholas Max de Lavison.

Back in Britain, on February 17th, the inquest on Margaret Spevick opened before the coroner, Dr A.C. Sommerville. With the inquiry being at such a delicate stage and no guarantee that Hepper would even be brought back to Britain, this was immediately adjourned for two months.

Two days later, on the 19th, the two British detectives travelled to San Sebastian where, the following day, they first interviewed Hepper. Satisfied that there was little else they could do until all the governmental paper work was complete, Bidgood and Lane flew back to Britain on February 22nd. Five days later, the documents were complete and the British Embassy in Madrid formally applied to the Spanish Foreign Ministry for the extradition of William Sanchez de Pina Hepper to face a charge of murder.

The wait must have seemed interminable but finally, on March 12th, the Spanish government announced that they had consented to the application. Four days after that, on March 16th, Bidgood and Lane were boarding a plane to travel back to Madrid. It was decided that Hepper would be brought back to Britain on the liner *Alcantara* which would be diverted to the west coast port of Vigo, and from there would sail for Southampton. On March 18th, Hepper, accompanied by officers of the Spanish police, was taken to Vigo where, on March 22nd, he was handed over to Bidgood and Lane and taken on board the *Alcantara*. The ship sailed the same night and finally, on March 23rd, Hepper once more set foot on English soil when the ship docked at Southampton.

On March 24th, Hepper appeared at Hove magistrates' court where evidence of arrest was given. Remanded for a week, Hepper was then driven to Brixton prison, claiming to have no memory of the crime with which he had been charged. There were a number of such remands. Hepper appeared in court on March 31st and again on April 8th. It was not until his fourth appearance, on May 4th, that he was committed for trial at the next Sussex assizes.

The trial opened at Lewes on July 19th, 1954, before Mr Justice Jones. The case for the Crown was led by Mr R.F. Levy, assisted by Mr R. Maxwell Turner. Hepper was defended by Mr Derek Curtis Bennett and Mr John McManus. The jury consisted of ten men and two women.

One of the most crucial factors was deciding exactly when little Margaret Spevick had actually died. She was certainly alive on February 4th, for on that date she was seen by Mary Holly. Hepper had called on Mary and told her that he was expecting a wireless to be delivered the next day and if he was out, would she be kind enough to take it in for him. Mary could see into Hepper's room as they spoke at the doorway and Margaret was inside, reading a book.

That same evening, Hepper received a visit from a friend, George Redvern Kemp Davey, a newspaper proof reader who often called on Hepper to discuss art. As they spoke a small, dark-haired girl was in the room and Hepper introduced her as his niece. It was in the course of the conversation between Davey and Hepper that the latter remarked that he had been hoping to book a passage to Gibraltar but the fare was £23. He had had £20 but had fallen asleep in a Brighton cinema and when he woke, found that the money had been taken from his pocket.

The likelihood is that Margaret was killed that same night. Miss Peggy Grace Harper lived in room number 3, on the second floor, and she recalled seeing Hepper walking down the staircase, carrying a suitcase, at 6.00am. She was not sure which day this was but knew that it was either the Friday, February 5th, or Saturday the 6th. Hepper's passport had been stamped at Dieppe on Friday, so it was impossible for him to have travelled on the Saturday.

To counter this suggestion, Miss Jennie Lines, who also lived in the flats, said that she had made an entry in her diary stating that on February 5th, she had seen Margaret at 11.45am. If this entry was correct, Hepper could not have been the killer as the only boat he could have caught on that day was the 12.30pm from Newhaven. There was therefore no way in which he could have killed Margaret after 11.45am and been in Newhaven in time to catch that boat. Under cross examination, though, Miss Lines admitted that when she ran out of space, her diary entries often overflowed to the next day. It was quite possible therefore that although it was written under February 5th, the 11.45am sighting might have referred to an incident which actually took place on the Thursday. In this way, it was determined that Margaret, if she was killed by Hepper, must have died late on the Thursday, or very early on the Friday morning. However, since the few clothes that Margaret was still wearing were day clothes, a short blouse, a woollen jumper, a bodice and a vest, it is almost certain that she would have died on the Thursday.

Elizabeth Spevick told the court the story of Hepper's repeated requests to take her daughter to his studio in Hove. He had told her that the child would be in the care of nurse Corcoran who had two rooms in his flat. Mary Corcoran, when she was called, stated that she was a State Registered Nurse, and lived in two rooms, numbers 15 and 16, at 112 Western Road. Hepper had told her that a young girl, his niece, was coming to stay with him and had even asked if it was possible for her to continue medical treatment at the local hospital, but that was as far as it went. She had never been asked to offer medical advice herself, or to take care of Margaret in any way. The most she did was tell Hepper which hospital to go to, and wrote the address down for him.

Medical evidence was given by Dr Leonard Robert Janes, the pathologist at the Royal Sussex County Hospital. Margaret Spevick had died from asphyxia following strangulation by means of a band placed across the neck. It was likely that her own sling was the murder weapon. The doctor added that Margaret had also been raped.

The prosecution also entered into evidence a letter written by Hepper to his daughter Margharita, on February 12th. In this he referred to a strange experience at his studio in Hove. In part the letter read, "...My wife came to see me in Hove ...I opened her purse and found a letter from her lover ...I struck her and she gave me one with a bottle. I hit her again and then we fought, body to body. I believe I left her unconscious on the bed. I tried to revive her with smelling salts ...then, as I love her with madness, although she was unconscious, I caressed her. In the morning I decided to flee to my beloved country." In that letter, Hepper was claiming that if he was shown to be responsible for Margaret's death, it must have been some sort of illusion and he had believed he was attacking his wife.

Hepper entered the witness box to tell his version of what had happened at Hove. Before that, he related some of his past history. Hepper had been born at Huelva in Southern Spain, on August 14th, 1891, making him 62 years old. His father had been born in Gibraltar whilst his mother was Spanish. He had married in 1919, and had five children, three daughters, and two sons.

From 1928 to 1939, Hepper had been on consular service at Oporto and had helped many people to escape the fascist Spanish police. After that period, he had worked as a translator in the Latin-American section of the BBC until, in July 1946, he had been involved in a road accident during which he sustained a head injury. From that he received £1,000 in damages, but he had never been the same man since. Since he also suffered from asthma, he had been forced to leave London's smoky environment and seek accommodation near the sea. From July 1952 to early December 1953, he had lodged at the home of Mrs P.M. Hewetson at Farm Road, Hove, until he had found the room at Western Road.

Turning now to the events of early February, Hepper said that he had felt strange since the Wednesday. On that day he remembered leaving Margaret alone in the flat, reading a book, whilst he went for a long walk on the sea front. He laid down on a bench in a shelter and fell sleep, not returning to the flat until some time between 3.00am and 4.00am. He did not see Margaret then, but she must have been there for he did notice her at 9.00am. He had been planning a trip to Spain for some time and only left when he did because he had a letter from his sister saying that their brother was dying. Margaret was still alive when he left Brighton and he had given her the train fare she needed to get back to London. Further, he certainly could not have been the man who raped her as he had been impotent for the past year. At one stage whilst he was giving this evidence, Hepper collapsed in the dock and the trial had to be adjourned for 20 minutes.

The proceedings came to a close on July 22nd and it took the jury just 85 minutes to judge that Hepper was guilty. Asked if he had anything to say he replied, "I think it is quite unfaithful…" Then he corrected his English and said, "…I mean incorrect. I did not do it."

On August 3rd, it was announced that Hepper would not enter an appeal but that representations would be made to the Home Office, asking for the sentence to be reviewed. Those efforts were in vain and the sentence was duly confirmed.

At 9.00am on Wednesday, August 11th, 1954, three days before his 63rd birthday, William Sanchez de Pina Hepper was hanged at Wandsworth by Albert Pierrepoint and Royston Rickard. A crowd of around 40 people had gathered outside the prison gates, waiting for the appointed hour and when they had departed it was seen that someone had left a small bunch of pink gladioli, wrapped in white paper. On an envelope was written, "In memory of Sanchez de Pina Hepper — Judge not that ye be not judged. From Margaret Evans of Chelsea."

CHAPTER 26

LEGS DIAMOND

THE morning of Thursday, November 10th, 1960, was little different to any other for the staff of Lloyds Bank, Goring Road, Worthing. Having opened the branch for business, two members of staff collected a leather case full of cash and prepared to drive out to open a sub-office at Field Place, Durrington, a couple of miles away.

Under normal circumstances, the cashier involved in opening the sub-office would have been Rodney Edgar James Pine, but on this particular day he was ill, so his place was taken by Andrew John Gordon Barker, a young man who had worked for the bank for just over a year. The other member of staff involved in running the Field Place office was John Henry Pull, a 61-year-old former postman who now filled the position of cleaner and guard at the sub-office.

John Pull was a well-known figure in Worthing. An amateur archaeologist, Pull was a former president of the Worthing Archaeological Society, had conducted excavations and had even had a book published on the flint mines of Black Patch. He had joined the bank only one month before, merely looking upon the job as something to fill his time since he had left the Post Office.

Barker and Pull arrived at Field Place a few minutes before 10.00am. The leather bag from the main branch was placed to one side on the counter, next to a Gladstone bag which contained papers, whilst Barker got his till ready for the day's transactions. At exactly 10.00am the doors were unlocked and one minute later, the first customer of the day, Mrs Davies, entered the bank but her transaction was finished in less than a minute. As she left the bank, John Pull walked into the cloakroom at the back of the bank. It was time to put the kettle on.

Next door to the bank was Alexander's greengrocer's shop, owned by Alex Alexander but managed by his son-in-law, Maurice Taylor. Both men were busy serving customers when, at about 10.10am, the alarm went off at the bank. At first, the two men thought that this was just another test. There seemed to have been so many such tests lately and no doubt, in a minute or two, the siren would stop. It was then that Andrew Barker ran into the shop, shouted that there had been a raid and asked someone to telephone for the police. Taylor and Alexander now rushed back into the bank with Barker, where to their horror they found John Henry Pull lying on the floor, his head a mass of blood.

Pull had been shot in the head at very close range and could hardly breathe since his nostrils were clogged with his own blood. Alexander, after calling the police, got cold compresses to place on Pull's head whilst Taylor cleared the wounded man's nostrils and removed his false teeth so that he might breathe more easily. It was all to no avail. Before any medical help could arrive, John Pull died in Maurice Taylor's arms.

The police were soon on the scene and although he was deeply shocked, Andrew Barker managed to tell the officers what had happened. A few minutes after Mrs Davies had left, two young men, each perhaps no more than 20 years old, had entered the bank. Without speaking one had walked past the counter and down a corridor which led to the staff area and the cloakroom. Barker asked the man what he was doing, at which a shot-gun was produced from underneath the man's coat. At that precise moment, Pull, still carrying the kettle, came out of the cloakroom, only to come to face to face with the man with the gun.

At this point the other man, who had thus far remained silent, demanded to know where the money was. Barker indicated the bags on the counter and the second man snatched the wrong bag. Meanwhile, Pull had lifted an arm, a mannerism he had when he was about to speak, and might also have touched the gunman on the shoulder. The armed man took a step back, lifted the gun to point directly at Pull's head, and fired. As the bank guard fell, the two men turned to leave. Barker, obviously in a state of terror, and fearful that the men might return, shouted that they had the wrong bag. The gunman then snatched the correct bag whilst his accomplice threw the other one to the floor. The robbers left and Barker ran outside in time to see a green car, one he thought might be an MG Magnette, speed off in a westerly direction. He had then set off the bank alarm and run to the greengrocer's shop for assistance.

A message went out to all police officers in the area, to be on the look out for two young men, possibly in a dark green car, though, of course, it was realised that this might already have been abandoned. The breakthrough came much sooner than anyone had expected.

Matthew 'Mac' Wilson, a taxi driver, was sitting in his car outside Worthing station, when two men got into his cab and asked to be driven to Western Row, a thoroughfare near the sea front. The fare for that journey came to 2s 6d but one of the young men had handed over a £1 note and told Wilson to take, '…half a sheet'. Wilson took this to mean 10s, and gave a 10s note in change. Now, whilst taxi-drivers might well expect a tip, one which is three times the basic fare, is unusual to say the least. It was now 10.25am and although Wilson had not heard about the bank robbery, the police constable he mentioned his big-tipping fare to, certainly had.

Another message was flashed to all police cars to watch out for two young men, especially near the sea front, and basic descriptions were given. Very soon afterwards, Sergeant Jack Grant and Constable Derek Randle were driving along Marine Parade when they saw two men at a bus stop near the junction of Queen's Road. They turned their patrol car around and approached the pair.

One of the men, who identified himself as 16-year-old Philip Tucker, said that he and his friend, Alan Alfred George Hosier, had come from Portsmouth and were now on their way back there. Both were asked to prove their identities and when they said they were unable to do so, it was decided to search them. In one of Tucker's rear pockets were 20 £1 notes whilst in the other were eight £5 notes. His compatriot, Hosier had a wad of £5 notes and claimed that he had saved this money over a period of time. Not satisfied with their answers, Grant and Randle took the two men into custody.

By the afternoon, Scotland Yard had been called in and it was a senior officer from there, Detective Superintendent Basil Acott, together with Detective Superintendent Alan Hoare, the head of the West Sussex CID, who interviewed Hosier and Tucker at Worthing police station. When Hosier was told that John Pull was dead and this was now a murder case, he was visibly shocked. He began to shiver and shake uncontrollably and had to be wrapped in blankets, placed near an electric fire and given two cups of hot, sweet tea. Both men then made statements admitting their involvement in the robbery and naming two more people.

Tucker, whose home was at Almand Road in Brentford, admitted that he was one of the men inside the bank, but he had not carried the gun. Hosier was the driver and had waited outside for Tucker and a man so far still at liberty, one Victor John Terry. As the car left the bank, Tucker had stuffed all the money into a blue BOAC bag but in the excitement, Hosier had taken a wrong turning and it was decided to abandon the car, with each man making his way back to an address in Western Row. Tucker, still carrying the money, left the other two and took a number 4 bus to the station. It seemed to take an inordinate amount of time to reach its destination and by the time it did, only Hosier was waiting for him. Travelling by taxi, these two eventually arrived at Western Row by about 10.30am where Terry and his girlfriend were waiting. It was decided that the four of them should split up and make their way to Portsmouth in pairs, travelling by different routes.

Tucker and Hosier would travel together. In due course they would meet up at Portsmouth Harbour Station and divide the cash up properly. In the meantime, Tucker was given £60 10s whilst Hosier got £120. These two left Western Row together at 11.10am, but five minutes later, were picked up by the police. Tucker told police that the man who had fired the gun was 20-year-old Terry, and said that the other person involved was Valerie Salter, Terry's girlfriend, who lived at 7 Western Row, Worthing. She had taken no part in the actual robbery, but had been at home, waiting for the others to return.

Hosier told much the same story, admitting that he was the driver of the car, which he had abandoned in Becket Road. Whilst sitting in the car, he had heard the sound of the shot and when Terry got into the vehicle, Hosier demanded to know what had happened and Terry had replied, "He got hold of the gun, wrestled with it and it went off, but I don't think it hit him."

Having left the car, he and Terry got on to the number 5 bus which got to the station before the number 4. It was these two who got into Matthew Wilson's cab and Terry who paid the fare to Western Row with a £1 note. After some minutes, Tucker had not appeared and, fearful that he might have been stopped, Hosier took another taxi back to the station to look for him. Tucker was found and the two went back to Valerie Salter's house where some money was handed out. In addition to the money Tucker had already mentioned, Salter was also given £120 which she took upstairs and locked away in her wardrobe. She had wanted no part in the robbery, and wanted none of the proceeds.

That same evening, police officers called at 7 Western Row, and searched Valerie Salter's room. The wardrobe was found to be locked and once the door had been forced, the £120 in banknotes which Valerie had hidden there earlier was discovered, as were two men's coats. In the pocket of one of those coats was discovered a cartridge extractor from a shotgun. Later still, Detective Inspector Albert Buckey examined the car found in Becket Road. It transpired that this was not an MG but a Wolseley 4/44 saloon. On the floor at the back he found a single-barrelled shotgun and, in a bag wedged between the seats, a bank cash balance sheet.

The search for Terry and Salter was widespread. Road blocks were put up to seal off Sussex, Surrey and the eastern part of Hampshire. All Automobile Association patrolmen were asked to be on the look out for a car containing the two fugitives and a description of Terry was published: 5ft 8ins tall, medium build, with light brown hair. On his right arm, he had four tattoos: 'Vic', 'Maureen', 'Knife', and 'Mabel'.

Unknown to the police, they had been very close indeed to Terry and Salter. As officers Grant and Randle were interviewing Hosier and Tucker at the bus stop, a number 31 bus had gone past. On the top deck, Terry and Salter had watched their two friends being spoken to. By noon, these two had arrived at Littlehampton and it was there that Terry bought a suedette lined coat for Valerie. If by now the police were looking for her too, then a description of the clothes she was wearing would also be circulated. With this new coat, she might not be identified as easily.

Terry and Salter now climbed into yet another taxi, this time driven by Arthur Flenley, and asked to be driven to Portsmouth. It was at the Stockbridge cross-roads, along the Chichester by-pass, at 12.50pm that the cab was stopped by Sergeant Stanley Bicknell. At this time, of course, officers had been told to be on the lookout for two men so Bicknell was not unduly suspicious of the man and woman in the back of the cab. They were holding hands and Terry said that his name was Weston, and he lived at Wiston Road, Littlehampton. The woman identified herself as Valerie Brown and gave an address in the same street. The couple said they were engaged and were going to do some shopping for the wedding, in Portsmouth. Sergeant Bicknell wished them all the best and waved them on.

At Portsmouth there was, of course, no sign of Hosier and Tucker, and Terry assumed that they had been arrested. He now bought a tartan hold-all to take the cash and since he and Valerie were by now rather tired, they booked into a guest house at Southsea. The landlady, Mrs Florence Barker, believed Terry's story that they were newly-weds and saw that they had signed in as Mr and Mrs Diamond, 22 Western Avenue, Greenford, Middlesex. The couple had breakfast the following morning and by 10.00am had left after paying their bill.

The following day, November 11th, Hosier and Tucker made their first appearance at a special hearing of Worthing magistrates' court. The proceedings began at 7.23pm and the magistrate, Jack Gentle, was called in from a dinner party which explained why he was wearing full evening dress. The hearing lasted only nine minutes, both were charged with murder and remanded in custody until November 18th. In newspaper reports of the day, Tucker was not in fact named since he was, of course, a juvenile.

Meanwhile, Victor John Terry was trying his best to escape the net thrown around the south of England. Having checked out of the guest house in Southsea, it was time to get another taxi, this time driven by Geoffrey Leonard Halstead. He was told to drive towards London and along the way was asked if he knew anything about getting to Ireland or the Channel Islands. He was also quizzed on the times of trains to Scotland.

This particular taxi ride was far from straightforward, though. Halstead was first of all asked to drive to Salisbury and here his male passenger bought a gun. This was confirmed by James Alfred Pyke of Macklin Road, Salisbury, who recalled selling the .410 Webley bolt-action weapon to a man fitting Terry's description. Terry tried to load the gun whilst sitting in the back seat of the cab. From Salisbury, they travelled to Fovant where the trio stopped at a public house whilst Halstead telephoned his employers, on Terry's instructions, and inquired about the price of a trip around Devon and Cornwall. Telling Terry that he would be driven wherever he wished as long as he could pay the fare, Halstead was now told to drive towards Yeovil but along the way, was told to turn right instead and following Terry's directions, ended up in London where the £15 fare was paid in £5 notes.

Having dropped off his fare, Halstead first rang his office to tell them what had happened and ask for further instructions. Having conferred with his boss, he then contacted the police, who ordered him to drive his cab to Worthing. Terry had left the single-barrelled shotgun, which he had been unable to load properly, on the back seat of the taxi, along with four boxes of cartridges and a copy of the *Daily Mirror* which gave details of the crime he was involved in.

A police watch was put on Terry's home at 10 Oldfield House, Devonshire Road, Chiswick, but there was no sign of the two fugitives. The time had come to publicise the details even wider so descriptions and photographs were put out in newspapers and on the television. It was the latter medium that led to the arrest of Terry and Salter.

Eunice Walker ran the Lynedock Hotel in Glasgow, and on the evening of November 12th, she saw Terry's picture flash on to her television screen. She instantly recognised him as the man in room 7 and contacted the police. In the early hours of the morning of November 13th, Detective Inspector Hector MacDougall went to the hotel and looking at the register saw that room 7 was apparently occupied by 'Mr and Mrs Carter, British, 22 Argyle Street, Manchester'. MacDougall knocked on the door and a male voice from within shouted, "What do you want?" Identifying himself as the police, MacDougall was admitted by the man. In the bed, the detective noticed a woman and MacDougall asked them both for some identification, telling them that he was inquiring into a murder in Sussex. Terry persisted in saying that his name was Carter until MacDougall asked him to roll up the right sleeve of his shirt. The tattoos would prove things one way or the other. 'Mr Carter' knew he was beaten and muttered, "Okay, I'm Terry." Both he and Salter were now taken into custody and when the room was searched, MacDougall found the tartan holdall which still held £918 10s in cash.

Flown back to London and then driven to Sussex, Terry and Salter appeared at Worthing magistrates' court on November 13th. Terry, who was represented by Mr John Bolland, was put into the box first and remanded on a charge of murder. Salter who made her appearance immediately afterwards, was represented by Mr William Hemming and faced a charge of receiving. She, too, was remanded, to the same date, November 18th. Two days later, on November 15th, John Henry Pull was laid to rest at Durrington cemetery.

The first time all four of the accused were in court on the same day was on November 18th. Terry, Hosier and Tucker were first brought up together. By now both of the other defendants had been successful in obtaining representation. Hosier's solicitor was Mr Thomas Gosden, whilst Tucker, still unnamed in press reports, was instructing Mr T.E. Bangor-Jones. Salter followed these three into the dock and was now charged, more specifically, with receiving £928, knowing it to be stolen. All four were remanded again, this time until November 25th, Although it was suggested in court that on that date, Mr Hemming might well apply for bail for Valerie Salter.

In the event, no such application was ever made and Valerie Salter remained in custody throughout the various remand hearings. There was, in fact, only one more hearing where no detailed evidence was heard and that was on December 2nd. On that date, all four were told that they would appear in court on December 7th, when the case against them would be heard. That hearing extended over to December 8th and continued the following week on December 15th and 16th. On this last day, the four were sent for trial at the next Sussex assizes.

On that final day at Worthing, an attempt had been made to transfer the case to the Old Bailey. Mr John Platts-Mills, who now represented Tucker, claimed that the four would not receive a fair trial due to public feeling in Sussex and that this represented an inordinate delay since the Sussex assizes were not due to open until March. Mr Bolland, for Terry, said he could not support this application as he would not be ready in time if the case were moved to London. At this, Mr Platts-Mills withdrew his application. The case would be heard at Lewes, in March.

In fact, it was March 20th when the trial finally opened, before Mr Justice Stable. The prosecution was led by Mr Geoffrey Lawrence, assisted by Mr Peter Crowder. Terry, the only one facing a charge of capital murder, was defended by Mr Alan King-Hamilton and Mr John Bolland. In addition to non-capital murder, Hosier and Tucker were also charged with aggravated robbery whilst Valerie Salter was now also charged with being an accessory after the fact of murder. There would be a total of 62 prosecution witnesses.

Although the three men were admitting their part in the robbery, witnesses still had to be called to verify what they had said. Albert Edward Hood, for instance, was the conductor of the number 4 bus. He identified Tucker as a young man who had boarded his bus at South Street, Tarring, and travelled to Worthing station. He also recalled that Tucker was carrying a blue BOAC holdall at the time.

Mrs Edith Tree had been a passenger on the number 31 bus to Littlehampton. She recalled seeing Terry and Salter sitting on top of that bus, looking intently at something outside. She then saw what had attracted their attention: Tucker and Hosier being interviewed by two police officers.

George Henry Baldwin had been the conductor on that 31 bus, which ran from Brighton to Littlehampton. He certainly remembered Terry for he had asked for two singles to Portsmouth, a journey that would have involved changing at Littlehampton. This was a most unusual fare and the only one of its kind that Baldwin had taken on that particular day.

Mrs Violet Mills, who lived in Melville Way, Goring, had travelled to Durrington on November 10th, to do some shopping. At around 10.06am she had been walking from Strand Parade to the greengrocers when she saw a dark green car come from somewhere behind the bank and come to a stop directly in front. A few minutes later she saw a man walk out of the bank carrying what appeared to be a rifle. He got into the green car which held two other men, and the vehicle then drove off at some speed.

Nellie Shorten lived at 5 Western Row, next door to the Salters. She reported that at around 8.00am on November 10th, she had seen a dark green car pull up outside her home. The car had three men in it and, in due course, she saw Valerie come out of her house and sit in the car. Later all four went into number 7.

Mary Salter told how a man had knocked on her front door a few minutes after 8.00am on the day of the robbery. A young man said he was 'Vic' and she took this to be Victor Terry who she knew her daughter had been seeing. He asked if he could see Valerie, who was still upstairs getting ready. A few minutes later, Valerie went out to the car, returning later to ask her if Vic and his two friends could have a cup of tea, whereupon all three were invited into the house. She and Valerie both worked at the same factory and Valerie now asked her mother to tell people at work that she was ill so that she could take the day off and spend it with Vic. By the time she left for work at 8.30am, her other daughter, Gillian, had already gone off to school leaving Valerie alone with the three men.

William Frederick West, a taxi-driver, testified that he had been sent to Queen's Road to pick up a Miss Brown. When he arrived, it was Hosier who climbed into his cab and West remarked that he was a very strange 'Miss Brown'. Hosier replied that she was just the woman who had rung for him and asked to be taken to Worthing station. Told to wait at the station, West saw Hosier return with Tucker and was told to return to Queen's Road. The fare came to 3s 2d and he was given a 10s note and told to keep the change.

Mrs Mary Wrigley ran the Square Deal sports shop in Chiswick High Road and she stated that on November 9th, three young men whom she identified as the defendants, came into her shop and said that they wished to buy a gun as they were going shooting on Dartmoor. Terry paid five guineas (£5 5s) for the 3-bore shotgun and some cartridges, asked her to clean it for him and came back for it later that same day. This was the weapon found on the floor of the abandoned dark green car and had been used to kill John Pull.

Dr Francis Camps, the Home Office pathologist stated that there had been a single wound inflicted on John Pull. Death was due to shock and haemorrhage of the brain, the gun having been fired from a distance of between 6ins and 9ins and the wound being over the right side of Pull's left eye. He further testified that even had medical expertise been instantly available, John Pull would not have survived.

Amongst the most telling evidence was that of the bank clerk, Andrew Barker. He repeated what he had already told the police but stated that at the time the gun was fired, there was no contact between Terry and Mr Pull and that Pull had not tried to grab the weapon at any stage. This was further underlined by the fingerprint evidence for whilst Terry's prints were found on the weapon, there was no sign of any contact prints from John Pull. The time came for the four defendants to tell their own stories. Between them they explained how, on November 3rd, the three men had met in the Crown public house at Chiswick to discuss Terry's plans to rob a bank in Worthing. Six days later, on November 9th, they had purchased the gun but Terry had stressed that this was just to frighten the bank staff into doing as they were told.

Later that same day, the three met up in another pub, the Jolly Farmer, at Hounslow, and it was in a street nearby, Spring Grove, that they stole the dark green Wolseley. This was deliberately chosen as it looked like a police car and so if it were seen speeding away from the scene, it would be less likely to arouse suspicion. The group now drove towards the south coast but stopped for the night just past Horsham. It was here that Terry insisted on trying out the gun and loosed off a shot into some trees.

Early the next morning they drove to Valerie Salter's house and from there, drove up to the bank, arriving outside just after 9.30am. They waited for the bank to open, Terry and Tucker going inside whilst Hosier kept the car engine running so that they could make a quick getaway.

In effect, Hosier and Tucker, who had now been named in the newspapers, were saying that they were guilty of being involved in the robbery but had nothing to do with the killing of John Pull. That, of course, was for the jury to decide but even if found guilty they would not face the death penalty since neither man had actually pulled the trigger. It was only Terry who faced the noose and so it was up to his defence to prove that he was not in control of his own actions when he fired that gun into John Pull's face.

Evidence had been given that Terry had worked at 11 different jobs since the summer of 1956, and the autumn of 1960. His own father, Alfred Terry, had once taken his son on as a painter but he had shown no interest in the work and soon left of his own accord. Harry Rogers was a director of the company which operated the Dome dance hall in Worthing. He had engaged Terry in September 1960 but later ordered the manager there to let Terry go as he was known to be heavily involved in the drugs scene. Once Rogers had visited the club and seen Terry throwing pills into the air and catching them in his mouth.

Melvin Phillips had worked with Terry at the Dome. He related one incident when Terry walked through the club carrying a gun. Concerned for his friend's safety, Phillips had followed Terry and taken the gun from him. It had turned out only to be an airgun but this was perhaps a sign of how unbalanced Terry could be when he was high on drugs. Other evidence showed that Terry had for some time been taking large quantities of drinamyl or 'purple hearts', along with other, similar drugs.

Perhaps the strangest part of the defence was Terry's claim that he felt that his mind and body had been taken over by the spirit of the American gangster, Legs Diamond. Terence Edwin Burns, a friend of Terry's from Chiswick, said how Terry had been subject to sharp changes of mood but could not have been described as a violent person but seemed to become a different person when he was on drugs. Burns also related how having seen a film about Legs Diamond, Terry had been enthused with interest and spoke about it for weeks afterwards. Finally, Terry's own mother, Mathilda, said that her son had told her he felt there was something in his body that was stronger than he was and that it was urging him to do things. It was now up to the medical experts to decide whether Terry really was not responsible or if he was faking these symptoms.

Dr Felix Warren Brown, a London-based consultant psychiatrist, believed that Terry was an extremely psychopathic personality, suffering from a severe abnormality of mind which substantially influenced his behaviour. Dr Brown believed Terry's story and felt that the young man really did feel possessed by Legs Diamond. For the prosecution, though, Dr John Pearce, a Harley Street psychiatrist, said that he felt Terry was perfectly sane and trying to build a picture of abnormality. It now all rested with the jury.

The trial came to an end on March 28th, 1961, when the jury retired and took two and a half hours to consider their verdicts. Phillip Tucker was found guilty of non-capital murder and since he was by now still only 17, was ordered to be detained during Her Majesty's pleasure. Alan Alfred George Hosier was adjudged to be guilty of non-capital murder and jailed for life. Valerie Salter was found guilty of harbouring Terry and was given 12 months' probation, the judge believing that she had been placed in an impossible position between her duty and the man she loved. Terry was found guilty of murder and since his hand had fired the gun, this was a capital offence and he was sentenced to death.

Hosier and Tucker decided not to appeal against their sentences, but Terry did.

The appeal was heard on May 8th, before the Lord Chief Justice, Lord Parker, and Justices Ashworth and Lawton. There were four main grounds: that there had been misdirection on the issue of diminished responsibility; misdirection on the issue of accident; that the judge did not properly or fully put Terry's case in his summing up; and that the judge did not properly sum up with regard to medical evidence concerning diminished responsibility. After due consideration, the judges decided that the summing up had been fair and the appeal was consequently dismissed.

There was one final twist to the story and this may well explain why Terry fired the gun on that fateful morning. He had been very friendly with a young man named Francis Forsyth, known to all as 'Flossie'. who had been sentenced to death along with Norman James Harris for a brutal murder at Hounslow. On the very morning that Terry had walked into the bank at Durrington, he had heard on the radio that Forsyth had been hanged.

At 8.00am on Thursday, May 25th, 1961, Victor John Terry was hanged at Wandsworth prison by Harry Allen and Samuel Plant. They were the same gallows which had claimed the life of his friend Francis Forsyth.

APPENDIX

List of all executions for murder at Wandsworth since 1900:

George Henry Parker 19th March 1901
Ernest Walter Wickham 13th August 1901
Charles Robert Earl 29th April 1902
George William Hibbs 13th August 1902
William Brown 16th December 1902
Edgar Edwards 3rd March 1903
George Chapman 7th April 1903
William Joseph Tuffen 11th August 1903
Edward Harrison 28th February 1905
Alfred Stratton and Albert Ernest Stratton 23rd May 1905
Alfred John Heal 20th June 1905
Frederick Reynolds 13th November 1906
Richard Brinkley 13th August 1907
Julius Wammer 10th August 1909
Thomas William Jesshope 25th May 1910
Frederick Henry Thomas 15th November 1911
Sargent Philp 1st October 1912
George Marshall 17th August 1915
Arthur Harold Victor de Stamier 12th February 1918
Joseph Jones 21st February 1918
Jack Alfred Field and William Thomas Gray 4th February 1921
Joseph O'Sullivan and Reginald Dunn 10th August 1922
Fredeick William Maximillian Jesse 1st November 1923
Jean Pierre Vacquier 12th August 1924
Patrick Herbert Mahon 3rd November 1924
John Norman Holmes Thorne 22nd April 1925
James Murphy and
Frederick Stephen Fuller 3rd August 1927
Sidney Bernard Goultier 6th January 1928
James Gillon 31st January 1928
Frederick Lock 12th April 1928
William Henry Kennedy 31st May 1928
William Charles Benson 20th November 1928
Albert Edward Marjeram 11th June 1930
Albert Probert and Frederick William Parker 4th May 1934
Leonard Arthur Brigstock 2nd April 1935
Percy Charles Anderson 16th April 1935
Raymond Henry Bousquet 29th October 1935
Frederick Herbert Charles Field 30th June 1936
George Arthur Bryant 14th July 1936
Wallace Jenden 5th August 1936
Alfred Ernest Richards 12th July 1938
William James Graves 19th July 1938
George Brain 1st November 1938
Harold Armstrong 21st March 1939
William Thomas Butler 29th March 1939
Leonard George Hucker 10th October 1939

Stanley Ernest Boon 25th October 1939
Arthur John Smith 26th October 1939
Edward Ernest Hammerton 27th March 1940
William Charles Cowell 24th April 1940
Stanley Edward Cole 31st October 1940
George Johnson Armstrong 9th July 1941
John Ernest Smith 3rd December 1941
Harold Dorien Trevor 11th March 1942
Cyril Johnson 15th April 1942
Gordon Frederick Cummins 25th June 1942
Arthur Anderson 21st July 1942
Patrick William Kingston 6th October 1942
Herbert Hiram Bounds 6th November 1942
Harold Dorkin 27th January 1943
Dudley George Rayner 31st March 1943
August Sangret 29th April 1943
Charles Arthur Raymond 10th July 1943
Charles Eugene Gauthier 24th September 1943
Terence Casey 19th November 1943
John Joseph Dorgan 22nd December 1943
Ernest James Harman Kemp 6th June 1944
Horace Beresford Gordon 9th January 1945
Andrew Brown 30th January 1945
Ronald Bertram Mauri 31st October 1945
Robert Blaine 29th December 1945
Michal Niescior 31st January 1946
Arthur Clegg 19th March 1946
Marian Grondknowski and Henryk Malinowski 2nd April 1946
Sydney John Smith and David Baillie Mason 6th September 1946
Frank Joseph Freiyer 13th November 1946
Sydney Sinclair 18th March 1947
David John Williams 15th April 1947
John George Haigh 10th August 1949
William John Davies 16th August 1949
Ernest Soper Couzins 30th December 1949
Albert Price 16th August 1950
Joseph Brown and
Edward Charles Smith 25th April 1951
James Virrels 26th April 1951
Frank Burgess 22nd July 1952
John Kenneth Livesey 17th December 1952
James John Alcott 2nd January 1953
Derek William Bentley 28th January 1953
John Francis Wilkinson 18th December 1953
Alfred Charles Whiteway 22nd December 1953
James Reginald Doohan 14th April 1954
William Sanchez de Pina Hepper 11th August 1954
Rupert Geoffrey Wells 1st September 1954
Sydney Joseph Clarke 14th April 1955
Gunter Fritz Edwin Podola 5th November 1959
Francis Robert Forsyth 10th November 1960
Victor John Terry 25th May 1961
Hendryk Niemasz 8th September 1961

BIBLIOGRAPHY

NEWSPAPERS

Brighton Evening Argus
Brighton Gazette
West Sussex Gazette
Mid Sussex Times
The Bognor Regis Post
Bognor Regis Observer
Hastings and St Leonards Observer
The Times

PUBLIC RECORDS

CRIM1 58/5 Masset
CRIM1 1501 Raymond
CRIM1 1524 Gauthier
ASSI 36/37 Mahon
ASSI 36/38 Thorne
ASSI 36/48 Probert and Parker
ASSI 36/57 Dorgan

INDEX